14—
4

MADAME DE MAINTENON

Françoise de Maintenon and her niece, Françoise d' Aubigné
Portrait by Ferdinand Elle

MADAME DE MAINTENON

Uncrowned Queen of France

CHARLOTTE HALDANE

CONSTABLE · LONDON

To Ruth
with love

Constable and Company Limited
10 Orange Street London WC2

First published in 1970
SBN 09 455750 0

Printed in Great Britain by
Cox & Wyman Ltd, London, Fakenham and Reading

Contents

List of Illustrations

Preface

The biographer in search of Mme de Maintenon's true personality inevitably turns first of all to her own correspondence. And there the enigma of this extraordinary woman immediately reveals itself. For although she wrote thousands of letters between the ages of fifteen and eighty-four, she burned almost the whole of her correspondence with Louis XIV. In consequence no direct evidence remains regarding her relationship with him either before or after their marriage. The fact that this did take place however is generally accepted.

Few if any women have played so important a part behind the scenes in their country's history. The only time Mme de Maintenon emerged from this political seclusion was during the War of the Spanish Succession, when Louis XIV was using her correspondence with the Princesse des Ursins as an ancillary channel of communication with the Spanish Court, independently of his official representatives there.

Until well into the nineteenth century, Mme de Maintenon was regarded as an unsympathetic figure. The libels propagated by Saint-Simon and the Duchesse d'Orléans in her lifetime were further enhanced by the forgeries of her correspondence by La Beaumelle, which were only exposed in 1865 by the scholarly researches of Lavallée.

My aim has been neither to strengthen the case of Françoise de Maintenon's hagiographers nor of her slanderers, but to present my readers with the facts as far as they are ascertainable, and leave them to judge for themselves. I hope that they will agree with me that she was neither a saint nor a devil, but one of the most remarkable women in European history.

The bibliography which is given at the end of this book contains the main sources, in addition to the correspondence, on which the evidence is based. I am grateful to the authors and publishers of these works for permission to translate and quote certain passages from them, in particular Editions Hachette for permission to quote from *Mme de Montespan et l'affaire de poisons* by Georges Mongrédien, and Editions du Seuil for *Mme de Maintenon* by Jean Cordelier.

As usual I am greatly indebted to the librarians and staff of the London Library for their loan of books. My gratitude is also due to my friends and readers, notably Miss E. G. Stephen, Miss Hilda Hyatt and Mrs Irene Lillicoe, and above all to my indispensable research assistant Ruth Jordan, without whose invaluable co-operation in the later stages, this book could not have been completed.

Part One

1   *The Little Indian Girl*

It would be difficult to invent a more inauspicious start in life for the baby girl born in the shadow of Niort Prison, in the province of Guyenne on 27 November 1635, who was to become the uncrowned queen of France.

Her paternal grandfather was Agrippa d'Aubigné, an implacable and ruthless Huguenot who for years was in the service of Henry of Navarre. When Henry returned to the Catholic Church in order to become King Henry IV, d'Aubigné would never have said to him, as his colleague Sully did, that Paris was worth a Mass. For he continued to fight the Catholics until at the age of sixty-eight he was condemned to death for conspiring against the government of Henry's son and successor, Louis XIII. He then fled to Geneva, the stronghold of Calvinism, where he died in 1630, in his eightieth year.

In 1583 Agrippa had the good fortune to marry a young heiress, Suzanne de Lezay, who brought him the properties of Surimeau and Mursay. They had five children of whom three survived, an only son, Constant, and two daughters, Marie and Louise-Arthémise.

Constant was born in 1585. His father gave him a sound Protestant education, and started him off in life as a page to the Baron de Neuillant, the Governor of Niort, conferring on him also the barony of Surimeau, bestowed on Agrippa by Henry IV. Constant, however, lacked none of the vices of his time; he was a born scoundrel, profligate, drunkard and gambler, murdered his first wife and her lover and between his bouts of debauchery dabbled in forgery, espionage and treason. Not surprisingly, his father disinherited him as 'the destroyer of the good name and honour of his family'. He was arrested for treason—conspiring with the English against the French crown —in September 1627 and imprisoned in the Château Trompette at Bordeaux.

Constant, however, possessed unusual charm, on which he traded all his life. In prison he used it so successfully that within three months this scoundrel, aged forty-three, became engaged to the sixteen-year-old daughter of the Governor, Jeanne de Cardilhac. Their marriage in 1627 could only be explained on the supposition that he found some means of seducing this innocent girl, although there was no actual evidence of the fact.

Their first two children were both boys, the third a girl. Jeanne de Cardilhac was well connected. The Governor of Niort, M. de Neuillant, was a distant relative. The register of the church of Notre-Dame at Niort contained the following entry:

The 28th day of November, 1635, was baptised Françoise, daughter of Messire Constant d'Aubigné, Lord of Aubigné and Surimeau, and of Dame Jeanne de Cardilhac, his wife. Her godfather was François de la Rochefoucault, Lord of Estissac and Maigno, son of *haut et puissant* Messire Benjamin de la Rochefoucault, and her godmother Demoiselle Suzanne de Baudéan, daughter of *haut et puissant* Charles de Baudéan, Lord-Baron of Neuillant, Governor for His Majesty of this town and castle.[1]*

The baby's godparents were themselves still children, a boy of ten and a girl of eleven. Their names looked well on the register, but they were not in a position to provide their god-

* Notes on the sources will be found on p. 289.

daughter with the worldly goods, care and upbringing which she needed. Nor, married to a convicted felon, was her mother.

Many years later, when reminiscing to her secretary Mlle d'Aumale, Mme de Maintenon remembered how, as a very small girl, she had played with the little daughter of the gaoler, at Niort. This child had a toy silver service, and as Françoise did not possess one, looked down on her for her poverty. But with lofty disdain Agrippa's grand-daughter made it clear that birth came before wealth. 'I am a lady,' she said, 'and you are not one.'

This was probably the earliest instance of Françoise's realistic understanding of the class distinction that ruled her period. The older she grew the more firmly she determined to hold her head high and stand well in the eyes of the world.

Of Agrippa's two daughters, the elder, Marie, married Caumont d'Addé, who in due course was to increase the misfortunes of his sister-in-law, Jeanne d'Aubigné. But Agrippa's favourite was his youngest daughter Louise-Arthémise, whom he fondly called '*ma douce, mon unique*', and for whom he found an eligible husband, the Marquis de Villette, giving her the Château of Mursay as part of her dowry.

Mme de Villette was as gentle and kind as her father claimed, the only being on earth who consistently stood by her appalling brother. She provided for her two little nephews, and when the baby girl was born helped Jeanne at her confinement. Although Françoise had been baptised in her mother's religion, her aunt nevertheless took the baby home with her to Mursay, where she remained for the first seven years of her life, tenderly and lovingly cared for.

Throughout her marriage poor Jeanne d'Aubigné never knew a moment's happiness. At the end of his life Agrippa, who left a considerable fortune, was to repent of his lack of affection for his elder daughter. By then she had died, yet he left three quarters of his property to her husband and children, Mme de Villette only receiving one quarter, and his outcast son, 'the destroyer of the welfare and honour of his house', not one sou.

Unfortunately for herself, Jeanne d'Aubigné attempted to recover some of the inheritance she considered due to her husband and children; she went to Paris and in a series of lawsuits she brought against Caumont d'Addé, she lost what little money she possessed as well as her peace of mind, becoming an embittered shrew. For women like herself, respectable although penniless, there was only one refuge—the convent, where she might get food and lodging for next to nothing. But Jeanne's worst calamity occurred when on Richelieu's death in 1642 her husband was released from prison and immediately set out for Paris to rejoin his wife, taking little 'Bignette', as the child was nicknamed, with him.

Mme de Maintenon said later that her mother, although devoted to her two sons, had never loved her; and had only kissed her twice throughout her childhood on her forehead. Jeanne was, apparently, a severe disciplinarian, but not necessarily more prone than the average mother of her period to give a disobedient little daughter a box on the ears. And of Bignette's disobedience on being returned to her family, Mme de Maintenon herself provided at least one instance.

She never ceased to love the kind aunt in whose home she had been so happy and undoubtedly resented being parted from her and taken to Paris by her father. Both her famous grandfather and her undistinguished mother had one trait in common, profound obstinacy, and of this Bignette had inherited her full share. Mme de Villette had brought her up as a Calvinist, for although France remained firmly and fervently Catholic, by Henry IV's Edict of Nantes in 1598, the Huguenots were accorded full freedom of worship. Françoise, however, had been baptised in her mother's religion, and when she rejoined her in Paris was naturally expected to conform to it. But the child's resentment at being taken away from her aunt was rationalised as a determination to stick to the Reformed religion she had taught her. When taken to church by her mother, Bignette deliberately turned her back on the altar, refusing to kneel to the Blessed Virgin. Quite simply, of course, this indicated her rebellion against Jeanne who not surprisingly requited it by a sound box on the ears, which was still ineffective in re-converting the stubborn child.

On his final release from prison after Richelieu's death Constant d'Aubigné was sixty, an age at which anyone who was not an incurably restless adventurer might have been about to settle down. But Constant had neither the means nor the intention of doing so. Having begged or borrowed all the funds he could from various patient relatives and friends and lost them in various gambling hells and brothels, he was obliged to look round for some lucrative employment. To have obtained a post in France might not have been easy for a man of his reputation. Nevertheless there was a tinge of almost admirable audacity in his decision to emigrate with all his family to the faraway and romantically attractive French West Indies.

The lesser Antilles, a group of islands in the Western Ocean, certain of which included Martinique, Guadeloupe and Marie-Galante, had passed into the possession of the French West India Company. Already they were populated by imported Negro slaves, under various French landowners hoping to enrich themselves by exporting to the mother country cotton and the new and exciting drug, tobacco, which in France was fetching the high price of such a luxury commodity. Since there appeared little competition for a post so mysteriously far away, even a man with d'Aubigné's record was able to obtain one with an imposing title, and he had no great difficulty—since his patrons were no doubt only too thankful to be rid of him—in being appointed Governor of one of the lesser islands, Marie-Galante.

Even Jeanne may have felt hopeful when in 1645 she embarked with her husband and children for such a tropical paradise, where every prospect was pleasing, forgetting that there, as elsewhere, only man was vile.

The three-months' voyage in a sailing-ship was hazardous enough. Françoise, aged ten, was so utterly exhausted by sea-sickness that the poor child finally lost consciousness and just escaped being buried at sea.

She owed her life to her mother. For when she was about to be thrown overboard, Mme d'Aubigné insisted on having a last glimpse of her. She found her pulse still beating and said: 'My daughter is not dead!' which saved her life.

When they finally did land at Martinique, it was only to discover that the post d'Aubigné had been assigned was already filled. He therefore decided to return home, leaving his family in Martinique until he, or one of his previous benefactors, could provide the necessary funds for them to rejoin him.

For Jeanne the present was turning out no better than the past: nor was there any cause for optimism regarding the future. In an utterly strange tropical environment, with three growing children on her hands, in a country where discipline was far laxer than at home, fearing for their health and even more for their morals, her educational methods apparently became positively savage. Not surprisingly, in later years Mme de Maintenon did not care to dwell on her memories of this brief period. According to Mlle d'Aumale, she only remembered her mother's harshness, verging on downright cruelty, as when once she combed her hair so roughly that she drew blood, and to punish the screaming child forced her out into the tropical sun where flies settled on the congealing wound. Another time the house they were living in caught fire and Françoise was scolded for weeping at the sight, because her favourite doll was perishing in the flames. Experiences of that kind when one is eleven or twelve tend to be traumatic. To protect their minds from moral contamination Jeanne forbade her three children to read any books save Plutarch's *Lives* and the Bible. Yet all around them were sunshine, tropical beauty, gaily flashing birds, dazzling trees, shrubs and flowers; in spite of their slavery the Negroes were carefree and gay, singing, dancing and making love with the insouciance so endearing in their race. But during the two years she spent in Martinique the charms of the island, the climate and gaiety, appear to have made no impression on little Bignette d'Aubigné. Nor at any subsequent period in her life did she show interest or curiosity in natural beauty. She was and remained singularly unimaginative; intelligent above the average but almost wholly concerned with the practical details of life.

From Martinique Jeanne wrote to her kind and generous sister-in-law, Mme de Villette, begging her to help her to educate her elder son, Charles, of whom she was very fond, for a military career, and to place the younger, also called Constant, as a page in one of the great houses, where he might make a social career. Like his father in almost every way, Charles was to turn into a profligate charmer. At the age of thirteen—he was a year older than Françoise—only the charm was already obvious. As for Bignette, her mother wrote, 'she has taken the liberty of writing to you, ashamed that she is forgetting every-thing, both on account of the great heat of this country and also the bad food. I cannot blame her too much for it; she is never happy, poor child, except when she can have some news of you . . .' which does not sound like the letter of a harsh and un-loving mother. Jeanne was in fact very conscientious, and in those exceptionally difficult circumstances still paid great attention to her children's education. Françoise was later to owe a great deal to this early training. She was a bright child, very quick at her lessons, but her younger brother, of whom she was extremely fond 'was very lazy' she told Mlle d'Aumale. 'He said to her, "sister, you do my lessons for me and during that time I will go out and get you some oranges as your reward" and as,' said Mme de Maintenon, 'I liked oranges and didn't dare go out like my brother, I was delighted to do his lessons for him.'

Jeanne finally succeeded in obtaining return passages for herself and her family. Their ship was apparently in danger of being captured by corsairs. 'She dressed her children in their best clothes, and put a large rosary around her own waist, not fearing thereby to advertise her religion. Françoise d'Aubigné whispered to her brother:

'"If we are captured we will soon console ourselves for no longer being with her."' And to mitigate this rather startling admission by her revered employer, Mlle d'Aumale hastily added: 'This was because Mme d'Aubigné did not love them. All her affection was given to her eldest son . . .'

Possibly that was another reason why Bignette resented her

mother, and if that was the case and jealousy was a cause of her undoubted but unadmitted dislike of her—except for this one instance—it would have been natural enough.

Within a few weeks of their arrival at Niort Jeanne suffered yet another blow when her eldest boy was accidentally killed; according to some accounts in a duel, to others by drowning. His mother's grief at his death was genuine, but his father's disappearance could only have been a relief to her. This, also, was a mystery. Whether to escape from his wife's nagging or his family responsibilities, soon after his return from the West Indies the ebullient Constant set out, in the completely opposite direction, for Turkey. His destination there is unknown, since he got no farther than the old Roman city of Orange, in Provence, where he died in 1647. All he left behind him were an appalling reputation, debts, a penniless widow, and that charm which had carried him through so many vicissitudes, his only legacy to his son and daughter.

For Françoise inherited her full share of it. When, at the age of twelve, to her great joy she was taken back to Mursay by her beloved Aunt Arthémise de Villette, she may still have retained some of her West Indian sunburn. With her remarkably fine dark eyes and glossy black hair she was an exceptionally pretty child. They nicknamed her 'the little Indian girl'. Possibly her relatives tried to draw her out on the subject of her exotic life in Martinique but, if they did so, with little success. Already her character was formed, and one of its strongest traits, which as she grew into young womanhood became more and more marked, was quite unusual reticence. A childhood such as hers —bandied about between mother and father, and, as shortly was to happen, from one aunt to another, from Huguenoterie to Catholicism and back again—with no stable home or security, would have been enough to account for this reserve, which in due course proved so invaluable to her career.

2 *Rebellious Convert*

Jeanne went back to Paris and her ceaseless lawsuits. Like any unfortunate litigant in *Bleak House* she wasted her time and energy on them, leaving none to spare for her family.

At Mursay Françoise was treated like a daughter, provided with a governess, and taught all the accomplishments of a young lady of her class, charity to the poor and visits to the old and ailing included. This was the life that she felt herself destined for, a life of willing service and response and obedience to loving kindness. Everything in her subsequently brilliant career reveals the influence of those few happy months. In Mme de Villette's affection Françoise's anxiety to be loved and wanted was gratified for the first time. The earlier years she had spent at Mursay —she was only seven when she was taken away the first time— she later claimed hardly to have remembered. But on her return she was rising fourteen. It was a life that might have seemed too good to last—and so it proved.

When shortly after her birth, Mme de Villette had taken the baby Françoise to Mursay for the first time, there was no reason to expect that fourteen years later she would be reclaimed for a second time by her Catholic relative, Mme de Neuillant, the wife of the Governor of Niort.

Whether or not her attention was drawn to the fact by her confessor, she now remembered that little Françoise d'Aubigné was her own daughter's godchild, and she had therefore the responsibility before God of ensuring that Françoise was brought up in the true Catholic faith, and not as a heretical Calvinist. But her predominant motive was a more worldly one. This laudable intention gave her an opportunity to draw the attention to herself, in this meritorious act, of the Queen Mother and Regent, Anne of Austria, the widow of Louis XIII, who was governing the country during the minority of the little king, Louis XIV, who was three years younger than Françoise. For, apparently, it needed an order personally signed by Queen Anne, to compel the Huguenot aunt to surrender the child to the care of her Catholic relative. The order was readily given.

Willy-nilly, Françoise was again on the move, this time from Mursay to Neuillant. She took with her an abiding devotion to her Aunt Arthémise and the governess she had given her, whom many years later she sent for to join her. As Françoise grew older she invariably showed the sense of gratitude to her protectors which was already one of her most endearing characteristics. Her memory was remarkably retentive. In her years of power she never forgave a real or imaginary slight, but neither did she forget the affection or kindness she had been shown in the past.

It was, however, out of the question that after the Queen Mother had signed the order placing the girl in the care of Mme de Neuillant she should remain at Mursay any longer. Mme de Villette accepted the inevitable and Françoise was compelled to do the same.

The household at Niort to which she was sent was a far less agreeable one than the happy home she left behind her. The aunt whom she loved and the great-aunt to whom she was confided differed in more than their religious beliefs. Mme de Villette was comfortably off, but nevertheless no more than a provincial lady of a family that could barely be described as aristocratic. Mme de Neuillant was the wife of a state official in

close contact with Paris and the Court. She was a woman of
wealth, yet as avaricious as any farmer's wife. According to a
later account given by Françoise—

> I remember that although she was rich enough to have a
> coach-and-six, I had nothing but clogs to wear, and except
> when there was company, never wore shoes. I also remember
> that my cousins and I, who were about the same age, spent
> part of each day keeping her turkeys. They put a mask on our
> noses, to prevent them getting sunburnt, and gave us a basket
> with our lunch and a little volume of Pibrach's quatrains,
> some of which we had to learn each day [These were sets of
> moral verses very popular at the time]. We were also given a
> large stick with which to prevent the turkeys from straying.[1]

A great deal of nonsense was subsequently written—part of
the legend of the future Mme de Maintenon—suggesting that in
this manner Françoise spent part of her early teens as a little
goose-girl or Cinderella, ruthlessly exploited by a mean and
wicked aunt. And since she was to marry, not merely a fairy
prince, but the Sun King, it must have been very tempting for
her adorers to give her earlier history this romantic twist. But
from the manner in which she herself told the story it seems
clear that far from suffering from these menial farmyard tasks,
she may well have enjoyed them. She shared them with her
cousins: they meant freedom in the fresh air instead of being
cooped up in classrooms; with her quick brain the learning of
Pibrach's quatrains would have given her no trouble, and one
can see the girls playfully chasing the straying gobblers and
having lots of fun whilst doing so.

Even more exaggerations were added to the legend when
Mme de Neuillant sent her young ward to the Ursuline Convent at Niort to be educated and re-indoctrinated in her baptismal faith. Nothing, in the circumstances, could have been
more natural and proper. But again the later panegyrists
attempted to turn this teenage girl into a religious controversialist. Allegedly Françoise, in spite of repeated attempted
discipline in the manner of her severe mother, beatings and the

rest, implacably refused to renounce the Huguenoterie of her beloved Aunt Arthémise. And finally, tired of her refractory obstinacy, the nuns returned her to Mme de Neuillant. The facts seem rather different. For Françoise was not, according to her own account, unhappy there. If the discipline was strict, with her usual passionate desire to be loved and wanted, she attached herself to one nun especially, Mère Céleste:

> I simply adored her. Nothing gave me greater happiness than to do everything I could for her. I spent whole nights starching the *pensionnaires'* uniforms, so that they should always look fresh . . . and when to her amazement she found that all her work had been done for her I was delighted. When I left the convent I thought I should die of grief. I prayed for her every day and never forgot her.[2]

The simple reason why the nuns refused to keep Françoise any longer was nothing more than a sordid financial wrangle. Mme de Neuillant, with her usual meanness, when placing her with them in the convent had instructed them to send the bills to Mme de Villette. This was adding insult to injury, and not surprisingly their recipient refused to pay them, although she remained still sufficiently fond of Françoise to send her presents of dresses and other personal things. When the amount owing for Françoise's fees—education and maintenance—reached a certain sum, seeing that there was little likelihood of this being paid, the Ursulines returned the girl to Niort.

At that particular time Mme de Neuillant, about to make a trip to Paris, and feeling that she had successfully broken the bond between Françoise and her Huguenot aunt, decided to take the girl with her. Her intention seems to have been to hand her back to her mother, who, living in a state of penury which her rich relative saw no reason to alleviate, was less than enthusiastic at her unwanted daughter's return. Who paid the fees this time is not clear, but once again Françoise was given in charge of the Ursulines, in the rue St Jacques.

Her distress on that occasion is recorded, since the poor little thing, abandoned by her Catholic mother and aunt, in desperation wrote her Aunt Arthémise at Mursay.

Remembering your great kindness and generosity to poor abandoned children, I am stretching out my hand to you, imploring you to take me out of this place, for my life here is worse than death . . . You cannot imagine what a hell this so-called House of God is to me, and the harshness and cruelty of those who have been given power over my body, though not my soul, for that they cannot touch. . . . I beg you once more to immediately take pity on your brother's child and your humble servant Françoise.[3]

This desperate cry from the heart remained, however, unanswered; not, one assumes, because of Mme de Villette's indifference to Françoise's misery, but simply owing to her fear of the consequences to herself, should she meddle any further in the upbringing of the Catholic child taken from her by royal command.

Françoise remained in the Ursuline convent, and with the resilience of youth accommodated herself to the rigorous régime. The simplest means of putting an end to the harshness and cruelty to which her defenceless body was exposed was, of course, her spiritual compliance. When with proud defiance she declared to her aunt that 'they' could not touch her soul, she had unwittingly portrayed herself as she already then was and would through her life remain. The inner core of her personality was already formed and inviolable. The number of young girls and women whose actions were governed, even in their maturity, by their heads and not their hearts must be fairly rare. Yet of this minority, Françoise d'Aubigné was the most supreme example, a feminine realist. Even at the age of fifteen she already understood quite clearly that a tolerable existence was only achievable if she followed the rules, and follow them she did.

Many years later the Ladies of St Cyr gave a highly dramatised account of her conversion, allegedly told them by Mme de Maintenon herself. It began convincingly enough. One of the kinder and more intelligent nuns first won the little rebel's confidence. She was then allowed to listen to a debate in the Ursulines' parlour between a Catholic priest and a Huguenot parson. The Huguenots had apparently been bringing considerable pressure to bear on the great Agrippa's grand-daughter not to abjure his faith. They did this by throwing notes to her over the school wall. On listening to the controversy, however, Françoise, young as she was, discovered certain discrepancies in the pastor's case and thereupon surrendered to the priest. The only condition she made was that she should not be asked to believe that the soul of her dear Aunt Arthémise would in due course be eternally damned.

Whether Mme de Maintenon's memory was at fault or the ladies' account of the story was highly coloured, it seems doubtful that the Ursulines would have taken so much trouble to convert a penniless young orphan, but of the conversion there is no doubt at all. Her mother and Mme de Neuillant were at last pleased with her and her existence immediately became less intolerable.

Nevertheless, as she was rising sixteen and her education was ending, new problems arose. It was time to leave the convent. Mme de Neuillant had discharged her duty by rescuing her daughter's godchild from future damnation in the next world, but by doing so had only landed herself with the responsibility of looking after her in the present one; another body to clothe, another mouth to feed. There was no further question, in the case of a growing young lady, of turning her out to mind the turkeys or carry hay to the horses, as she had previously done. Mme de Neuillant was now also preoccupied in launching her own daughter—the girl cousin with whom Françoise had shared these childhood duties—into society. The ritual was laid down: first, presentation at Court, then a début with a view to as rich and brilliant a marriage as possible. That was the accepted method of placing a well endowed girl in the great world. In the case of a penniless dependant, however, the picture was a far less hopeful prospect. Françoise might be exceptionally intelligent and even exceptionally pretty. But she was an orphan, with a mother living miserably from hand to mouth, who could not possibly support her, with not an influential friend and relative other than Mme de Neuillant, and not a *sou* to call her own let

alone a dowry; a friendless and dowerless unwanted young
woman.

She was well aware of it. Almost from birth Françoise had
been dragged up or pushed around from pillar to post. Where
would this life end? She must have wondered, dreading and
revolting against the obvious answer to that question. For it was
as simple as it was unbearable to her—the convent.

Vocation she had none, and all her youthful vitality protested
against such a fate; with all the ardour of her fifteen years, her
radiant youth and superb health, she wanted to live, live, live.
To her, as she had written to Mme de Villette, the convent was
a fate worse than death; any other, she felt, would be preferable.
But if, metaphorically, Françoise had started life as a little
Cinderella, no fairy godmother brought a handsome young
prince knocking at the door to ask for her hand. The godmother
she did have was hard and mean, and the suitor who most
extraordinarily came to her rescue could not have been less
romantic nor more revolting in appearance, and when she was
taken to his house for the first time Françoise burst into tears.

3   *The Chivalrous Cripple*

Reader who has never seen me, I am going to tell you as nearly as possible what I am like. My figure was well made, although small. As a result of my illness I have shrunk at least a foot. My head is rather large for my body. My face is full, whilst my body is that of a skeleton. My sight is fairly good, although my eyes protrude, and one of them is lower than the other on the side on which my head is bent. My legs and thighs formed at first an obtuse, next a right, and finally an acute angle; my thighs and body form another, and with my head bent down on my stomach I look like the letter Z. My arms and legs have shrunken, and my fingers as well as my arms. To sum up, I am a condensation of human misery.[1]

This was the self-portrait of the future husband of Françoise d'Aubigné.

Scarron was the son of a councillor to the Paris Parlement, nicknamed 'the Apostle' because on the least pretext he would quote St Paul. Probably boring and pompous, the old gentleman was quite well connected and financially prosperous. When Paul's mother died the boy was only three and his father's second wife was the sort of woman that type of man so often marries, mean, spiteful, the typical cruel stepmother of the fairy-tales. Paul was able to defend himself, however. From the age of nineteen onwards he was so riotously sowing his wild oats that the councillor stepped in and insisted that he entered Holy Orders. From his friend, the Bishop of Le Mans, Scarron senior obtained for his son a membership of the chapter of the cathedral of St Julian, with the prospect of becoming a canon in due course. Having been banished from Paris and its pleasures, young Scarron found no compensation in accompanying his bishop to Rome, on which he wrote a disparaging sonnet. At twenty-six he received his canonry, but had to wait another three years for the post to be vacated and the income to be paid him. Nevertheless, like so many young men unwillingly forced into the priesthood as a career, Holy Orders in no way impeded him from continuing the roystering life he had previously enjoyed. But suddenly all this came to an end when Scarron developed a mysterious, intensely painful, and incurable disease.

La Beaumelle, a thoroughly untrustworthy chronicler of the life of Mme de Maintenon, who never hesitated to distort the facts if by doing so he could make them appear more salacious, gave a fantastic account of the source of this illness. According to him, at carnival time, Paul Scarron wished to make a particularly gay impression. Instead of wearing fancy dress he smeared his body all over with honey, then tore open his featherbed and rolled in the down until he was completely covered in feathers. Going out thus adorned, he amused himself by accosting the pretty girls. But their escorts, annoyed by his impudence, began to pull off the feathers by handfuls and Scarron, before he was stripped completely naked, had no refuge but to jump into a bed of rushes along the riverside. As the result of the chill he then caught his lifelong martyrdom began. Those earlier biographers who rejected this Boccaccian account found only one alternative —venereal disease. But although in view of Scarron's dissipations this can hardly be ruled out, his symptoms point quite obviously to some form of acute rheumatoid arthritis. He showed none of the mental degeneration that would have developed with tertiary syphilis, but remained vigorously intellectual, witty and amusing to the end of his life. In fact it was only after the onset of his disease that he wrote the verse and prose that made him one of the most popular humorous writers of his day.

Scarron's misery was increased by his lack of funds. On his father's death the 'Apostle's' money went to the children of the second marriage; all that remained to Paul was the small income from his canonry. At that stage, before he was completely crippled, Scarron became a confirmed beggar. His charm of manner and personality still remained to him. Marie de Hautefort, a fallen favourite of King Louis XIII, having retired to Le Mans, became a friend or possible admirer of his gifts; at any rate, when on the King's death she returned to Court, she spoke to Anne, the Queen Regent, about this extraordinarily amusing character, who promptly petitioned Her Majesty to appoint him her *Malade de La Reine* or Queen's Invalid, a bitter but amusing variant on the theme of the traditional Court jester. Anne did so, granting him a pension of 500 *livres*. Scarron became the fashionable entertainer of his day. The Court laughed delightedly at his biting verses and comedies, and since he was in royal favour he could dedicate various of his works to noble or aristocratic patrons who would pay for the honour.

His rheumatoid arthritis did not affect Scarron's mind or his enjoyment of life, particularly his palate. In fact the one pleasure remaining to him was gastronomy. Seated in his immovable boxed-in wheelchair at the head of his table, in the Yellow Room in his fashionable apartment at the Hôtel de Troyes, he presided over nightly banquets to the most elegant company of the period. Soon they became similar to the 'bottle parties' given by artists and writers three hundred years later. For Scarron, even in his heyday, could not afford to keep open house on that scale. With his usual brash wit he dubbed his apartment the *Hôtel de l'Impécuniosité*, and those who took pleasure in dining or drinking with him were invited as usual, but expected to provide the victuals and wine. Since they were assured of an excellent evening's entertainment, they were more than willing to do so.

Naturally enough Scarron, who was still only in his thirties when his disease struck him, tried frantically to find a cure for it. A Parisian 'doctor'—for those of the period were mostly quacks —prescribed mercury pills that half-poisoned him and merely aggravated his pain. He made several pilgrimages to various watering-places, with no more effective results. By 1648, when he wrote the self-portrait describing his physical misery, he was almost helpless, yet mentally at his most creative and active.

At the death of Louis XIII in 1643, the little Dauphin, who was then five years old, succeeded to the throne as Louis XIV. During his long minority his mother, Anne of Austria, became Regent. Louis XIII's principal minister had been the great Cardinal Richelieu, who died in 1642. Richelieu had discovered a young Italian, Mazzarini, born in the Abruzzi, in 1602. After having served as an officer in the papal army, Mazzarini had switched from a military to a diplomatic career and, although not in holy orders, was appointed papal nuncio in Paris. Richelieu, impressed by his remarkable ability, attached him to his personal staff. Mazzarini then adopted the French spelling of his name. Richelieu, a year before his death, obtained a cardinal's hat for him and from that time onwards he was known as Cardinal Mazarin.

The Thirty Years War had been dragging on in Europe during the previous reign and the childhood of Louis XIV. Originally a partly political partly religious war, over the rulership of Bohemia, it gradually involved all the leading European powers. Although Anne of Austria was the sister of King Philip IV of Spain, during these long conflicts France was three times invaded by the Spanish, who in 1636 came as close to Paris as Compiègne, and in the following year threatened both Dijon in Burgundy and the province of Languedoc.

This exhausting war was finally ended by the Peace of Westphalia, in 1648, a triumph for Mazarin's brilliant diplomacy. The Italian Cardinal, however, had little experience of French domestic politics, and here almost met with defeat.

In 1648, when Louis XIV was ten years old, civil war broke out, due to the revolt of the French against Mazarin's internal financial policies. This war, which was known as the *Fronde*, developed in two phases: the first, the Old *Fronde*, lasting from 1648 to 1649; and the second, the New *Fronde*, from 1649 to 1653. It took its name from a game, *la fronde*, played by the children of Paris. The Old or Parliamentary *Fronde* was led by the Paris Parlement, the Cardinal de Retz and Prince de Conti. Scarron was already famous as the sharpest controversialist wit in Paris; Cardinal de Retz and his supporters were frequent guests at the poet's banquets in his Yellow Room at the Hôtel de Troyes. This soon became the headquarters of the Frondeurs, and Scarron their propagandist. With almost absurd imprudence he launched into a violent diatribe against the powerful Cardinal, *Les Mazarinades*. All it brought Scarron was ephemeral publicity and, as anyone more prudent might have anticipated, the loss of his pension as the Queen's Invalid.

A neighbour of Scarron's at the Hôtel de Troyes was Cabart de Villermont, who was connected with the French West India Company. Presumably from him the suffering poet heard of the superlative climate of the isles, the perpetual sunshine, the air free of the bitter winds, rain, sleet, snow, frosts and fogs of Paris in winter, which so greatly increased his sufferings. In his chosen role of Court Invalid or Jester, he would be entertaining his fashionable visitors with a series of jokes, witticisms, and what nowadays are termed wisecracks, when suddenly a sharp stab or twinge of unendurable agony would make him scream with pain. Yet, still optimistic, he dreamed of escape; could he reach the islands and settle there he might recover. He bought shares in the West India Company and took the keenest interest in the expedition it was fitting out to sail to Guadaloupe and which he intended to join.

At this stage in the lives of the girl nobody wanted and the crippled poet coincidence (the novelists' bane but the biographers' boon) came into play. For Cabart de Villermont had already been to the West Indies and there had met the d'Aubigné family, befriending them and helping them to return to France. He had remained in touch with them, at La Rochelle

Madame Scarron
Engraving from the portrait by Petitot

Paul Scarron
Engraving by E. Desrochers

and Niort, and also with the Governor of that city, M. de Neuillant, their rich aristocratic relation.

Undoubtedly Françoise was becoming a problem to Mme de Neuillant. Preoccupied as she then was in arranging the marriage of her daughter, a maid-of-honour to the Queen, to the Duc de Navailles, she had neither time nor money to spare for the girl, whom she took with her to Paris, intending to return her to her mother. But Jeanne was struggling along on a miserable pension of 200 *livres*, and could not possibly keep her daughter with her. So Françoise remained with Mme de Neuillant at the house of a relative, M. Tiraqueau, Baron de Saint-Hermant, in a suburb of Paris near the Porte St Michel, at the top of the hill from which in later times the Boulevard St Michel was to run down to the river. This house was next door to the Hôtel de Troyes, where Scarron was then living, looked after by a former mistress, who had become an elderly nun. It was presumably their mutual friend Cabart who first told Scarron that Mme de Neuillant's ward was a pretty little creature whom he had known as a child in the West Indies, and who was still nicknamed the young Indian girl. In spite of his physical incapacity Scarron's sexual interest and curiosity were aroused. It was by his own invitation that Mme de Neuillant came to visit the crippled poet, accompanied by her niece, Jeanne d'Aubigné, and Françoise.

In spite of Scarron's own description of his 'protruding eyes' one of which was lower than the other, his portraits show them to have still been extremely lively, malicious, and expressive. The Yellow Room was as usual crammed with fashionable ladies and gentlemen in elegant dresses and costumes when the three women were shown in; Mme de Neuillant no doubt suitably arrayed, Jeanne as well as possible, and the little girl of whom those sharp eyes had their first glimpse, in his own words, 'in a frock much too short for her, and who, for some reason unknown to me, began to cry'.

The explanation for those tears was a simple one; Françoise, a child of only fifteen still, was terrified at being surrounded by all those smart people who looked at her far less kindly, probably

B

with smiles of contempt and wondering what on earth she was doing there. Knowing herself so shabbily and unsuitably dressed, probably in some cut-down and discarded frock of her rich young godmother's, the kind she had been obliged to wear ever since entering Mme de Neuillant's avaricious care, brought tears of mortification into her eyes. These might also have been induced by pity at the dreadfully sad appearance of her host, the helpless cripple shut up in his little box-chair. Certainly, a strange current of mutual sympathy was immediately established between them, both in their respective ways so unloved and unwanted. Scarron had also noted that in spite of her scant dress and mental distress the little girl was remarkably attractive, with beautiful dark eyes that shone through her tears, and a charming figure. He may well have bitterly regretted—as he more than once said he did—that his paralysis made it impossible for him any longer to seduce a pretty girl.

Nothing further is known of this first visit, after which Mme de Neuillant took Françoise back to Poitou. Jeanne returned there also.

During her stay with the Saint-Hermants, Françoise had made friends with the Baron's daughter. This was the first instance of her talent for finding women friends who in one way or another might be useful to her. Her method was to ingratiate herself with them, by little services or tactful gestures which would be remembered. Françoise was unusually liked by other girls and women, from the governess whom Mme de Villette had given her, the nun, Mother Céleste (both of whom she remembered and kept in touch with throughout their lives), to ladies of the highest society. From the country she began a correspondence with Mlle de Saint-Hermant, who found her letters so entertaining and witty that they were shown to the literary cripple next door.

Mademoiselle,   From Niort 1650
   You flatter me too much and treat me almost as if I were of a different sex from yours. I am much more flattered by your praise than by M. de M's, who expresses his with more passion but less tenderness, and I would be very wary of allowing

a lover to enter my heart with as much success as you have done.[2]

This M. de M. was apparently Georges Brossin, Chevalier de Méré, Françoise's first admirer. Mme de Neuillant had allowed him to give her lessons to round off her education. In later years he claimed the credit for having developed her considerable intelligence and admitted that he had fallen in love with his attractive pupil. Young as she was, however, his attentions did not in the least turn Françoise's cool little head.

> I would not be missing Paris if you were not there. You were more important to me than anyone else I liked there. I shall never forget the tears you shed with me, and every time I think of it I shed some more. Each time I sit down on that chair you embroidered with your own hands I love it more, and when I try to write I am dissatisfied with my expressions and my thoughts, unless I use your pen and your paper. I beg you to forgive me for not filling up the whole page. I have neither enough boldness nor enough wit to do so; I promise to send you half, and the remainder when I am as witty as M. Scarron. I am very fond of Mlle de Neuillant, and please tell her so from me, and thank her for the service she did me in giving me a friend like you, who would console me for being parted from my mother, if anything could do so.[3]

This, the only surviving letter from Françoise to her friend, seems to the modern reader rather stilted and composed, partly in the manner of the period, but also because Françoise was already picking up the style of the so-called *Précieuses*, the female high-brows or blue-stockings of whose circle she would soon become a member. How deliberate, one wonders, was the reference to Scarron? Did she hope that he would be shown her letter to correct his first impression of a gawky girl overcome by shyness to the point of tears?

Whether deliberately or not, the letter was shown to him. Scarron's interest was sufficiently stirred for him to write to her directly:

Mademoiselle,
    I have always suspected that the little girl who came to see me six months ago, in a dress that was too short, and who

burst into tears, I really don't know why, was as intelligent as she seemed to be. The letter you wrote to Mlle de Saint-Hermant showed so much intelligence that it made me dissatisfied with my own lack of observation, that had not immediately convinced me of it. To tell you the truth, I never thought that one might learn, either in the American Isles or at the Convent in Niort, to write so well, and I cannot imagine why you should have taken as much trouble to hide your gifts as others do to reveal theirs. Now that you have been discovered you should make no difficulties about writing to me as well as to Mlle de Saint-Hermant. I shall do my best to turn out as good a letter as yours; and you will have the pleasure of seeing that I shall have to make an effort to show as much wit as you do. Such as I am, I remain your life-long very humble and very obedient servant.[4]

Most of the subsequent letters allegedly written by Scarron to Françoise were discredited by later historians as forgeries by the egregious La Beaumelle. Scarron was known to have amused himself occasionally by writing gay, slightly lascivious, and bitterly regretful letters to some of the pretty young women whose interest he could capture in no other way. One very long letter, which apparently was not altogether spurious, contained some interesting lines, since in it Scarron reproved Françoise for having made him fall in love with her:

I do not know whether I should not have done better to beware of you the first time I saw you . . . But what reason was there to suppose that a young girl would disturb the mind of an old bachelor? [Scarron was forty-two.] And who would ever have suspected her of causing me such distress that I should regret being unable any longer to avenge myself?

And all that because I love you more than I ever expected to. Dammit it, how I love you! And what stupidity to love like that! At any moment, my life's virtue, I'm longing to leave for Poitou, and in this bitter weather, too. Isn't it madness? Oh, come back, for God's sake come back, since I am crazy enough to be longing for absent beauties. I should know myself better and remember that it is quite enough already for me to be crippled from head to foot, without needing to suffer as well what is known as *impatiently longing to see you.* ...

The letter rambled on in this semi-facetious, semi-self-pitying style:

> Tell me, my *mignonne*, are you a Christian? On my honour you are a Turk; I'm an expert and you are one of the worst Turks. Rich and honourable Turks, moreover, are great alms-givers, but as I know you, you would not do good for an empire, even to those who love you. You are therefore worthless, although you are entirely lovely and good; more than anyone else in this world you are an instance of the proverb that says '*All that glitters is not gold*' and you are as much a little devil as you are spotless. So now you know what it is to be beautiful and more than anyone on earth I am your very humble and very obedient servant.[5]

This letter is important as self-revelation. No doubt it was not meant to be taken too literally, yet in these jesting references to her attractiveness and cruelty Scarron revealed his innate lasciviousness and may well have been testing Françoise's reaction to himself and his misfortunes with an ulterior motive.

Françoise returned to Paris unchaperoned; wearing a yellow serge dress and carrying a basket containing rye bread and eggs to eat on the journey. On arrival she was met by the old family friend and Scarron's neighbour, Cabart. Pending further arrangements for her future she returned to the Ursuline convent. Staying, she visited Scarron, and by then had apparently lost her shyness. A curiously tender and perfectly honourable relationship gradually developed between them. Françoise was determined as ever not to become a nun. Scarron offered her a 'dowry' should she wish to enter the convent as a boarder, but this she was too proud to accept.

According to one version of what followed, Scarron then said to her, 'Well, my dear, the only alternative is for you to marry me!'

Scarron may well have said so, but if he did, the tone of voice in which he made his startling proposal would have been of considerable significance. One inclines to think that he generally did speak half in jest, half in earnest, and genuinely fond of Françoise as he was—madly in love with her, to judge from his letter—he may have put it to her deliberately in a manner that would give her an opportunity to reject him without causing him too much loss of face if she did so. In fact, whether those words were ever spoken or not, Françoise accepted him, almost with alacrity.

Several of Mme de Maintenon's biographers have made out Mme de Neuillant to have been a vile character, little better than a procuress, who deliberately engineered this fantastic marriage in order to rid herself of an unwelcome responsibility, disposing of her unwanted ward by marrying her off to a dirty old man, a lascivious monster. But, as Voltaire pointed out, no such melodramatic interpretation is necessary: 'It was,' he wrote, 'a lucky chance for Mlle d'Aubigné to marry that man, handicapped and impotent as he was, and none too well off.'[6]

At sixteen and a half, Françoise d'Aubigné was mature beyond her years. She was not merely shy but intensely reserved, with a streak of innate priggishness inherited from her Huguenot ancestors, which she never lost. According to her own statement to Mlle d'Aumale, 'she often said that nobody had been more frantically anxious than she was to be of good repute and to be generally admired, and that she had suffered martyrdom on account of it. "Perhaps it was to punish me for it," she said, "that God allowed me to rise so high, as if in His anger he had declared—you wanted praise and general esteem, you shall have enough of it to bow you down."'[7] Partly this exaggerated self-respect and secret desire to be admired by everyone was due to the strict training her mother had given her in childhood, never mitigated by a gesture of tenderness, a hug or a kiss. And partly it may have been due to an unusual characteristic in addition to her inbred puritanism, a definite sexual frigidity. More than one of those who knew her testified to this; in later years she was said never to have been in love, and seemed in fact terrified at the mere suggestion of sexual passion. Now here was a man proposing to her who even then made it quite clear that he would be unable to consummate their marriage. She may already have known, since it was a commonplace of her day, girls of her own age who again and again were forced into marriages abhorrent to them by insensitive parents who of course legally owned their daughters body and soul. Their wedding nights, the legitimate raping of such helpless virgins by brutal, revolting, drunken husbands, were nightmares. By marrying Paul Scarron Françoise knew that she would be spared such a ghastly experience; far preferable to be merely a nurse to a helpless but kind invalid. That Scarron was kind to her is indubitable, and kindness was the surest way to Françoise's affection. There is not the slightest doubt that almost unbelievable as their union was, there was from the very beginning a mutual attraction between them. As her letter to Mlle de Saint-Hermant proves, even at fifteen Françoise was intelligent enough to appreciate Scarron's brilliance. She also had sufficient social sense to appreciate the advantages of being married to a man who entertained the *gratin* or cream of Parisian society in his large and comparatively luxurious apartment; of becoming hostess to most of the leading aristocrats and intellectuals of both sexes of the day. Her own father had been a profligate, constantly abandoning her mother, her brothers and herself; but a husband chained to an invalid's chair would never escape her. At last she would have a home of her own, security, the status of a married woman and the relative independence that went with it.

Looked at from this eminently practical point of view—and Françoise was nothing if not practical—there was a great deal to be said for this marriage, and no need at all to postulate wicked machinations on the part of Mme de Neuillant to bring it about. Scarron, hoping more than ever to be cured in order that he might be able to have normal intercourse with his lovely young bride, still clung to his plan to emigrate to the West Indies and far from opposing it, when the time came, Françoise was perfectly willing to embark on the voyage there with her husband.

When the date for signing the marriage contract was fixed, it was necessary to obtain Jeanne d'Aubigné's authorisation for it, since her daughter was still a minor. This was sent by her to Cabart de Villermont, the bride's principal witness, on 19 February 1652. Françoise never saw her mother again, for prematurely worn out by struggle and suffering, she died soon after the marriage.

Nor was Mme de Neuillant present on 4 April in that year, when the contract was signed at the house of M. de Saint-Hermant. Possibly Françoise's friend, his daughter, may have been her bridesmaid, but there is no mention of any feminine witness on this occasion. Husband and wife agreed to endow one another with all their worldly goods. In Mme Scarron's case this was merely a legal fiction, since she had none. Scarron was already in financial difficulties, having lost his lawsuit to recover his father's property from his step-brothers, and his pension as the result of his notorious *Mazarinades*, attacking the Cardinal.

Where and when the religious ceremony took place is unknown. It was alleged that when the priest officiating asked the bridegroom—cruelly enough in the circumstances—whether he was capable of consummating the marriage, Scarron snapped back, 'That is my business and Madame's,' but since this extraordinary union of a sixteen-year-old bride and a cripple nearly three times her age was the talk of Paris—most of it maliciously sneering—he may have said no such thing. Queen Anne, on hearing of the match, remarked that if there was one superfluous piece of furniture in Scarron's house, it was a wife.

Yet by the irony of fate Scarron won himself a place amongst the leading figures in French seventeenth-century literary history, not on account of his own light satirical works, but owing to this extraordinary marriage to the future Mme de Maintenon.

4 Madame Scarron

With Mazarin's return to power at the end of the *Fronde*, Scarron, who had so viciously lampooned the Cardinal in his *Mazarinades*, thought discretion the better part of valour. His marriage had by no means deterred him from his intention to visit the Western Isles in search of a cure. But whilst he and Françoise were preparing to join the expedition its departure was delayed again and again and when it did finally leave it came to grief.

For years Scarron had been engaged in an extremely expensive lawsuit against his step-brothers and sisters over the Apostle's will. Finally he did manage to have awarded to him by the courts some small properties in Touraine that had belonged to his father. So, on the pretext of visiting these, the crippled author and his young wife quietly left Paris for the countryside.

There they lived very contentedly until the autumn of 1653, congratulating themselves when they learned of the disasters to the expedition they had had the good luck not to join. Scarron gave up his dream of tropical adventure. Meanwhile the political situation had calmed down. Although Scarron's former pension was not restored to him, Mazarin, far from wishing to avenge himself on his lampooner, appeared to have forgotten him contemptuously. Not so, however, the Parisian public, with whom his burlesques and other ribald writings were still immensely popular. Like most good Parisians, Scarron could not bear to leave the capital for any length of time, and as theatrical managers and publishers still had plenty of work for him, he returned there with his bride in the spring of 1654.

The most fashionable quarter in the city was the Marais, conveniently near the theatres, and containing some residences. The exquisite Place des Vosges—known then as the Place Royale—remains a monument to the architecture of the period. In later centuries the Marais went out of fashion and degenerated into a sordid slum, but in the twentieth the wheel has turned once again, and it has become as it was in the Scarrons' day, a favourite residential quarter for successful artists, writers, and other rich intellectuals.

The Scarrons set up house in the rue Neuve-Saint-Louis, later known as 56, rue de Turenne. The house was only a small one, but contained two large rooms, one on the ground floor, one above it. The lower of these was Mme Scarron's bedroom, more than luxurious when compared to those Françoise d'Aubigné had previously occupied when she lived in poverty with her mother or in the convents of Niort and Paris.

The walls 'were hung with tapestries representing scenes from the Old Testament; on one was an oil-painting of the Magdalen in a gold frame, and over the mantelpiece a Venetian mirror two feet high'—a rare possession in the seventeenth century for a young married woman not of the wealthy aristocracy. Françoise slept in a large four-poster bed; her clothes were kept in a pearwood cupboard; the room was also furnished with four armchairs embroidered by their owner in tapestry, similar to the one given her by Mlle de Saint-Hermant. There were also six other chairs and six folding stools, all upholstered in yellow damask and probably used in the Yellow Room at Scarron's former residence in the Hôtel de Troyes when he entertained company. This setting must have seemed the acme of elegance to its young owner. Behind Françoise's room was a smaller one, where the furniture was covered in red brocade with yellow flowers, and where the grand visitors who were soon crowding the little house may have left their plumed hats and ornate coats.

The reception–dining-room was on the floor above; hung with English tapestry and containing in the centre twelve chairs and the large table at which the famous nightly supper-parties took place. Against the walls were a sofa, an ebony cabinet, and two bookcases, containing Agrippa's *Histoire Universelle*.

Scarron's own little bedroom was behind this salon, with the small four-poster in which his wife gently put the poor cripple to bed after the visitors had departed, and where he could drop the jester's mask and shed tears of agony when, as his disease immobilized him more and more completely, he was even unable to turn from side to side.

During the early days of their marriage, however, and when his sufferings gave him some respite, what was the conjugal relationship between Paul and Françoise?

At the time of their wedding Scarron was alleged to have remarked blithely that, 'I shall not indulge in any nonsense with her, but I shall teach her plenty'. Since his disease had not affected his appetite nor his digestion, it might well have left his sexual urge equally unimpaired. Obviously, crippled as he was, he could not consummate the marriage in the normal manner, by deflowering his bride. But he was still able to touch, caress, stroke and kiss the delightful young body belonging to him. In his youth he had been a rake; his knowledge of various alternative means of gaining sexual satisfaction would have enabled him to teach Françoise to give it to him. Her own reaction to such nights of ignominious pawing-about by the unfortunate cripple who owned her could not have been less than disgust, even if it was merely the normal reaction of a healthy young body to a diseased one.

Many years later she wrote to her brother that 'you will perhaps find it odd that a person who was never married nevertheless gives you so much advice on marriage'. There was never any doubt that she was legally married to Scarron, so presumably she was referring to the sexual act which he was unable to perform. She also in later years told the young lady pupils at St Cyr, the girl's college she founded, that wives were 'obliged to accept every whim and every strange kind of behaviour on the part of their husbands' and that 'it would be difficult to foretell to what lengths they might go'.

But although Scarron's lovemaking must have revolted her, Françoise was an exemplary wife and endured it without a word of complaint. She seemed, in fact, as happily contented with her station as any other young married woman of her day.

As soon as the Scarrons were re-installed in Paris, his former admirers of both sexes thronged to the little house in the rue Neuve as they had formerly done to the Hôtel de Troyes. At first young Mme Scarron was excessively shy. Like their host, an ex-canon, most of his guests were Catholics only for form's sake, freethinkers by predilection. In their gluttonous dining habits they made no distinction between Fridays and any other day of the week, Lent or otherwise. But whilst they gorged themselves on the rich dishes she had, as a dutiful housewife and hostess, prepared for them, she herself would sit demurely at her end of the table, with downcast eyes filleting the herring she ate with bread, butter and salad for her own supper.

'I admit,' she later told Mlle d'Aumale, 'that in those days I had a very good opinion of myself'. Mme de Caylus, her niece, wrote that Françoise would then 'immediately retire to her room, because she realised that if she had behaved less correctly and austerely the young men would have taken every kind of liberty, and her reputation would have become tarnished'.

It was this reputation that she cherished as her greatest treasure.

As she told her young ladies many years later, but obviously recollecting her aims and intentions with absolute clarity:

I did not want to be loved by anyone in particular, but I did want to be liked by everybody, have nice things said about me, cut a fine figure, and earn the approval of the best people; that was my ideal . . . there was nothing that I would have been incapable of doing and suffering to that purpose. I held myself on a very tight rein, but it cost me nothing, provided that I kept my good name; it was that I cared about, madly. (*C'était là ma folie.*) I was not interested in being rich, I was a hundred degrees above self-interest, but I wanted to be respected.

This passion, since it was hardly less, that Françoise had for her 'honour' may have been due to natural frigidity, or a sublimation of the normal instincts of a girl of her age, disgusted with sex as she had learned it from her husband; more probably a combination of both. Whatever its origins, in this extraordinarily intense desire to be universally liked and respected lay the seeds of her secret ambition leading to her later amazing career. Mme Scarron could have had no idea then of the grandeur that lay in store for her, yet it was as if she were already holding herself in reserve for it. Her character was, in fact, completely formed by the time she was in her early twenties.

In 1680, when she was forty-five, she described herself in a letter to her confessor:

> I have a morale and good tendencies which prevent me from doing harm; I have a desire to please and to be liked which puts me on guard against my passions; therefore I hardly ever have to reproach myself for anything I have done, but for very human weaknesses, a great deal of vanity, considerable frivolity and dissipation, great freedom of thought and judgment, and a degree of verbal restraint that is only due to natural prudence.

This might just as well have been a self-portrait by Françoise when she was twenty years younger. Her marriage to Scarron and her life with him for eight years afterwards introduced her to a libertine circle and an unusually broadminded setting for a young woman of her time. But she combined this innate wariness with a natural gaiety and highspiritedness against which she had to guard her tongue. The amazing thing was that she should already then have realised this. For as she expanded into young womanhood she really enjoyed life, in spite of the handicaps her marriage had inflicted on her; in spite of her rocklike passion for respectability she was flattered by the adulation of her would-be lovers, and even to some degree flirted with them and encouraged them in the *Précieuse* tradition, allowing them possibly to hope for greater favours which she not for one moment intended to grant them.

There was something touching and almost pathetic in this frank self-portrait of a sincere and charming young person, full of natural vitality, torn between her inclination to enjoy herself and the necessity to suppress it in the cause of that extraordinary subconscious ambition which was to carry her to such incredible heights.

In an age and a society in which only relatively few young married women—Scarron's wife in particular—could escape slanderous gossip, Françoise came out of her peculiar ordeal unscathed. The libels on her behaviour were not spread until a much later date. Of her two bitterest detractors, Saint-Simon and Madame, Louis XIV's sister-in-law, the former was not even born when Mme de Maintenon was still Mme Scarron; the latter did not know her until she was the uncrowned queen of Versailles. La Beaumelle's forgeries of her alleged correspondence were not made until the middle of the following century.

Françoise gradually lost her early shyness and began very successfully to act as her husband's hostess. Out of respect for her the conversation at their parties became less equivocal and lewdly allusive, but no less witty and entertaining. The Duchesse de Lesdiguières wrote to the Chevalier de Méré for some information about this young woman.

'You wish me' [he wrote in reply],

to tell you about this young Indian girl, whom you call my pupil, and I may say, Madame, that she is one of those people well worth teaching. Had you taken her with you as you intended and she expected, if her husband could have spared her for so long, she would have changed completely and become a masterpiece. I assure you also, Madame, that your voyage would have been that much more agreeable, for in addition to being very lovely and most pleasing in appearance she is gentle, grateful, reserved, faithful, modest, intelligent, and to crown it all she only uses her intelligence to entertain or make herself liked by people. And what I particularly admire in such a young person is that she receives all her admirers on the strict understanding that they abide by the rules, and following this principle she does not seem to me to be in any great danger, although the handsomest men at Court and the most powerful in the financial world lay siege to her on all sides. As I know her, she will hold out for a considerable time before surrendering, and because she is so easy-going and receives so many people they need not think they will get the better of her, as this is only a proof that she feels perfectly able to handle them. I will, however, admit to you that what annoys me is that she is too conscientious, in spite of all those who would cure her of it. I noticed this horrible defect in her recently, when her husband, who cannot turn from one side of his bed to the other, took it into his head to go to the Indies, imagining that a stay there would restore his health. I know they were going to leave, and that this young woman, who should have been happy enough in France, was prepared to go there with him and revisit America. I therefore think that a great Queen who always expresses herself so wittily and has such good judgment, did not know her very well when she told the invalid that 'his wife was the most useless piece of furniture in his house'.

There were other witnesses to Françoise's virtue and charm. It was also no exaggeration that her admirers included men of all ages and the highest standing. As she grew out of her teens she became a really beautiful young woman. It was generally agreed that she had brought about a great improvement in Scarron's appearance—he was always spotlessly clean and neatly dressed—and manners. Their salon was the rendezvous of women, as well as men. Françoise undoubtedly far preferred members of her own sex as friends and companions, was neither jealous of them nor, until much later, aroused their jealousy. Her regular visitors included three of the most brilliant women of her day, whose company undoubtedly greatly influenced her manners, giving them that social polish which once and for all set her at ease even in the best society. These three, all of whom were to become famous in their own right were Madeleine de Scudéry, the *Précieuse* authoress; the Marquise de Sévigné, the mother who wrote her daughter newsletters which ever since have remained classics of their kind, and Ninon de l'Enclos, the courtesan whose beauty and charm were to become legendary.

Mlle de Scudéry and her brother were aristocratic *littérateurs* —the Sitwells of their day. They belonged to the set known as the *Précieux* and *Précieuses* who gathered at the Hôtel de Rambouillet, where its owner, the Marquise, had founded a literary salon. Their affected imitations were later satirised by Louis XIV's favourite actor and playwright, Molière, in his two comedies *Le Bourgeois Gentilhomme* and *Les Précieuses Ridicules*.

Mlle de Scudéry was the most widely read woman novelist of her day and the characters in her enormously long novels were mostly people she knew, described under neo-classical pseudonyms. She frequently visited the Scarrons, and was entranced by Françoise, who in due course appeared in her novel, *Clélie* as 'Lyriane', whose dark eyes were the loveliest in the world, and who, with the most charming smile was able to keep her most ardent admirers at a distance. Françoise had already learnt to express herself simply and effectively.

Scarron became proud of his young wife's intelligence and took pleasure in developing it; improving her vocabulary and even teaching her the rudiments of Italian and Spanish. He was then at the zenith of his own success and was writing comedies of which the Parisian public could not have enough. As his hands became progressively more crippled Françoise acted as his secretary; apparently occasionally making useful suggestions which he accepted, and endeavouring to tone down his lewder jokes and double meanings. Another of her admirers, Somaize, who did Mme Scarron the honour of including her in his *Dictionnaire des Précieuses*, said that she could write verse and prose, and had she only known what she had been taught by Scarron, would have done as well as most of the other female highbrows.

Mme de Sévigné was not a pretentious blue-stocking, although she, too, was a member of the Hôtel de Rambouillet côterie. She was Marie de Rabutin-Chantal, of a distinguished family, wealthy, and extremely well educated socially and intellectually. She was no great beauty, but as portrayed by the fashionable painter Mignard—another member of the Scarron circle—delightfully pretty and attractive. She had a large dowry when in 1644 she was married to a Breton nobleman, the Marquis de Sévigné, by whom she had a son and a daughter. The son, Charles, never meant a great deal to his mother, whose passionate maternal devotion was concentrated on her daughter, who married the Comte de Gringnan, Governor of Provence. It was to this adored child that Mme de Sévigné wrote the letters on which her fame is based; keeping her informed almost day by day of all the latest Court news and town gossip.

Like so many of his contemporaries M. de Sévigné was a rake and even for those days glaringly unfaithful to his charming little wife. The first of the two great loves of his life was Ninon de l'Enclos; the second, Mme de Gondran, another lady of easy virtue, known by the nickname *La belle Lolo*. On 4 February 1651 de Sévigné fought a duel with the Chevalier d'Albret, one of his rivals for Lolo's bed, was severely wounded and died rather ignominiously, leaving Mme de Sévigné a widow at the age of twenty-five. Whether or not she consoled herself for his loss by having an affair with the leading statesman, Fouquet, Mme de Sévigné was circumspect and discreet; she never married again. Her husband's liaison with Ninon de l'Enclos was public knowledge, and as Ninon was an intimate friend of Scarron's, Mme de Sévigné did not too often risk meeting her by visiting the rue Neuve. She did, however, go there from time to time and both liked and respected Françoise. Undoubtedly as Mme Scarron grew into her twenties she learned a lot from this charming, witty, discreet and highly bred lady.

Ninon de l'Enclos seduced both Mme de Sévigné's husband and, much later, her son. Ninon was wellborn but, as the little Indian girl had been, without a dowry and faced with the same choice between the convent and the world, but no Scarron was available to give her a setting of respectability. It is tempting to speculate whether, had their positions been reversed, the future uncrowned queen of France would have followed the same profession—the so-called oldest in the world—as her friend. For they did become intimate friends. No doubt Françoise would have been saved from such a career by her innate puritanism, for Ninon said of her that although she tried to teach her, Mme Scarron had no aptitude for the arts of love. Rather contemptuously she added later that 'Mme de Maintenon was virtuous because she lacked courage to be otherwise; I tried to cure her of it, but she was too godfearing'. Yet Ninon's references to Françoise after she became Louis's morganatic wife must be treated with considerable circumspection. Although Mme de Maintenon kept in touch with her occasionally during their later years, it would have been natural enough for Ninon to have been envious of that insignificant little Mme Scarron who was to attain a higher position than any other Frenchwoman not of the Blood Royal. As Mme de Sévigné wrote to her daughter—'Who would ever have believed it?'

Mme de Maintenon's detractors tried to insinuate a lesbian relationship between Ninon and Françoise because, they alleged, the two women used from time to time to sleep together in Ninon's bed. But as was pointed out by less prejudiced commentators it was quite a normal thing in those days, even at Court, for two people of the same sex to sleep together without any suggestion of a homosexual relationship between them.

Ninon was a courtesan, but by no means a vulgar tart. Her career more nearly resembled that of Aspasia, the famous mistress of Pericles in ancient Athens. All the most brilliant and wealthy men of the day gathered in her salon, and from among them she would select as her lover the man who at the time most attracted her, and to whom the privilege of keeping her was assigned. When the attraction waned, the lover would be relegated to the status of friendship, and accepting the situation quite happily, remain her friend ever afterwards. Ninon herself rarely fell in love. She did so, however, with Louis de Mornay, the unusually handsome young Marquis de Villarceaux, so much so that for three years she abandoned Paris and all her admirers to live with him at his country seat. She was bombarded with letters, in prose and verse, imploring her to return, which she did in 1655, their affair presumably having ended, either then or a little later, but as usual, in Ninon's case, with no rancour on either side.

Villarceaux also visited the Scarrons, and it was not long before he was madly, head over heels, in love with the crippled entertainer's young wife. Françoise was then twenty. Her portrait by Mignard four years later shows how successfully the poor little orphan girl had flowered from the days of her first appearance at the Hôtel de Troyes in a frock too short for her. She is shown full-face, in *grand décolletage*, with a dress or cloak of some rich material, possibly velvet, draped around her almost bare shoulders, over an edging of fine cambric and lace. She wears long jewelled earrings as her only ornaments. The head is proudly poised on a rather short but pretty neck, with, already, the slight hint of a double chin. The eyes are as large, dark and expressive as they were described by Mlle de Scudéry, and the full lips are determinedly closed. The expression is remarkable, almost severe, uncompromising, with a definite hint of sadness under the well-marked arched eyebrows. Another portrait of the same period, a miniature by Petitot, shows her also in *décolletage*, with pretty sloping white shoulders. Her hair is less severely dressed, with a few curls at the back, and into it and around her neck is woven a strand of pearls, whilst the lace of her gown is held up at the shoulder by a large pearl brooch, to match her pearl drop-earrings. But here again the expression in her eyes does not match the rather elaborately glamorous costume; there is the same unsmiling almost suspicious glance, a seriousness which all who then knew her recognised, for they said that she rarely smiled or laughed, and put this down to her sad childhood and the marriage which tied her to a hopeless invalid. This seems an exaggeration. For since Françoise had lost her shyness she apparently became a delightfully entertaining and witty young hostess, at times almost a chatterbox, although continuing to keep her admirers at a proper distance.

When in due course Mme de Maintenon became the most powerful woman in France her enemies feverishly tried to rake up some scandal in her past, during her marriage to Scarron and subsequent widowhood, to damage her reputation. The only one of such stories that has a faint basis in reality is the allegation that Françoise did allow Villarceaux to seduce her and take her virginity. This is based on the flimsy evidence of a passage in a letter from Ninon de l'Enclos to her friend and former lover, Saint-Evremond, then in England:

'Scarron,' she wrote, 'was my friend; his wife's conversation gave me the greatest pleasure, but at the time I found her too *gauche* for carrying on a love affair. As for the details, I never knew anything, nor saw anything, but I very often did lend my Yellow Room to her and Villarceaux.' As Jean Cordelier commented on this passage, 'one does not'—and especially Ninon did not, presumably—'lend a room to a couple in order that they should say their prayers there together'. But as he also confirmed, this letter came from a collection that contained many forgeries, and might therefore equally have been one. It is also possible that in her old age Ninon might have wished to damage the reputation of her former young friend, whose subsequent glory had so greatly surpassed her own.

The suggestion that Françoise did have an affair with Villarceaux, is supported by some further 'evidence' that might have been far more damaging. It was incontrovertible that Villarceaux was for a time madly in love with her, so much so that in his château there hung the portrait of a beautiful young woman, emerging naked from her bath, the face of which was Françoise Scarron's. This portrait did really exist; the question was, did the alleged subject in fact sit for it? If this was the case, it was a flagrant contradiction of all else that is known and fully authenticated, of Mme Scarron's character and behaviour. The theory of her physical frigidity immediately goes by the board, as well as her attested modesty, ostentatiously paraded. Would a young woman who carefully covered up her body in her oldest and shabbiest clothes when visiting Fouquet, the powerful minister who was a notorious womaniser, in order that he should not be attracted by her, have blithely stripped for such a compromising memorial? The young woman who, as she herself repeatedly stated later, cared for no one, caring only that her

reputation should remain above suspicion and that everyone
should like her?

Saint-Simon of course pounced on this spicy morsel of scandal
and even claimed that Mme Scarron spent several summers at
Villarceaux's château as his mistress, in spite of the fact that the
Marchioness was in residence there. And finally, her friendship
with his wife makes it almost unthinkable that Françoise could
have lent herself to such a scandalous manner of deceiving her.
Women unmercifully and intuitively ferret out the weaknesses
of one another. Françoise's attested popularity with all the great
ladies whom she met after her marriage to Scarron makes such
behaviour on her part more than unlikely. The general con-
sensus of opinion today is that Villarceaux either commissioned
or himself painted—since he was an amateur artist—this picture
of a nude body, and had Mme Scarron's features added to it or
himself painted them in from memory.

In a very short time the most distinguished members of the
aristocracy who were providing the food and drink for those
nightly dinner-parties at the *Hôtel de l'Impécuniosité* were bringing
their wives along as well, to meet the charming young hostess.
They included the Marshal d'Albret, whose wife was to become
one of Françoise's most devoted protectors, treating her almost
as a member of the family; and other ladies of the highest
reputation, such as Mme de Montchevreuil and Mme de
Montataire.

Even during Scarron's lifetime his attractive young wife
began to be invited out into the best society and by then
appeared in the salons of these great ladies sufficiently at home
and quite capable of conversing with the company in the best
Précieuse style. It was, after all, understandable that a delightful
young woman in her early twenties should occasionally emerge
from the bedside of the cripple to whom she was tied and enjoy
some social relaxation. Scarron was at first flattered by the
attentions paid to his wife, but during the later years of their
marriage as his health worsened he became more and more
tetchy and there were occasional arguments between them. As
Scarron's fame gradually waned, their situation was not eased

by increasing financial difficulties. There were days at the *Hôtel de l'Impécuniosité* when, if no visitors and victuals turned up, the unfortunate host and hostess were actually short of food, and shivered in front of an empty grate.

To add to Françoise's difficulties, even then Scarron had not given up all hope. As was the fashion, he began to experiment in all kinds of alchemical nonsense, spending money he did not have on buying chemicals to discover the philosopher's stone or to make some gold potion by which he still hoped to be cured. They were burdened with further financial difficulties, when, her brother Charles d'Aubigné, an utter wastrel like their father, turned up and even succeeded in borrowing from Scarron, who at that time had managed to obtain a little capital by the sale of his small estates in Touraine. This brother was Françoise's heaviest responsibility, which with admirable loyalty she never attempted to throw off, but bore with exemplary patience, although sometimes she could not refrain from writing to him pretty sharply.

Towards the end of his life Scarron had one more brief moment of glory, when he was taken to the Louvre to be presented to the Queen Mother's guest, the eccentric ex-Queen Christina of Sweden, who after her abdication loved to visit France and was staying at Court. Curious of all the later social and intellectual Parisian fashions Christina wished to meet this extraordinary jester, and 'Queen's Invalid'. She received him kindly, and also sent for his wife and Ninon de l'Enclos.

But Scarron knew that his life was ending. With that devotion and affection that had marked his behaviour towards Françoise from the day of their first meeting, he told his friends that 'my one regret is that I have nothing to leave my wife, who possesses infinite merit and to whom I have every imaginable reason to be grateful'. He even wrote a burlesque will, in rhyme, in which he gave her permission to re-marry after his death and apologised for having caused her to suffer those years of abstinence from the pleasures of love, yet begging her not to forget him. He died on 6 October 1660.

It would have been natural enough for Scarron's poor

crippled body to arouse disgust and repulsion in Françoise. Throughout their marriage, however, she consistently showed him tenderness, compassion and gratitude. She never spoke of him except with gentle affection, never complained of the wearying hours she had spent nursing and caring for him. And on his death her sorrow was genuine.

She arranged for his burial in the church of St Gervais where, later when she could afford it, she had a monument erected to his memory and perpetual masses said for the repose of his soul.

In spite of his ribaldry, gluttony, endless pestering of his friends and patrons, Scarron died with dignity. His short self epitaph is still worth a farewell glance:

> *Celui qui cy maintenant dort,*
> *Fit plus de pitié que d'envie,*
> *Et souffrit mille fois la mort*
> *Avant que de perdre la vie.*
> *Passant, ne fait pas de bruit,*
> *Garde bien que tu ne l'éveille,*
> *Car voici la première nuit*
> *Que le pauvre Scarron sommeille.*

5 *Françoise Steps Forward*

In their marriage contract Scarron had left all his worldly goods to his bride. But he left no will. As soon as he was dead, Françoise requested the official receiver to seal off the house and make a complete inventory of all its contents. This inventory (given in full by Boislisle) contains some fascinating details, including a list of all Mme Scarron's clothes and effects—even her chemises and handkerchiefs. Some of her dresses were quite pretty, including a skirt of pink satin and two black velvet corselets, worn over white blouses. There was another one of flowered satin trimmed with fur; there were two lace scarves and a neck kerchief of Genoese lace, probably a present and the one she wore in her portrait by Mignard; it was valued at sixty *livres*. She had only six chemises, one camisole, four nightcaps, four handkerchiefs, six pairs of socks, and the same number of stockings. The list of her personal debts at the time of her husband's death showed that Mme Scarron owed money to the tailor who provided her mourning outfit, to the shoemaker, haberdasher, glovemaker, as well as a thousand *livres* which she borrowed to pay for Scarron's funeral, but which were never repaid.

Immediately the poet was known to have died his creditors rushed to the house to seize what they might, in compensation for the money owing to them. Those already there included the servants, whose outstanding wages were still owing—the valet, housemaid, cook, and three more female helps. When all Scarron's goods and possessions were sold up his widow was left with only a few thousand francs. Two letters from her at this time reveal her plight. They were written to her Aunt Arthémise and M. de Villette, with whom Françoise had always kept in touch and for whom her affection was as warm as ever.

The first was a brief and anxious note to her aunt at Niort:

I have been so overwhelmed during these last few days and M. Scarron's death caused me too much grief and too many worries to be able to write to you. Even now I have no time except to ask you to send me an extract from my baptismal certificate which I urgently need. [In connection, no doubt, with the legal procedure concerning her claims to the estate.] Send it to me as quickly as you possibly can, and believe me, my dear aunt, that whatever condition I am in, I am entirely yours.

The Villettes were still as fond of Françoise as she was of them, and in reply to this letter M. de Villette wrote to her for more information regarding her situation. Françoise answered either towards the end of October or at the beginning of November:

I have had too much evidence of your kindness and friend- ship not to realise that your wish to know the state of my affairs is not due to mere curiosity; but to tell you the truth, my condition is so deplorable that I would like to spare your feelings by not giving you too many details of it.

M. Scarron left ten thousand francs, and twenty-two thou- sand francs of debts; according to my marriage contract I am entitled to twenty-three, but it was so badly drawn up that although I am supposedly the estate's first creditor and therefore should have an advantage over the others, it only means that I shall have to carry a large proportion of their claims so that when the estate is settled I shall have to divide my share with them, and if I go to Court about it and win, I shall have all in all four or five thousand francs.

Françoise did not in fact do so, but left the whole estate to be divided up between the other creditors, but there were still not sufficient funds to pay them in full. She continued:

> That is all that was left by that poor man, who always had some fantastic scheme in his mind, and who wasted all his ready money on the philosopher's stone or some other equally imaginary idea. He had made some suggestion to *M. le procureur* [the minister Fouquet] that I am trying to have accepted, and if I succeed I hope that it will bring me in enough to set my mind at rest.

In view of her future, which had she then been foretold it, might have seemed as fantastic to Françoise as any of her late husband's wildcat notions, the last paragraph of this letter is fascinating:

'So now I've informed you about my affairs, as you asked me to do. From what I've said you will agree that I am not destined to be happy; but those of us who are devout call this kind of experience a visitation by the Lord, and we place ourselves at the foot of the Cross with complete resignation. I hope that there will be greater prosperity at Mursay'—perhaps M. de Villette had written how sorry he was that they could do nothing to help her—'the home of those whom I love and respect more than anyone else in the world.'

When Scarron died Françoise was twenty-four, a very attractive young woman with whom some of the most brilliant and dashing men of fashion were in love. But apart from the suggestion that she had been Villarceaux's mistress there was never a hint that she was then in love with anyone, nor that she intended to provide herself either with a rich lover or a husband. Instead, whilst waiting for her affairs to be settled, she went to live in a convent, where she remained even after she was able to pay her way there.

In those days convents were the only refuge of the poor, the aged and the sick, but in addition they were also frequently used as retreats by wealthy or distinguished persons in need of a rest from the strenuousness of Court and society life. Such ladies, and occasionally gentlemen, would hire a room from the nuns and furnish it themselves, living rather as those of their class might in later centuries live in residential hotels; well looked after, and even entertaining their friends there in a quiet manner.

Mme d'Aumont, Scarron's cousin, kept such a room for herself in the Convent of the Hospitalières in the Place Royale, known as the *Petite Charité* and almost around the corner from her own stately home. This room she lent to Mme Scarron. A malicious gossip of the period Tallement de Réaux wrote that 'the Marshal's wife at first sent her everything she needed, even clothes, but she told so many people about it that the widow became annoyed, and one day sent her back in a cart the firewood she had had delivered in the convent courtyard.' If this anecdote was true, it shows an unusual side to Françoise's character. She was certainly proud; she had refused Scarron's charity before marrying him, but she was not usually ungrateful or ill-mannered, and this tiny incident appears to have made no difference to her friendship with Mme d'Aumont.

Françoise's own cousin, the former Mlle de Neuillant, had become Duchesse de Navailles and a lady-in-waiting to the Queen Mother. She also took an interest in helping her poor relation. The Queen was informed that her late Royal Invalid, the poor Scarron, had left a beautiful, intelligent and virtuous young widow in direst poverty, and it was suggested to Her Majesty that she could not do a more deserving act of charity than to return to her the pension she had withdrawn from her husband when Scarron had so foolishly published his *Mazarinades*. The sum was only 500 *écus*, but when the Queen inquired the amount she was informed that it was 2000 livres. She then ordered that Mme Scarron should receive this income and that the first payment should be taken to her at once, to relieve her distress.

Having at last a small but certain income Françoise was able to pay her own way in the convent and was even able to employ a personal maid. The girl she engaged then was called Nanon Balbien. If women are to be judged on their capacity to keep their servants—and this has always been an important criterion for other women—Mme Scarron passed the test of kindness and consideration with the highest marks. For Nanon was to remain in her service, as her closest companion and confidential maid, for the rest of her life. In due course, when Mme de Maintenon was the most influential woman in France, Nanon was a close second. She imitated her mistress's hair styles and way of dressing, her manner of speech and her religious devotion, and 'she was half a fairy godmother; the princesses were happy when they had a chance to talk to her and kiss her, daughters of the king though they might be; the ministers who worked at Mme de Maintenon's apartment bowed very low indeed to her'.

Meanwhile their joint environment was an extremely modest one. Françoise still had no religious vocation and not the least intention of taking the veil. But during her marriage she had begun to become increasingly devout, whether as a means of self-protection against the importunities of her lovers, or because she genuinely felt so.

Her confessor was the Abbé Gobelin, in some ways as severe as a pastor. He rebuked her for being too well dressed, not because her dresses were made of silks and satins, but because of the amount of material in them. 'But sir,' Mme Scarron ventured, 'I only wear quite ordinary materials'. 'That's true,' he admitted, 'yet I don't know what it is, dear lady, but every time you kneel down I see such a quantity of stuffs falling at my feet around you that I somehow feel it's too much'.

Françoise did, in fact, dress very simply all her life and for preference wore plain black, with only a touch of real lace at the neck and wrists. Nor did she care for jewels, even when she might have had the most magnificent collection. Yet she was as fashion-conscious as any young woman of her time and enjoyed helping her friends to dress up, without ever showing the least envy.

After the death of her beloved Aunt Artémise, she wrote to her cousin, the young Mme de Villette, that she was sending her by messenger a box containing 'lace for your white skirt; I have had your kerchief laundered and am keeping the other one. Never have so many pinafores in English embroidery been worn as at present, but I would like your armbands and cuffs to be the same, for nothing is better than trimmings that match . . .'

Françoise's girlhood and young womanhood were behind her. Yet she was never troubled, apparently, by sexual longings and had no desire for a husband and family of her own. Nor did she envy Mlle de Pons, a niece of the d'Albrets, when she was married to the Marquis d'Heudicourt, but spent an infinite amount of time and trouble in helping her with her trousseau and looking after her like a mother, right up to the actual ceremony. 'I remember that when she got married,' Mme de Maintenon said later, with some amusement, 'I forgot all about myself and let everyone who came to the wedding see me, as untidy and neglected as a servant girl. I was promptly taken into a room so that I might dress myself properly in my turn, and when I came back, neither Mme de Montespan nor anyone else recognised me. I did all that quite naturally, as I always did, to give pleasure to my friends, not from self-interest, for I was expecting nothing, and in those days I was far from imagining that after God Mme de Montespan would be the first cause of my great good fortune.'

Like so many of Mme de Maintenon's later statements and stories to the young ladies of St Cyr (all of which were as piously treasured as Holy Writ) this passage is not a tissue of lies, but of half-truths. She did undoubtedly at that period devote herself wholeheartedly to her women friends. She also said later that it had been the most delightful time of her life, since she had no ambitions, nor any of those passions that might have disturbed the happiness she enjoyed in the environment she had chosen.

But to say that she had no ambition was an over-simplification.

When Françoise was still married to Scarron his powerful visitors, like Marshal d'Albret, had introduced her to their wives, certain proof, said the Ladies of St Cyr, that he had recognised her virtues, since in those days husbands did not care that their wives should know women of doubtful reputation. Mme d'Albret was an estimable woman, but stupid. Françoise realised however that it was far more useful to her to be bored by a lady of the highest aristocracy than amused by women friends of lower rank. And when Mme d'Albret went to the theatre to see the fashionable plays of the period, with their classical allusions, Françoise accompanied her to explain their meaning to her.

The Abbé Gobelin, her confessor, shrewdly realised that if Mme Scarron had no sexual vanity, she did pride herself on her wit and intelligence. He imposed on her the penance of ceasing to parade them in company; of appearing dumb, or stupid. This she scrupulously endeavoured to do until the Abbé Testu, a member of this fashionable circle, observing this odd conduct on her part, persuaded her to relax and continue to be herself. For in these aristocratic drawing-rooms Mme Scarron was often the most entertaining member of the company. She excelled at the party games that were in fashion; from Scarron she had learnt to write simple flowing verse of trivial content. But one of her poems of that period is of more than drawing-room interest. That same socialite Abbé Testu had compared the charming Mme Scarron to a gaoleress, whose admirers were all her prisoners. She thereupon answered him in the following lines:

> Il le faut avouer, le métier de geôlière
> Est un fort pénible métier :
> Il faut être barbare et fière,
> Faire enrager souvent un pauvre prisonier
> Et ce n'est pas là ma manière.
> Si ceux qui sont dans ma prison
> Se plaignent, ils n'ont nulle raison,
> Je les prends sans vouloir les prendre.
> Je ne cherche point les moyens
> De les mettre dans mes liens.
> Ce sont ceux qui vinnent s'y rendre.
> Mais comme, sans faire la vaine,
> Je les prends sans combattre et sans rien hasarder
> Sans me donner beaucoup de peine,
> Je sais comme il faut les garder.

Whether or not these lines were a typical example of preciosity, there was not a shred of evidence to disprove them. For

Françoise had not changed; by then her ambition, her secret but still most powerful ambition to be generally esteemed and liked, had, if that were possible, increased. She may have been only half aware of it, or may have been deliberately making herself not merely agreeable but indispensable to those great ladies whose patronage she was enjoying, and in whose homes she was spending most of her time. She also had so many visitors in her little room at the *Petite Charité* that, according to Tallement, the nuns complained of the 'furious' number of visitors she was receiving, and asked her to leave. Whether for this reason or not Françoise did move—back to the Ursulines with whom she had originally stayed before her marriage.

She did more for her aristocratic women friends, however, than entertain them and their guests. In view of the appalling muddle in which Scarron's affairs were at the time of his death it is rather surprising to find his widow, so soon afterwards, revealing such competence that she was more or less running the households of Mme d'Albret, the Duchesse de Richelieu, and Mme de Montchevreuil. Not only did these ladies trust her and consult her, she became a kind of super-housekeeper to them.

'I used to go constantly,' she reminisced, 'to my good friend Mme de Montchevreuil,' at whose country seat she spent her summers. 'I took care of her household and looked after her accounts and all her housekeeping. One day when I had sold a calf for fifteen or sixteen francs I brought back the money in deniers [small change] because the good people to whom I sold it hadn't any other cash . . . I always had Mme de Montchevreuil's children around me and I would be teaching one of them reading, the catechism to another, and tell them all I knew.' She managed to save up enough from her small income to take them loads of toys as well.

This is the first time that Mme Scarron appears in the role of nursery governess, in this instance unofficially and unpaid, but foreshadowing the career she was shortly to enter.

The great ladies' lordly husbands also noticed that this obliging little woman had an old head on her young shoulders and took to consulting her. According to a remark she made much later she occasionally found this very flattering attitude on their part oppressive and would have preferred them not to have considered her so sensible and practical. 'I would rather,' she said, 'have been laughing with Mlle de Pons and Mlle de Martel,' girls who were not so much younger than herself. And there was more than a shred of truth in this retrospective wistfulness, for Françoise d'Aubigné had never known the lighthearted youthful gaiety enjoyed by these young ladies.

For several years the little widow led this busy and cosy life, with her convent background for security, emerging early in the morning to visit and make herself useful to her grand friends, sometimes staying too late to return in time for vespers, and spending the night with them. She said later that she had regretted it many times, as a duck might miss her pond. It would be too fanciful perhaps to suggest that Françoise was an Ugly Duckling destined to become a swan, yet it was entirely due to the excellent impression she made in these distinguished circles that her whole life was shortly to undergo a tremendous change, one which she herself at first resisted and almost resented.

Queen Marie-Thérèse, wife of Louis XIV, in 1683
Portrait attributed to Beaubrun

Louis XIV, King of France
Engraving by Nanteuil

6 First Glimpse of Glory

As Louis XIV began to grow into manhood, he became exceptionally handsome. He was tall and well built, towering above most of his contemporaries. His brown hair was thick and glossy, worn long in the fashion of the period, and he did not take to wigs until middle age. His eyes were dark and expressive and his features well formed.

The young king's upbringing and education, closely supervised by the Queen Mother and Mazarin, were careful and thorough. He was intelligent and diligent, and from an early age divided his attention between the tasks of war and peace, which he assumed on attaining his majority. Early in life he followed a strict rule of working daily with his ministers. But his chief passion was the command of his armies and his favourite relaxation, when not at war, the chase. He was quite exceptional and, curiously, far more like an Englishman than a Frenchman, in his love of fresh air.

Yet during his adolescence Louis, who in maturity became an impassioned and voluptuous lover, was intimidated by women. Not until he was sixteen years old did he lose his virginity. His seductress—and this no doubt gave him confidence—was a woman of forty, no lady of high degree, but the Queen's seamstress, Catherine Henriette de Beauvais. One evening, when he was returning from his bath, this woman who was by no means beautiful, but still attractive, initiated her young lord and master into the pleasures of sex. Louis, who throughout his life showed his mistresses, and even his wife, great kindness and consideration, gratefully rewarded Mme de Beauvais with a pension and a residence in the then highly fashionable quarter of Paris called the Marais.

During the following years, however, the young King's love affairs were not so simple and straightforward.

At the age of seventeen, Louis had fallen passionately in love with Cardinal Mazarin's Italian niece, Marie Mancini, who was a year younger, and she with him. Their affair was a pure and tender idyll, and had it not been for the difference in their stations, it might have ended in a perfect love match. Mazarin and the Queen Mother had, however, other plans.

A king's marriage was not a love match but one of policy. The small state of Savoy was of considerable strategic importance as a buffer between France and the Spanish possessions in Italy. Mazarin therefore planned a match between Marguerite, daughter of the Duc de Savoie, and his royal master. Louis, the Queen Mother and the Court had travelled to Lyons to meet this princess. But Mazarin's plans suddenly changed when an envoy arrived in France from Philip IV of Spain, Anne's brother, offering his daughter the Infanta Maria Theresa as future queen of France. The importance of this alliance far outweighed the possible advantages of the Savoie match. Those negotiations were therefore broken off, and Mazarin proceeded to haggle with his Spanish opposite number over the future queen of France's dowry, which was to amount to half a million gold *écus*. The marriage contract having been agreed upon, a peace treaty between France and Spain, the Treaty of the Pyrenees, was drawn up in 1659. Although Mazarin professsed no doubts that the Infanta's dowry would be paid, he inserted in this treaty a precautionary clause, stipulating that if

it were not paid, the Infanta would retain her rights to the
Spanish throne and the Netherlands possessions.

Louis was still passionately in love with Marie Mancini, and
she with him. But both knew by then that a match between
them was out of the question, and the young King submitted
without protest to his forthcoming marriage. The Cardinal
sternly banished Marie from Court to the remote little south-
western town of Brouage, opposite the Ile d'Oleron, not far
from Niort, Françoise d'Aubigné's birthplace. As a parting
present Louis gave Marie a small puppy named Friponne.

Mme Scarron was then already a member of Mme d'Albret's
circle, and it may have been through one of those ladies that
Marie Mancini came in contact with this bright little woman,
who might be persuaded to leave her crippled husband for a
time, in order to become a paid companion to the lovelorn
exile. Inquiries were made. Scarron had not met Mlle Mancini,
but was highly flattered that she should choose his wife for this
post. As he regretfully wrote to M. de Villette, however, she was
unable to accept it:

'Mme Scarron is very unhappy that she has neither sufficient
means nor transport available to go where she would like to,
when she is offered such a great pleasure as an invitation to
Brouage by Mlle de Mancini . . . I hope that when the Court
returns to Paris she will be compensated for so great a disappointment and that she will have the honour to be acquainted
with this incomparable Roman lady,' a wish that remained un-
gratified, since the Court had gone to meet the Spanish Infanta
and Marie's banishment was permanent.

On 9 June 1660 Louis XIV, aged twenty-two, was married to
his cousin, the Spanish Infanta Maria Theresa (immortalised by
Velazquez's portrait of her). On 26 August the bridal couple
made their entry into Paris. Ever since his childhood the
Parisian populace had adored their young King, charming,
handsome, and promising the most brilliant reign France was to
know. The marriage to the Spanish princess set the seal on the
Treaty of the Pyrenees, as the result of which France, for the first

time in forty-one years, was at last enjoying peaceful relations with all the other Great Powers.

For this triumphal entry into the city, the Parisians had cheerfully voted the colossal sum of more than ten million *livres*. The procession was due to enter by the rue St Antoine, where a triumphal arch was erected. The Queen Mother, Princess Henrietta, Queen of England, the Princess Palatine (Louis's sister-in-law), Cardinal Mazarin, surrounded by the whole Court, awaited Their Majesties on a specially built stand and balcony there. Quite near to this perfect vantage-point were the windows and the balconies of the mansions of Mme Scarron's protectresses, packed with ladies whose male relatives and lovers were taking part in the magnificent cortège.

Little Mme Scarron was privileged indeed to be invited to one of these windows to see this superb procession. And the thrill it gave her vibrated in every line of the very long letter describing the unforgettable scene she wrote soon afterwards to Mme de Villarceaux in the country, the wife of the Marquess who allegedly was then her lover. This letter was for a long time preserved in the archives of St Cyr. It is remarkable both for its spontaneous liveliness, its striking descriptiveness and for showing its writer in an unusual light—still bubbling over with excitement at this breathtaking spectacle:

> Paris, 27 August 1660.
> . . . I do not think anything so beautiful could ever have been seen, and last night the Queen must have gone to bed well satisfied with the husband of her choice . . . I cannot tell you anything in the right order because I can hardly yet disentangle all I saw yesterday during ten or twelve hours. . . .

After describing the sumptuous pageantry of the immensely rich Cardinal Mazarin's suite, and that of Monsieur, the King's younger brother, much less impressive, Françoise continued

> and then the King's, truly royal . . . you cannot imagine the beauty of the horses, mounted by the pages of the great and small stables, cantering and most beautifully handled. Then followed all the musketeers, with their different plumes; the first were white, the second yellow, black and white, the third

blue, white and black, the fourth green and white. Then came the pages of the chamber, wearing tunics of flaming red velvet, covered all over in gold. . . .

After them appeared the gentlemen of the Household, including certain of the habitués of the rue Neuve . . .

a very large number, all equally magnificent, amongst whom I was looking for my friends: Beuvron was one of the first, with M. de Saint-Luc, who was seeking me, too, but in the wrong place . . . I was looking for M. de Villarceaux, but his horse was so mettlesome that he was only twenty paces from me before I recognised him. He looked very well to me, one of the least magnificent but very elegant, and he had a superb horse, which he rode well; he was well in evidence and people were admiring him as he went by.

If Villarceaux was indeed then her lover Françoise must have been either quite innocent of passion for him or an arch-hypocrite to have written so ingeniously to his wife about him.

The Comte de Guiche walked alone, covered with embroideries and precious stones that flashed admirably in the sun . . . he looked splendid in green and white, which suited him extremely well.

The marshals of France preceded the King, over whom a brocaded canopy was borne . . .

There followed an abrupt break in the letter. In her edition of it Mlle d'Aumale stated that 'a sheet of four pages is missing here and has never been recovered; in it she described the lords, their suites and the King's magnificence' of which the only remaining lines contained the sentence 'with amazing grace and majesty'.

How this sheet came to be missing is unknown. It might simply have become detached from the rest of the letter and lost. Yet the suggestion was made that Mme de Maintenon herself destroyed it in later years. Certain commentators also made rather heavy weather with her opening sentence—'Last night the Queen must have gone to bed well satisfied with the husband of her choice'—as if little Mme Scarron was obliquely comparing herself and her unfortunate marriage with the Spanish Infanta's. Françoise's reaction at the sight of the Sun King was probably typical of that of all the young girls and women who saw their glamorous monarch on his wedding day. The King was no ordinary man; he was the Lord's anointed, the absolute ruler whose word was law, semi-divine and semi-human as was the Emperor of China, the Son of Heaven, to his millions of subjects. For Mme Scarron to have imagined herself in his bride's place would have been a form of presumptuous day dreaming. Such fantastic visions would have been quite out of place in a character so unimaginative and tactful as hers. The first glimpse of Louis was simply a gorgeous spectacle which, in common with thousands of his other humble subjects, she treasured and remembered.

Like his grandfather, Henry IV—the dashing and romantic Henry of Navarre—Louis became a great lover, admired and secretly envied by those Frenchmen who, unlike their absolute monarch, could not raise to the rank of royal mistress—*maîtresse en titre*, a rank only second to the Queen's—any lovely young woman on whom their choice fell. Louis's affairs during the years of his early manhood were the subject of the keenest interest, the liveliest gossip, in France and Europe. From his coronation on 7 June 1654, the King lived almost his whole life in public, his courtiers attending him from the moment of his rising, his *lever*, until the favoured one holding the candlestick at his undressing and bedding, his *coucher*, handed it to his chief and confidential valet, Alexandre Bontemps. The only privacy he was able to enjoy was when, as the result of considerable planning and intrigue, he visited the mistress in current favour. After his reluctant parting from Marie Mancini Louis did not again fall in love seriously until he was a married man. His only brother, Philippe, Duc d'Orléans, 'Monsieur', had been married to the Princess Henrietta-Anne, a Stuart, daughter of Charles I of England and Henrietta Maria of France. But Philippe was homosexual and although consummating his marriage as his station and duty required, preferred to spend his time with his two powerful *mignons* and favourites, the Chevalier de Lorraine and the Marquis d'Effiat. Madame, so conspicuously neglected by her effeminate husband, began to flirt with her brother-in-law. By then the Queen Mother had been obliged to accept the fact that the King was unlikely to remain faithful to his podgy, stupid little Spanish wife, and in order to prevent a possibly incestuous affair between him and his sister-in-law, with Machiavellian prudence she selected three of the prettiest girls at Court to engage his interest. The ruse worked and Louis was soon madly in love again, with Louise de la Vallière, Henrietta's maid-of-honour, extremely pretty, with curly ash-blonde hair and violet eyes. She was country-born and bred, and shy by nature, modest as a violet. Yet after only two weeks' ardent courtship by the King in the gardens of Fontainebleau, riding and hunting in the surrounding forests—Louise was an admirable horsewoman—or during the nightly magnificent masques, balls and fêtes at which Louis danced with incomparable grace, the King seduced Louise at a house lent to him for their rendezvous by one of his courtiers.

Louise was officially lady-in-waiting to Madame and her first quarrel with her royal lover occurred over her mistress. Henrietta was consoling herself for Philippe's indifference by a flirtation with the Comte de Guiche—the nobleman whose splendid appearance in the royal wedding procession had been so much admired by little Mme Scarron. Louis insisted that Louise should tell him the truth about this affair. But with the loyalty that was in her family tradition Louise refused to incriminate Madame. The King left her in anger; in desperation Louise fled during the night to a convent at Chaillot. Next morning whilst immersed in matters of State the King was told that Louise was about to become a nun and instantly dropping everything else he rushed off, mounted his horse, and galloped to the convent where he found her lying on the parlour floor sobbing brokenheartedly. He forgave her and brought her back to Court, for he was still as young and romantic as he was powerful and passionate.

During Anne of Austria's lifetime there was a severe and straitlaced Catholic faction at the Court in spite of the increasing luxury, ostentation and magnificence the King was introducing there. Even Louis was not immune to his mother's disapproval. He was also, and throughout his life remained, a sincere Catholic. Yet it was certainly naïve of Queen Anne to imagine that her son's passion for Louise de la Vallière might be immunised by the Lenten preaching of a rising young prelate called Bossuet, who was then beginning to emerge as the greatest clerical orator in France. The King appreciated the powerful style of Bossuet's denunciatory sermons but nevertheless, since he could not give up his adulterous passion for Louise, that year he omitted to perform his Easter duties.

As was inevitable Louise in due course became pregnant. The Royal mistress was installed in a small house in the Palais Royal, where in the greatest secrecy she gave birth to a son in December 1663. A second boy was born in January 1665, but both these babies died in infancy. Two years later Louise had a daughter, Marie-Anne, who survived and was acknowledged by her father as Mlle de Blois (and also known as Mlle de Bourbon).

Louis's genuine passion for de la Vallière lasted nearly six years, those of his early manhood, when he began to express his regal majesty by staging fêtes of such splendour that they became the talk of Europe. The most famous of these was the great tilting match on the huge space in front of the Tuileries, which ever afterwards was known as the Place Carousel. It was as the result of this gorgeous entertainment that an antiquary designed for the King an emblem that depicted the sun rising over the globe, with the motto *Nec pluribus impar*. Ever afterwards Louis XIV was the Sun King to all his subjects and countrymen.

An even more gorgeous open-air entertainment took place on 5 May 1664 at Versailles, the country seat which the King had not yet transformed into the famous and enormous palace which was to be his principal residence, but which he already favoured. Amidst the most splendid pageantry the King appeared, wrote Voltaire later, 'all the diamonds belonging to the Crown flashing on his costume and the horse he was riding. The Queen and three hundred ladies seated under triumphal arches witnessed his entrance.' But 'as all eyes were fastened on him, the King only sought those of Mademoiselle de la Vallière. The fête had been staged for her alone and she enjoyed it, lost in the crowd.'

It was on this occasion that the first three acts of a new play were performed by the company of the King's favourite actor-playwright, the son of the royal bedmaker, whose professional named was Molière. The play was *Tartuffe*, a virulent satire on religious hypocrisy.

But, Voltaire pointed out, in spite of his splendid amusements the young King was continually working at the tasks of the monarchy. Had he not done so, he 'would only have been able to hold Court, but not to reign. . . . No aspect of internal government was neglected, and abroad his government was also respected, the King of Spain being obliged to give him precedence, the Pope forced to give him satisfaction, Dunkerque added to France by a deal that brought glory to the buyer and shame to the seller; in fact all his policies, since he had taken over the reins, were either noble or useful; after that it was fine to give great entertainments.'

Louis's principal Minister and assistant in statesmanship, with whom he daily spent many hours at his desk, was Jean-Baptiste Colbert, one of the greatest statesmen France has produced. Fouquet, the Finance Minister, had exceeded his brief, swindling the Crown and the State of vast sums. Louis and Colbert laid a trap for him and after Fouquet's fall they administered the country with brilliant success for the next seven years. Like his master, Colbert was also a patron of the arts, sciences, and literature; authors like Molière, Racine and Quinault (the librettist of the opera composer, Lully); musicians, painters and architects were protected and subsidised. No detail seemed too trivial for the King's personal interest. 'To distinguish his principal courtiers,' wrote Voltaire, 'he invented blue tunics embroidered in gold and silver, permission to wear them being a great honour for men imbued by vanity . . .'

Anne of Austria, the Queen Mother, died in agony of cancer in January 1666. Louis had been a loving and dutiful son, but his unfaithfulness to Marie-Thérèse inevitably caused his pious mother great grief. As soon as her obsequies were over, only a week later in fact, de la Vallière, the reigning mistress, at last appeared publicly at Court by the King's command, side by side with the Queen. Contrary to Mme Scarron's impression, the poor little Infanta had small joy of her glamorous husband, although he treated her with punctilious courtesy and when she was in labour, bearing the heir to the throne, compassionately sat by her bedside all night, holding her hand.

Louis was both lecherous and sentimental, with an oddly uxorious side to his nature and a great love of all his children, whether legitimate or not. Considering that there were never less than three hundred girls and women at Court, including the loveliest in the land, avid to step into her shoes, he had been surprisingly faithful to his adoring mistress.

Yet in October 1666 the inevitable happened; the King began to notice a lady-in-waiting to the Queen who was also a friend of de la Vallière. Her name was Françoise de Montespan. It was she who failed to recognize Mme Scarron at the Hôtel d'Albret when that helpful young person had changed into a suitable dress for the wedding of Mlle de Pons, over whom she had been so busy that she was taken for a servant.

Mme de Montespan was also a relative of the d'Albrets, very well born and highly bred. She was one of the three daughters of the Duc and Duchesse de Mortemart.

The Mortemarts invented a kind of family turn of speech that, wrote Voltaire, was a blend of joking, naïveté and subtlety. In the same spirit Mme de Montespan, who had been baptised Françoise, considering the name too common, chose for herself the fancifully classical one of Athénaïs.

Athénaïs, who was in attendance on the Queen, gossiping in Mme d'Albret's drawing-room about the reigning mistress, told the other ladies with completely candid air that 'if I had the misfortune of being the King's mistress I would never have the insolence to appear in the presence of the Queen', knowing perfectly well that it was by the King's command that poor Louise, the violet who so much preferred to remain in the shadow of his glory, was obliged to show herself on such occasions.

Louise's beauty was beginning to fade; she had never been a witty talker, but had enchanted the young King by her simplicity and sincerity. As Louis grew into his early thirties, however, more and more successful in war abroad and administration at home, he needed a more powerful emotional stimulant.

Montespan, wrote Saint-Simon after her death, was 'mean, capricious, very moody. Her wit spared nobody, not even the King.' But it was precisely this high-spirited persiflage that he found irresistibly amusing, even—at first—when it was directed at himself. 'The courtiers avoided passing under her windows, especially when the King was with her. They said it was running the gauntlet, and this expression became proverbial at Court.'

As usual when Louis was beginning a new affair it had to be wrapped in conspiracy and intrigue to avoid public scandal as long as possible. For that reason poor Louise was retained, to throw the wool over the courtiers' eyes. When she begged the King to be allowed to retire to a convent he refused to permit it. After Mme de Montespan succeeded her, the Queen, wrote Saint-Simon, 'could hardly bear her haughtiness, which was very different from the consideration and respect of the Duchesse de la Vallière, whom she always liked, whilst she often said of the other one—"That whore will be the death of me"'.

Louis had bestowed the rank of Duchess on the woman he no longer loved and who took it, not as a mark of favour, but of dismissal. Mme de Montespan's triumph was complete when the King set out on his Flanders campaign against the Spaniards in 1667. War had again flared up between France and Spain. Mazarin's suspicion that the Queen's dowry would not be paid appeared to be confirmed. So, basing his claim on the marriage contract which stipulated that in such an event the Infanta would retain her rights to certain Spanish possessions in the Netherlands, Louis began what came to be known as 'The Queen's War'. In addition to certain parts of the Netherlands, he annexed the Franche Comté. This was a small but important strategic Spanish stronghold, bordering on Eastern France, Switzerland, Savoy and Germany.

This annexation was celebrated by a great banquet at Versailles. Among the three hundred ladies privileged to watch the King dining there on that occasion was Mme Scarron. She had been taken along by one of her aristocratic patronesses, the Duchesse de Richelieu. This appears to have been her second glimpse of the Sun King, who, however, was at that moment supremely unaware of her presence.

His departure for his Netherlands campaign was incomparably described by Voltaire.

> The ruin of the Dutch was planned during this voyage, in the midst of entertainments. It was a continuous fête in a setting of the utmost splendour.
>
> The King, who until then had made all his military expeditions on horseback, this time travelled for the first time in a coach with glass windows; post-chaises had not yet been invented. The Queen, Madame his sister-in-law, and the Marquise de Montespan were in this superb vehicle, followed by many others, and when Mme de Montespan travelled alone four lifeguardsmen were stationed at the doors of her coach. The Dauphin and his Court followed, Mademoiselle— the King's cousin—with hers . . . The most beautiful furniture was taken from the Court to the towns where the parties spent the night; in each one there was a masked ball or fireworks. The entire military establishment accompanied the King, the whole household organisation preceded or followed him and the tables were spread as at St Germain. In this magnificence the Court visited all the conquered cities . . . The cost in gratuities alone was several times more than fifteen hundred golden louis daily . . .

All these honours, all this homage, were for Madame de Montespan, excepting those that duty compelled to be paid to the Queen. But Voltaire was almost certainly wrong when he stated that this lady was not in the secret.

It was at Avesnes, where Mme de Montespan was being allegedly chaperoned by Mme de Montausier, the Queen's principal lady-in-waiting, that she surrendered. For although she had long before determined to suffer the misfortune of becoming the Royal mistress, Athénaïs played her hand most cleverly, in no hurry, since she knew she had plenty of time. Perhaps, also, she was secretly more afraid than she admitted of her jealous and fiery Gascon husband, who created so much scandal at being cuckolded by His Majesty that he had finally to be banished to his estates. Nor, surprisingly, did Louise de la Vallière accept the situation with her usual humility and resignation. In one final upsurge of uncontrollable emotion, not having been invited to join the royal expedition, she nevertheless set out in her own coach from St Germain, and when on the heights above Avesnes she saw the King's encampment, losing all self-control, in spite of the outrage to etiquette this involved, ordered her coachman to drive helter-skelter across the fields to join it. She was shattered, but could hardly have been surprised by her reception.

'Madame,' the King coldly replied, 'I do not like having my hand forced.'

Yet he still would not allow Louise to retire from Court, counselling her to continue her role as mistress-in-chief to mask his new love-affair from the world. Glamorous, beautiful, and intelligent as she was, it is impossible not to use a modern vulgarism to describe Mme de Montespan; bitch is the only appropriate term. Louise's suffering was almost unbearable when the woman whom she knew had supplanted her showed her in public every sign of the greatest friendship and affection, which she, for fear of irritating the King still further, was obliged outwardly to reciprocate. It was not until seven years later, in 1674, that her former lover finally permitted her to follow the vocation she increasingly felt, and retire to a convent. This was the second occasion on which Louise de la Vallière asserted herself both touchingly and dramatically. Throwing herself at the feet of the Queen—the helpless witness of the King's infidelities, and as unhappy as the departing mistress whom she had always liked—Louise begged her forgiveness. Finally she was obliged to attend a farewell dinner with her former lover and her triumphant successor. Next day she at last left Court, accompanied by the two surviving children she had borne

Louis, to whom she said good-bye for ever before entering the strict Carmelite convent in the rue de l'Enfer, where she lived for more than thirty years as Sister Louise de la Miséricorde.

If as was stated, Louis's eyes filled with tears when he and la Vallière parted, his consolation was sufficiently close at hand to dry them up. But new problems were arising. Mme de Montespan, like her predecessor, inevitably became pregnant.

7 *The Mysterious House at Vaugirard*

When the Queen Mother died Mme Scarron's modest pension ceased, but her influential friends induced the King to renew it. Yet her future was still insecure. She was offered the post of lady-in-waiting to the young French Queen of Portugal, but although there seemed to be no better alternative prospects at the time, on consideration she declined it. Her girlhood and young womanhood were behind her; she was in her early thirties, an age at which in those days a widow in her circumstances could hardly count on a suitable marriage or any other permanent and respectable form of security. Yet Françoise was perfectly contented, apparently, busy as ever, constantly in and out of my lady's chamber, in and out of the grand houses where she was so welcome. No, she decided, her life in Paris suited her excellently and she was not prepared to give it up.

In 1667, she spent three months visiting her relatives in the south-west. Her beloved aunt, Mme de Villette, and her uncle, had died, but Françoise was still in close touch with her cousins. Nor, with her usual loyalty to those who had been kind to her during her unhappy youth, did she forget to pay a call on her dear Mother Céleste, the nun who had befriended her in the convent at Niort.

Philippe de Villette married in 1662 and had three children, two sons and a daughter. But his daughter—later to be Mme de Caylus—of whom Mme de Maintenon was to take charge in rather peculiar circumstances, had not yet been born. The family were still living at Mursay, where Philippe, who was then thirty-five, able and intelligent, was fretting at wasting his life in provincial inactivity. But although Mme Scarron loved him like a brother and did her best to help him, she had little success. A letter to him, written in 1668, showed how, in spite of her affection she was invariably capable of taking a cool, critical look at any situation; nor did she hesitate to state her views to him, though as kindly as she could:

'I would like you to be employed, and I do understand that with all your intelligence it must be cruel to be ineffective and to spend your life in the provinces, but being forgotten as you are, and having no patron at Court, I doubt whether you will find any employment. Peace is expected this summer, but even if this does not happen, people ruin themselves in the service, which is not a career for a married man. If you were not one, I would advise you to sell Mursay and to take a chance to make your fortune. But you are no longer in a position to take such decisions and I think the best advice I can give you is to go on living quietly at home.'

And referring to one of their second cousins and his wife, the Fontemorts, of whose intrigues at the time she disapproved, 'it is a dirty business, and I shall tell them my opinion of it quite frankly.'[1]

Yet, perhaps on account of her d'Aubigné charm, Mme Scarron's frankness did not make her enemies, and her sound common sense won her increasing respect.

In her unwelcome pregnancy, Mme de Montespan remembered this sensible, reliable, tactful and obliging little woman, who was five years older than herself. From their first meetings at the Hôtel d'Albret they had got on extremely well together. No other woman in that circle of elegant and precious ladies had so intelligently and quickly appreciated the Mortemart wit, the gay irony, the sly jokes and half-hints with which Athénaïs enlivened it. Mme Scarron herself could also be amusing and witty, but above all she was unusually discreet.

It was even more essential for Mme de Montespan than it had been for Louise de la Vallière to conceal her pregnancy from the world. Louise had been retained at Court as an alibi for her affair with the King, but even so Athénaïs's jealous husband had made matters extremely awkward and if she had a bastard child born in wedlock—since there was never any question of a divorce—his reaction was unpredictable, but might certainly be dangerous. Louise's babies had been secretly taken away from her house in the Palais Royal by Mme Colbert, the Minister's wife, and put out to nurse. A similar procedure had to be found for those of her successor, even more urgently and secretly.

When Mme de Montespan chose Mme Scarron for this service, she approached her not directly but through Mme d'Heudicourt, that Bonne de Pons whom Mme Scarron had so devotedly attended before her wedding, and who remained one of her intimate friends.

According to Mlle d'Aumale—'Mme de Maintenon told me so herself'—

she refused, saying that she would not bring up the children of Mme de Montespan; if they were the King's, however, and it was his wish, he himself would have to ask her to do so. This the King did, and she then agreed to take charge of them, which she would never have done otherwise. I put this on record because many people condemned her for it. But it seems to me that she could take on this duty, without by doing so approve of the King's passion for Mme de Montespan.[2]

This paragraph in Mlle d'Aumale's recollections of her mistress is crucial. When in later life Mme de Maintenon told her secretary of this incident, either she was distorting the facts or Mlle d'Aumale did. Yet the same version is given in the account of Mme de Maintenon's life by Mme de Caylus,

Philippe de Villette's daughter, her cousin, but who passed as
her niece, and whom she had living with her at Court for many
years:

'Mme de Maintenon said that she would not take charge of
Mme de Montespan's children; but that if the King ordered her
to take care of his, she would obey. This the King requested of
her, and she took them to live with her.'[3]

The elderly Mme de Maintenon clearly forgot, whether
accidentally or deliberately, the original request made to little
Mme Scarron. For in 1668 or 1669 there was no question of her
raising the King's and Mme de Montespan's family. All she
was asked to do was secretly to take away from Mme de
Montespan a new-born infant, place it with a suitable wet-
nurse, and keep an eye on it. In those days of high infant
mortality such a baby might quite easily die soon after birth;
that particular little girl did so at the age of three. There might
not have been others. So the request made of Mme Scarron
would not at first seem to have meant anything more than taking
away this child, had it lived.

In order to ensure the least possible scandal the story was
spread at Court that Mme de Montespan's lover was the Duc de
Lauzun, one of the King's most trusted friends at that time. It
would have been natural for Mme Scarron to feel no inclination
to bring up a child that was the offspring of Mme de Montespan's
adultery with him. It was, however, extremely unlikely that
either she or Mme d'Heudicourt believed this transparent alibi
to be true, and this was endorsed by Françoise's alleged condition that the King himself must order her to take on the task
before she would do so. Even her confessor whom she no doubt
consulted on this tricky problem would not have dissuaded her
from accepting it. Yet at that stage neither Françoise nor anyone
else could have foreseen that, as Mlle d'Aumale added, 'this
employment was the beginning of her good fortune, as well as
her troubles and worries'.

During the next eight years, Athénaïs had six more children
by Louis. When Mme de Montespan was about to begin labour,
wrote Mlle d'Aumale,

Mme Scarron would be fetched. She carried away the infant wrapped in her cloak, she herself wearing a mask [as wellborn ladies generally did when travelling from home] took a fiacre and returned to Paris, not without being in great fear that the secret the King had asked her to keep would be discovered . . . She herself has spoken of the very great troubles this charge gave her, her ceaseless attentions and vigils, sometimes getting up fourteen or fifteen times in a night, minding the children in order that one of the wet-nurses might sleep, and all the time she was hiding them, in order that they should not be discovered, she was seeing her friends as usual, going from one to another during the night and arriving in the morning as if she had slept well, in order that they should suspect nothing. All this caused her a great deal of worry, especially as she was naturally shy, blushing very easily, and as people were beginning to suspect what was going on, as soon as a word was said seeming to lead up to the subject, she would become scarlet. In order to overcome this tendency to blushing she had herself bled, but it made little difference.[4]

At first, however, the babies were not living with her, but with wet-nurses in different places in the vicinity of Paris.

One can imagine the starry-eyed circle of the young ladies of St Cyr, the famous girls' school she founded many years later, when their revered patroness told them how

this rather strange honour [of bringing up the royal bastards] gave me infinite trouble and cares. I would climb ladders to do the upholsterers' work, because they could not be admitted to the house [so she herself had to hang the curtains or take them down]. The wet-nurses would not lift a finger for fear of tiring themselves and spoiling their milk. I would often go from one to another, on foot, in disguise, carrying clean linen or meat under my arm and sometimes, if one of the children was ill I would spend the night there, in a little house outside Paris. In the morning I would return home by the back door and after dressing enter a coach at the front door, to drive to the Hôtel d'Albret or de Richelieu, in order that my social circle should not suspect that I had a secret to keep.[5]

Her friends did notice, however, that under the strain Françoise was growing pale and losing weight.

The baby girl first entrusted to her, whose name by some

historical freak is unknown, soon had a little brother, Louis Auguste, Duc du Maine, who was born on 31 March 1670. This time the secrecy was even more stringent. The infant was taken from Mme de Montespan's room before there was even time to swaddle him, and given to M. de Lauzun, since it was thought too risky to have Mme Scarron come and fetch him there. The Duke hurried with his charge to the gates of St Germain, where he handed the baby over to Mme Scarron, who was waiting in a cab.

The gossip might possibly have been diverted or damped down. Unfortunately, a year later Mme d'Heudicourt had the appalling indiscretion to betray the secret of the royal bastards to her lover, the Marquis de Béthune.

The King, quite naturally infuriated at this betrayal, banished Mme d'Heudicourt forthwith, the greatest imaginable disgrace.

'Mme d'Heudicourt', Mme de Sévigné wrote, 'has left in indescribable despair, having lost all her women friends and convicted of every betrayal in the world, everything that Mme Scarron had been protecting . . .'[6]

And in a letter to M. de Villette at Easter, Françoise wrote, 'I was very much upset at having been obliged to break with Mme d'Heudicourt, but I could no longer continue to see her without doing a great deal of harm to my reputation and career.'[7]

Before this malicious indiscretion, however, Mme d'Heudicourt had handed over her own small daughter to Mme Scarron to live with her in the little house she then had in the rue des Tournelles, in order to provide an excuse, should callers chance to notice the nurses and maids.

A year later when Mme de Montespan gave birth to another baby boy, who was in due course to become the Comte de Vexin, it had become impossible for Mme Scarron to keep rushing every night to the various hide-outs where the royal babies were installed with their wet-nurses. So a large house with a garden was bought for her in the village of Vaugirard hidden away behind high walls. As Paris gradually spread out, this house became 25, boulevard Montparnasse. None of Mme

Scarron's friends were ever admitted to it. Mme de Sévigné's letters give us a glimpse of Francoise's life at that time. On 26 December 1672:

> We dine together every night, Mme Scarron and I. She has an amiable and marvellously clear mind; it is a pleasure to listen to her discussing the horrible upheavals of a certain country she knows well, and the despair of that d'Heudicourt, at the time when she seemed so miraculously well-placed; the constant rages of little Lauzun; the black misery or sad boredom of the ladies of St Germain, from which even the most envied is not always exempt.[8]

A year later, on 20 March, Mme de Coulanges, another member of their circle, wrote to Mme de Sévigné:

> At last we have found Mme Scarron again, that is, we know where she is, because to see her is not easy. I am sure you will think that a pension of two thousand *écus* is not much, which I agree, but it was done in a way that leaves hope for more favours to follow. The King was looking through the list of pensions; he saw two thousand francs for Mme Scarron, crossed it out, and inserted instead two thousand *écus*.[9]

On 4 December 1673 Mme de Sévigné wrote to her daughter:

> Yesterday we dined again with Mme Scarron and the Abbé Têtu at Mme de Coulanges . . . We thought it would be pleasant to take her home at midnight, right at the end of the Faubourg St Germain, much beyond Mme de la Fayette's, almost at Vaugirard, in the country; a splendid large house, which one does not enter. There is a big garden, fine and large rooms. She has a coach, servants and horses; she dresses modestly yet magnificently, like a woman who spends her life with persons of quality. She is amiable, beautiful, kind and informal.[10]

Françoise had taken on this heavy responsibility from a sense of duty and service to His Majesty. But in it she found her true vocation. She never had a child of her own, nor, apparently, did she long for one. 'To preserve one's honour,' she once said, 'the first thing one has to give up is pleasure.' This she had done. But now she lavished on those half-royal children all her pent-up maternal love. She adored the little Duc du Maine and throughout their lives he loved her as wholeheartedly, never showing any affection for his mother. Nor could he be blamed if another anecdote of this period is true.

One day the nursery chimney began to smoke. In such a crisis, when a woman of lesser fibre might have lost her head, Mme Scarron's chief anxiety was that if the wooden rafters caught alight, the secret she was so carefully guarding might be revealed to the men whom she might have to call in to put out the fire. Whilst she quietly set about dealing with the emergency she thought it wise, nevertheless, to send a messenger to Saint-Germain, to ask Mme de Montespan what she had best do in that case? The reply she received was—'I'm very glad to hear it; tell Mme Scarron that it's a sign of good luck for the children.'

No English nanny could have shown greater devotion than Françoise, whose theories on bringing up children were well in advance of her time. Nor did her interest in infant welfare ever die. When she was seventy-two she wrote, 'if I were not so old I would have liked to try bringing up children as they do in England, where they are all tall and well built, and as we have seen them brought up at St Germain'. This was a reference to the exiled court of King James II of England, at whose disposal Louis had generously placed this palace. 'When they are two or three months old,' continued Mme de Maintenon, 'they are no longer tightly swaddled, but under their dress they wear a wrapper and a loose nappy, which are changed as soon as they are soiled, so that the infants never remain, as ours do, tightly swaddled in their own mess. In consequence they never cry, are upset, suffer from sores or even have their little limbs deformed . . .'[11] Regular hours and plain wholesome food were her basic principle.

After the baby girl who died, came the Duc du Maine in 1670. The next was another boy, the Comte de Vexin, born in 1672, who died when he was eleven years old. There followed three daughters, Louise-Françoise, Mlle de Nantes, born a year later; Louise-Marie, who died when she was five; and in 1677 Françoise-Marie, Mlle de Blois. The last child was Louis-Alexandre, Comte de Toulouse, born in 1678. As they grew older Mme Scarron became the family's governess, teaching them their letters and catechism, as she had once taught them to the children of Mme de Montchevreuil.

We are not told if or when Mme de Montespan visited Vaugirard, but the King did so several times. Louis was as paternalistic as he was promiscuous; in this he took after his grandfather, Henry of Navarre. Both of them dearly loved their bastard children and would gladly have made them their heirs. With the exception of the Dauphin, all the Queen's babies died young. Louis's only legitimate son was as dutiful as any monarch could wish; he was also dull and lethargic, lacking his father's brilliance in every way, whilst the Duc du Maine inherited his charm and intelligence.

Mme de Montespan did keep in close touch with Mme Scarron and was constantly urging the King to do something to reward the little woman for her devotion. Louis is said once to have remarked rather irritably: 'Am I never going to hear the end of Mme Scarron?' and not until four years after she had entered his service so secretly did he increase her small pension. No doubt it was with a twinkle in her eye that much later Mme de Maintenon recalled that the first impression she made on His Majesty was far from favourable. 'He did not like me at all to begin with,' she said. 'He considered me a *précieuse* who was only interested in perfection, and who was very difficult in every way.' Françoise certainly was, in her quiet way, a perfectionist, and tenacious as well. For years she had been a *précieuse*, and the conversational subjects and manners of those ladies no doubt seemed pretentious and affected to the point of boredom to Molière's royal protector. Louis even told Mme de Montespan that he did not like her '*bel esprit*', a view that the reigning mistress could not have found altogether displeasing. But how long did he continue to hold it?

Louis's visits to Vaugirard were quite unofficial; he would drop in to see the children when he had a little time to spare and it suited him. And on one occasion when he did so, apparently, he found Mme Scarron holding one of them—probably the eldest, the little girl who died when she was three—by the hand, with the second, the Duc du Maine, in her arms, and the baby, the little Comte de Vexin, asleep in her lap. Mme Scarron, who still looked remarkably young and pretty, might easily have been the mother of this little family.

Louis, who was as sentimental as he could be ruthless, was delightfully moved by this charming picture. For, whether or not Mme Scarron was a pretentious highbrow, it was clear that she was a woman with all the requisite feminine instincts, who really adored her small charges. 'She knows how to love,' the King was said to have remarked afterwards, 'and it would be pleasant to be loved by her.'[12] But what were Françoise's own secret feelings about her master, to whom she owed everything, the considerable luxury in which, as Mme de Sévigné wrote, she was then living 'like a woman who spends her life with persons of quality'?

In March 1672 Louis XIV began his major attack on the Netherlands. The King joined his army on 27 April, setting out almost unaccompanied, and not immediately for the front. For he first drove in great secrecy to the Château de Genitoy, at Nanteuil, to rejoin Mme de Montespan, who was again pregnant. Mme Scarron and the two older babies were with her, and it was there that on 20 June the third child was born.

The Minister, Louvois, was in the King's confidence, and it[13] was through him that Françoise had obtained a commission in the Army for Charles d'Aubigné, that wastrel brother of hers, of whom she remained so fond. After the conquest of Holland he was given the governorship of Amersfort, a small stronghold near Utrecht. On her return to Paris in September, Françoise was writing to him as affectionately as usual, but acutely aware of his shortcomings, pleading with him—'in God's name, my very dear brother, do everything to earn the King's esteem . . .' and 'I am very glad that you seem pleased at what the King has done for you; I do not consider the governorship of Amersfort as a very permanent post, but it is the means to another; do your best, therefore, in the service of a man who deserves it, and by whom I believe you are even more charmed than I am, because you have seen more closely what he has done in this campaign. It must be a pleasure to serve a hero, and a hero to whom we are so close.'[14]

'A hero'—that was how Louis then appeared to her. But as a man? The alleged letters of Mme de Maintenon later published by La Beaumelle in due course proved to be forgeries. Yet they were so cleverly put together by quoting and adding to certain phrases that she had written that they occasionally contain grains of truth. This was particularly the case regarding the notorious letter which she was supposed to have written to either Mme de Coulanges or another friend, Mme de Saint-Geran, at the beginning of 1673, when she had returned with the three little children to Vaugirard.

By 1673 it was known that certain very privileged persons were admitted to the house at Vaugirard. Nobody would have dared mention His Majesty's name, but if he visited any woman at all, gossip immediately assumed that she was his mistress. The story was spread around that the reason Mme Scarron was living in this remote retreat was the fact that she was pregnant by the King. La Beaumelle's letter suggested how Françoise might have been dealing with such rumours. It very artfully simulated the wit and ironic gaiety with which a *précieuse* would have done so:

> Tell me everything people are saying, everything you think. What a pleasure to be incarcerated for the reason you give! Is it possible that Mme de Lafayette does not credit it, and finds it difficult to believe that I have supplanted my friend? . . . I am very well, shut up in a very lovely house, a very large garden, only seeing those who wait on me, ecstatic, enchanted by my latest adventure. Every evening I see your fat cousin [Louvois] who tells me something about his master and then leaves, for I would not want to talk to him for very long. That master sometimes comes to see me, in spite of myself, and leaves in despair, but without having been rejected. You can well imagine that when he goes home there is someone for him to talk to. As for me, I remain tranquil because I know I am doing the right thing. That, Madame, is a brief outline of my life; I wanted to give it to you, but please let it go no further.[15]

The lightheartedness, the underlying sense of triumph in this letter, in which almost every sentence has a double meaning, are clues to the enigmatic personality of Françoise Scarron which merit careful consideration. For even if it was a forgery it was based on incontrovertible facts; the fact that the King was visiting Vaugirard and that his previous dislike of Mme Scarron appeared to have changed into something much more similar to affection.

To say that at that period Louis was in love with Françoise would be entirely incorrect. He was and remained for several years longer in love with Mme de Montespan. He was also inconstant and frequently unfaithful to her, for he was as highly sexed as the barnyard fowl that became the emblem of his country, but none of these passing affairs had any lasting significance.

Madame de Montespan was brilliant as a diamond, certainly as hard. As their affair developed she became prouder and more capricious; and her extravagances cost the Royal Treasury millions. Mme de Caylus wrote:

In spite of the King's infidelities, I have often heard it said that Mme de Montespan would have kept her hold on him if she had been less temperamental and if she had counted rather less on the ascendancy she thought she had over him . . . For in Mme de Maintenon he found a woman who was always modest, always mistress of herself, always reasonable, and who in addition to such rare qualities was also witty and a good conversationalist.[16]

Taking La Beaumelle's letter line by line, it is not difficult to disentangle the blend of certain phrases which were entirely in Mme Scarron's character and the titillating inventions added to them by this literary forger.

The rumour that she was pregnant by Louis obviously appealed to Françoise's sense of humour, and the phrase in which she referred to it was clearly ironical.

'What a pleasure to be incarcerated for the reason you give! Is it possible that Mme de Lafayette does not credit it, and finds it difficult to believe that I have supplanted my friend?'

As Mme Scarron, who had spent so many years amongst them knew perfectly well, the explanation that Louis was merely visiting his children at Vaugirard, was much too simple for the scandalmongers of the day. And in this sentence she was making fun of the absurd rumours they were spreading. The last sentence in the letter which may also be taken as genuine fully bears this out: 'as for me, I am tranquil because I know I am doing the right thing.' But so innocuous an explanation did not satisfy La Beaumelle. And so he added in between these two sentences a paragraph on which the whole legend that Françoise was at that time Louis's mistress, was based.

'Every evening I see your fat cousin [Louvois] who talks to me about his master . . . That master sometimes comes to see me, in spite of myself, and leaves in despair, but without having been rejected.'

The allusions in this famous letter dealt with two separate points. The first was the rumour of Françoise's pregnancy by Louis, which was sheer nonsense. The second reference was to the attentions the King was then apparently paying her, when he visited Vaugirard. As Françoise herself said, her conscience at that time was clear. Yet indubitably Louis's attitude towards her at that period did begin to change from antipathy to sympathy, admiration, and perhaps a little more. The only known evidence of this change was his apparent remark, when seeing the affection she was lavishing on his children, that 'it would be pleasant to be loved by her'. Yet, as she had written to her brother, to her His Majesty was a hero, and to receive even the slightest signs of his benevolence would have been sufficiently flattering. Had the King at that stage made serious advances to her, she would have been placed in a situation that she would not have referred to in such light-hearted terms. Had he, however, merely been testing how far he could win more than her loyalty and devotion by so playful verbal or physical an advance, she would have had no difficulty in coping with him. She had learned early in life and in a hard school kindly but firmly to turn down her more pressing suitors who came to the Scarron household. The method was peculiarly her own, making her lifelong friends and no enemies. A little coquetry, flirtatiousness, 'perhaps one day' sent them away, possibly as La Beaumelle put it, in despair, but without having been completely rejected. It seemed a sexual technique that would have worked particularly well on a man of Louis's temperament, and there is no reason to suppose that if at that time he did make any definite advances to Françoise, she might not have used it as successfully as in the past.

Whether this account of Françoise's and Louis's relationship at this stage was truth or legend, one certainty remains. They shared an indissoluble bond which was to endure throughout their lives, their deep affection for and devotion to the children.

8 Governess at Court

Whilst the Sun King continued to visit the little family at Vaugirard, he decided that it would be pleasant to have the children at St Germain. Louis was becoming more and more attached to the three-year-old Duc du Maine and, apparently, sufficiently interested in his devoted governess to arouse the first stirrings of jealousy in Mme de Montespan. As yet these were only very faint, for it must have seemed almost incredible to the gorgeous, spoilt reigning mistress, who barely paid lip-service to the insignificant Queen by whom she was ostensibly employed as lady-in-waiting, that His Majesty could so much as look at their children's governess. How, when he was admittedly still so much in love with herself, acknowledged the most beautiful woman at his Court and therefore in all Europe, would he have spared even a glance for Mme Scarron, a widow in her late thirties, quite well preserved for her age, but employed strictly for her usefulness, her acknowledged devotion to their children? And yet the Mortemart eyes, which were not only very beautiful but as sharp as the Mortemart tongue, did notice the seemingly incredible. His Majesty appeared to take pleasure in the company and conversation of the woman whom he had once disdainfully called to her 'your precious friend'.

For the time being, however, Mme Scarron was much too useful to be discarded, and when bringing their children to visit them she behaved with her usual rather shy decorum, showing the expected friendly deference to her friend and patroness, their mother, and punctilious respect to His Majesty, their father, who occasionally deigned to notice her and speak a few friendly words to her.

Athénaïs de Montespan was again pregnant in May 1673 when the King left to visit his armies during the siege of Maestricht. As usual, this military activity was also a social one. His Majesty was accompanied by the Queen and poor Louise de la Vallière, still being used as a shield for his later affairs although by then the secret of the house at Vaugirard was mere fiction. Everyone knew that Mme de Montespan had three bastards by the King—the eldest of whom had died the previous year—and that she was again pregnant. Yet it would never have done for the King to take her with him whilst leaving the Queen and de la Vallière at St Germain. Louis's cousin, Marie-Louise d'Orléans, known as 'La Grande Mademoiselle', wrote that 'she did not see the Queen until two days before they left'—when the favourite's condition must have been pretty obvious. The Duchesse de la Vallière was staying with the Queen in her usual apartment. 'The Queen suffered a great deal from the vapours at Tournay.'[1] And certainly her sufferings were not lessened by the fact that Mme de Montespan was lodged at the King's command, not with those ladies but in the citadel, where she was accompanied and attended by the faithful Mme Scarron when on 1 June she gave birth to her fourth child, a baby girl, and who was to be called Mlle de Nantes.

It was from there that on 16 June Françoise wrote to her brother, d'Aubigné. He had been deprived of his command at Amersfort, and was as usual pestering her to have him appointed to another post. She reassured him on that score:

You may be sure that I shall not forget you, whatever happens, and I have good news for you. M. de Louvois is doing marvellously at every opportunity, and we are greatly indebted to him. I admit that I shall be delighted to meet you in Paris. But do not expect an account of my journey here; the citadel of Tournay is too boring for me to make a good story of it, but I shall have other things to tell you that will please you as much. I am very well indeed; very contented, and with good reason . . .[2]

This letter reveals a tone of unusual self-confidence and contentment. Françoise was not normally given to light optimism. But by then she knew herself to be in a particularly good position to help her brother and other relatives and friends, all of whom did not fail to take advantage of it. The King had shown his gratitude and indebtedness to her when he had so greatly increased her emoluments. Her requests to him were made either through Mme de Montespan, to whom she was so indispensable, or through Louvois, the minister whom she had known for some years and who was one of the few who had the entrée to the house at Vaugirard, where he frequently visited her and no doubt dealt with her household accounts.

After her confinement Mme de Montespan returned to Paris with Mme Scarron and the babies, who were once again installed at Vaugirard. From there Françoise wrote on 9 October to her cousin, M. de Villette, whose interests she was also furthering, although with little success. As he was a Huguenot, in spite of his ability, his chances of advancement were not very bright. On the 31st she wrote to her brother, of whose conduct at Amersfort Louvois had complained to her. Thanks to Françoise's influence, however, he was promised a post in Alsace:

'I shall see you when you change places, and I am looking forward to it with great pleasure, although it is somewhat clouded by hearing that you have not given complete satisfaction, and think more of your own interests than of pleasing the King . . .'[3] She begged him, neither for the first nor the last time, to amend his conduct. Françoise's letters to Charles were partly those of a loving sister to a dear brother, partly of a governess admonishing a naughty child. But she was more to be admired for her loyalty to him than blamed for her restrained but justified disapproval of his behaviour.

By then Mme Scarron's influence at Court was so well known

and established that Bussy-Rabutin, who had fallen out of the King's favour, did not hesitate to write a letter to her friend, Mme de Sévigné, which was deliberately meant to be shown her. Nor was there any insincerity in his reference to her generosity, honesty and virtue, which would be unspoilt by the corruption at Court. Mme de Sévigné replied that Mme Scarron had received his request very kindly and that if ever she had an opportunity to do him a favour she would gladly take it.[4]

Such occasions for using her influence were now on the point of becoming far more frequent.

Louis returned in triumph from his war against the Dutch. He was idolised by his people; he had a firm grip on external and internal affairs; his ministers were capable and devoted to him. Only the Church frowned on his open liaison with Mme de Montespan, which by then had lasted for more than five years and appeared to be as stable as ever. But at that moment the Sun King felt himself powerful enough to override such ecclesiastical grumblings. Apart from the Dauphin, his heir, none of his legitimate children survived. He was therefore determined to legitimise the two sons and the baby daughter his mistress had borne him. This important event took place on 20 December 1673.

'The King,' wrote la Grande Mademoiselle, 'declared himself the father of three children born out of wedlock; two boys, one of whom is called the Duc du Maine, the other, the Comte de Vexin, and a girl, Mademoiselle de Nantes. In their legitimisation their mother's name was not stated.'[5]

At last Mme de Coulanges and Mme de Sévigné had the satisfaction of visiting their friend in her hitherto mysterious grand house at Vaugirard, although by 1 January 1674 they had still not been allowed to meet the children.

For Françoise, the year 1674 was a crucial one. Since he had officially recognised the existence of his bastards, Louis wished to have them permanently under his own roof.

The house at Vaugirard was closed down, and the family moved into St Germain. There was never any question in their parents' minds that their governess should not reside there with them. But for Françoise there were two points at issue. The least important was her dislike of the Court and everything concerning it, from the strict protocol and ritual that dominated everyday life, to the extravagance and luxury, the dissipation and gambling, the constant spiteful intrigues and calumnies that made up its daily chronicle. She had not, after all, been brought up to Court life; in her wildest dreams she would never have aspired to play a leading role in it. She had entered St Germain by the back-door, in a highly secret and humble role, a role of which her employer, Mme de Montespan, was soon sharply and constantly to remind her. From that year onwards her correspondence and reminiscences, whether from St Germain or Versailles, contained an endless string of complaints, moanings and groanings about the intolerable conditions she was obliged to endure.

Yet there was a still more important reason against her remaining in her post. Religion as such did not mean a great deal to her. Françoise Scarron had never had a religious vocation; passion of any kind, even mystical communion with God and the saints, was ruled out by her fundamentally rational nature, in which there was more than a streak of her implacable Huguenot grandfather d'Aubigné's hardheadedness. She worshipped God in the most conventional manner; in fact to Françoise God was the divine incarnation of human propriety. If adultery had been prescribed and not proscribed in the Ten Commandments she might well have approved of it. But it was not; it was a major sin against religion and the God of convention. She had no need to concern herself directly with the Deity, however. For the purpose of interceding with Him on behalf of His weak human flock God had provided an infallible instrument, His Church. Françoise therefore practised the simple and satisfying rule of laying all responsibility for her own behaviour on her confessor. It was a neat solution. For if she did wrong, he and not she would be to blame; if his instructions went against her own inclinations she would find some means of reconciling the two.

D

From that year onwards she kept up a detailed correspondence with her confessor, the Abbé Gobelin. Its main theme throughout was the question, should she or should she not remain at Court? For from the Church's point of view her position was an invidious one; by bringing up the King's bastards, although they were now legitimised, she was condoning or appearing to condone his adultery. Her first letter to the Abbé sets the pattern of all later ones:

> . . . I do not know how long I shall be here, but since you have wished it I am resolved to let myself be led like a child, to try to become completely indifferent to all the places and ways of living to which I am destined, to detach myself from everything that might disturb my peace of mind, and to seek God in all I do . . . You will bear in mind, please, that it was you who wished me to remain at Court, which I shall leave as soon as you advise me to do so.[6]

But for both personal and public reasons the Abbé wished her to remain. He knew that the King already liked her since Mme Scarron had informed him of the royal visits to Vaugirard.

The Church was seriously alarmed by the King's dissipations, by his continued liaison with Mme de Montespan and his other sexual lapses. Whether or not the Abbé was already under orders from his superiors to introduce a steadying influence in Louis's life, in the person of the virtuous governess—as was later given out by Mme de Maintenon herself and maintained by all her hagiographers—it appeared highly desirable that she should remain in a post which gave her such constant access to His Majesty.

In any case at that moment, she could hardly have resigned. For the little Duc du Maine, whom she adored, was in greater need of her than ever. He had been a healthy baby, but when he was three years old he had what appears to have been an attack of poliomyelitis, with the result that one of his legs was considerably shorter than the other. It was decided that Mme Scarron should take him to a famous quack at Antwerp, a bonesetter, who, however, only succeeded in giving him a permanent limp, as well as causing the poor child excruciating pain. Mme

Scarron was his devoted nurse and comforter and this early experience was no doubt the reason why the Duke, when he grew up, continued to love his foster-mother with a devotion that never wavered.

When they took up residence at St Germain, the governess and her charges living in the favourite's private apartments, Françoise and her employer had the first of the bitter quarrels that were to make her life a real misery throughout the following four or five years. The ostensible reason for these was the usual difference of opinion that inevitably arises between a mother and a governess over the children's upbringing. Mme Scarron insisted on regular hours and a strict diet; Mme de Montespan ignored these rules, overfed the children and kept them up late. When they fell ill, she blamed Mme Scarron and, far worse, constantly complained of her to the King. On 16 July Françoise wrote her confessor:

> I have wanted to write to you for a long time, but my days pass in a slavery that makes it impossible to do as I would like; I am always depressed and matters are taking a turn that does not suit me. I have not enough self-control not to suffer, but I am willing to suffer and it is perhaps a sign of progress that I am no longer impatient but only pained. I do my best to seek consolation in God.[7]

The letter continued with an entirely new theme:

> That is all I have to tell you about my spiritual condition; let us now pass to the temporal. I have a great longing to buy some land, but cannot succeed. M. de Montchevreuil [her old friend] is in Paris and I have asked him to work at this matter and find out everything there is for sale.

And she asked the Abbé to do likewise.

Françoise's new plan was due to the fact that in return for bringing up the royal children she had been promised a sum of 100,000 *livres*. And banking on receiving it she had formed the scheme, so natural as to be almost inevitable in the case of any Frenchman or Frenchwoman, of buying herself some property to which in due course she might retire. To Françoise, brought up in penury, never knowing any real financial security until she entered the royal service, this must have seemed a breath-taking possibility. It would certainly never have been a sin in her stern confessor's view had she admitted that she was not remaining in her very difficult position at Court for love of God, but for mercenary reasons, natural enough though they were.

Her next letter, written on 12 July, concerned the Abbé's nephew, the Abbé de Ragois, whom Mme Scarron succeeded in having appointed as tutor to the Duc du Maine. It was therefore not altogether against Abbé Gobelin's own family interests that she should remain in the influential position she was occupying.

On 24 July a very long letter to her confessor contained some startling news:

> The Duchesse de Richelieu and Mme de Montespan are trying to arrange a marriage for me that will not take place— with a rather unsavoury and beggarly Duke: this would put me in a state of displeasure and embarrassment which I would find unendurable; I've already enough trouble in my unusual and enviable position without seeing more in a condition which causes the unhappiness of three quarters of the human race.[8]

The Duc de Villars-Brancas was a former admirer of the royal mistress, old, decrepit, and debauched, who had already been married three times. Françoise was outraged at the suggestion, and her general condemnation of marriage as such was a genuine cry from the heart, as sincere as it was bitter.

The motive for this proposed match between Mme Scarron and the Duke of Villars-Brancas was primarily social. Since Louis had legitimised his bastards, to whom Françoise in a letter of that year to her brother referred as 'my little princes', protocol appeared to demand that the woman in whose care they were placed should be a lady of title. In offering to make her a duchess, Mme de Montespan would naturally have thought that she was conferring a very great honour on the widow Scarron. And when this distinction was indignantly refused, Athénaïs could hardly be blamed for considering Françoise extremely ungrateful. The next passage in Françoise's letter showed where her real love was given.

M. the Duc du Maine is still ill, and although I do not think he is as yet in any danger, I am still unhappy about him and it is always terrible to see someone one loves suffer. It makes me very unhappy that I do not love this child any less than the other one [the baby that died] and this weakness of mine makes me so angry that I cried throughout Mass; nothing is so stupid as to love to such excess a child that is not mine, that I shall never call my own, and who will in due course give me enough trouble to kill me and displease those to whom he does belong. It really is senseless to remain in such a disagreeable position; one must be a slave of habit not to make a change that would give one peace.

Françoise was enduring an almost unbearable emotional conflict between her passionate love for the little Duke, her unstinting loyalty and devotion to her hero, the Sun King, and her growing antagonism to Athénaïs.

The Abbé had been twice to visit her at Versailles, not yet the superlative palace that was Louis's creation, but his father's former hunting-lodge in place of which it was to be built, and of which he was already extremely fond. In this letter Françoise went on to refer to these visits and asked the Abbé for further spiritual directions. In spite of herself, she was being drawn into Court life and entertainments. The King had commanded her attendance at his *Media Noche*, a midnight feast at the end of Lent.

Throughout August and September Françoise's letters informed the Abbé of the steadily worsening relationship between herself and Mme de Montespan. On 6 August—'I told her that ... I could see, without doubt, that I was on very bad terms with her and that she was setting the King against me ...' The King, however, would not hear of her retiring. The reason was clear enough, for throughout those months the Duc du Maine was ill, and needed his foster-mother's loving care more than ever. He sent Louvois to reason with her, and matters were patched up between the two women, but not for long.

At the end of August, when the child was better, Françoise left

Versailles for a short rest in Paris, to recover from a fever, to see her friends, and attend to her business affairs. Her principal interest at that time was to obtain from the King a larger grant, since the 100,000 *livres* would not suffice to buy the property she was seeking.

She returned to Versailles at the beginning of September and a fortnight later, on the 13th, was writing to the Abbé: 'Today Mme de Montespan and I had a very heated discussion, and as I am the injured party I cried a great deal.' In fact, she was then so desperate that she even thought of becoming a nun, although she admitted that she had no vocation. But 'I cannot believe that it is God's will that I should endure Mme de Montespan'. 'She talks to the King about me as she likes, and is making me lose his esteem ... I dare not speak to him directly, because she would never forgive me for doing so, and if I did, what I owe to Mme de Montespan'—the 100,000 *livres* and further favours she was hoping to obtain through her—'would not permit me to speak against her; there is therefore no remedy for my sufferings.'[9]

But the remedy was at last applied, for at the end of that month to her great delight, the King presented Mme Scarron with the second 100,000 *livres* she was needing. According to Mlle d'Aumale, it was to the little Duke that his governess owed this reward:

> One day, the King wished to see the Duc du Maine all alone in his room, without his governess nor any member of his suite. He was very young, but he stayed in the King's chamber without calling out, or crying or asking for anyone else, talking and answering the King so intelligently that he (his father) was astonished that he was behaving so well, without his attendants. He praised his good sense, to which the Duc du Maine replied, 'How should I not be sensible when I am being brought up by Reason in person?'[10]

It seems a little hard to believe that a child of four or five would have said anything so pompous. Yet the little Duke was a prodigy, extremely bright and attractive and almost as much adored by his father as by his governess. Whether or not it was the child who coined the name, in later years Louis constantly referred to Mme de Maintenon as Mme La Raison.

But her correspondence in the autumn of 1674 expressed no more than the gratitude and elation to be expected at the King's generous gift. On 16 October she wrote a short note to her brother, who by then was governor of Belfort: 'I am negotiating for an estate for which I am offering two hundred and forty thousand francs, but say nothing about it as yet; one should never boast, as it is both unlucky and ridiculous. Adieu, dear brother, I think we shall have a pretty happy old age, if there is such a thing.'[11]

From this letter it is clear that Françoise was already becoming ambitious. She was in her fortieth year and aware of the fact, never dreaming that time was still on her side, wanting, quite naturally, to provide as well as possible for her approaching retirement, which she thought imminent. But in spite of the King's generosity and her pleasure at it, she was still suffering acutely. To the Abbé Gobelin on 30 October:

> I suffer from not having been in touch with you for so long but when I want to write to you I find nothing to say that I have not said a hundred times already. I am bowed down by melancholy; they are killing those poor children in front of my eyes without my being able to prevent it; my affection for them makes me unendurable to those to whom they belong, and the fact that I cannot hide my feelings makes those with whom I am spending my life hate me, and whom I would not wish to offend even if they were not who they are.

This was an obvious reference to Louis, whom by then Mme de Montespan appeared to have won over. The letter continued:

> I sometimes make up my mind not to be so insistent, and to leave these children to their mother's treatment, but then I fear to offend God by abandoning them to her and I start nursing them again, which increases my affection for them and by shutting me in with them makes me suffer a thousand times over. This is the state I am in, full of trouble, and nothing will give me peace except to find myself a property which I cannot succeed in doing . . . My life is being torn in two opposite directions, which, as you know better than I do, is entirely

against acquiring the peace of mind and vigilance one needs in order to find salvation. . . . God be praised for everything for if I had found happiness in human beings I might never have thought of Him.[12]

This candid admission has a slight ambiguity in French. For the phrase used by Françoise, 'si j'avais été satisfaite des *hommes*' could refer only to the male sex. From the general tone of the letter, however, it is surely plain that it was not the children's father but their mother who was causing her such acute distress.

The poor little Duc du Maine was constantly ill and being dosed and treated by all the doctors at Court—even an English one—only to increase his misery and sufferings. And as Françoise wrote to the Abbé in November, 'I cannot get over my terrors which I think are justified by the remedies they are making him swallow.'[13]

But on 10 November she wrote to her brother that a mutual friend might have told him she was buying a property, 'but perhaps he does not yet know that it is Maintenon, and that the price is 250,000 francs. It is fourteen *lieues* from Paris, ten from Versailles, and four from Chartres; it is beautiful, a noble edifice, and will bring me in an income of ten to eleven thousand *livres*.'[14]

It was indeed an enchanting property, a small but perfect fairy-tale castle, with pepper-pot towers, lovely grounds and a lake. Françoise bought it from its owner, the Marquis de Maintenon, on 27 December 1674, and was absolutely delighted with it. But it was far more than she could afford, and throughout December she was having difficulties in raising the rest of the purchase price, since her 200,000 was not enough. Nor did the prospect of this splendid new possession immediately solve her dilemma. All three children were ill, the Duc du Maine was 'a pitiful sight' with a high fever, a severe cold and 'an open abscess on his bottom which gives him terrible pain when it is dressed, and which I, his very devoted mother, share.' And 'the poor child is in the hands of doctors and surgeons of whom only half would be enough to kill him.'

Finally on 17 January, Françoise informed the Abbé that the

purchase of Maintenon was concluded and that she was most anxious to go there, but that the children's ailments kept her from doing so. It was not until the following February that she was able to write that she had spent two days there that had passed like a moment. It reminded her of Mursay.[15] Later she was to tell the ladies of St Cyr how, when she went there for the first time 'I looked up with the greatest pleasure to the window of the room I imagined was the main bedroom, thinking that it was there I would end my life. I had no other plan than to live there peacefully among my peasants, but whilst I was looking forward to this, God willed otherwise.'[16]

9 *Royal Soul in Peril*

The news that the King had conferred the estate and title of Maintenon on Mme Scarron naturally aroused keen and envious interest among her friends. She was well aware of it. In reply to Mme de Coulanges's eager inquiries she wrote:

> It is true that the King has entitled me Mme de Maintenon and that I am fool enough to blush at it . . . My husband's friends are wrong in accusing me of having arranged my change of name with the King. They are either spiteful or envious of me, for a little happiness attracts a great number of enemies.[1]

Possibly the main advantage of her rise in the social scale was the fact that Françoise might now address His Majesty directly. Yet this did not put an end to the conflict between the King's mistress and the royal governess.

'One day,' wrote Mlle d'Aumale, 'when Mme de Maintenon was alone with Mme de Montespan, having a violent quarrel, the King walked in, and seeing them both in such an excited condition, asked what the matter was. Mme de Maintenon answered him with great self-control—'If Your Majesty will come into the next room, I will have the honour of explaining it to him.' The King did so, followed by Mme de Maintenon. She concealed nothing from her royal master, and gave him a detailed account of Mme de Montespan's harshness and unkindness, and of all she feared for the future—presumably for the children's future, since she ascribed most of their ailments to Mme de Montespan's constant interference. As the King still loved Mme de Montespan he tried to justify her, and in order to prove that she was not so hard-hearted (wrote Mme de Caylus) 'he said to Mme de Maintenon: "Have you not noticed that when one tells her of some generous and touching act her beautiful eyes fill with tears?"'[2]

So His Majesty endeavoured to patch up their quarrel. But whilst the indignant little governess was telling him her side of the story Louis noticed that her eyes also filled with tears and were, as Mlle de Scudéry said, remarkably beautiful, large, dark and lustrous. No doubt under the stress of her emotion Françoise was blushing as usual, and she had a very clear complexion. Although Louis was not yet ready to admit it, he was beginning to tire of Mme de Montespan's constant tantrums and really vicious temper. And as he looked down on this dear little woman, so remarkably well-preserved still, who for years had been obliged to put up with his temperamental mistress day by day, for his sake and his children's, he may well have felt more than a sense of gratitude.

Mme de Montespan's outbursts of temper at that period were due not merely to her disagreements with Françoise about the children. No doubt this was a pretext for venting the alarm and despondency she was then feeling regarding her relationship with Louis. It is doubtful whether she was then as jealous of his affection for Mme de Maintenon as Mlle d'Aumale claimed. Certainly it was not the fear that Françoise might supplant her that was causing her this deep uneasiness. The fundamental reason was that with the return of Lent both the King and his mistress were confronted with the necessity of performing their Easter duties, and the great obstacle to this religious obligation, which neither of them ever questioned, was their adulterous relationship.

By then the Sun King was supreme. A short essay he wrote a few years later, entitled *Reflections of the Profession of Kingship*, contained the following paragraphs:

One must be on guard against oneself, control one's inclinations, and always be on guard against one's own nature. The profession of King is great, noble and delightful, when one feels oneself worthy of all that it requires; but it is not free from trouble, fatigue and disquiet . . . When one has the State in mind, one is working for oneself. The well-being of the former provides the glory of the latter. When the former is happy, successful and powerful, he who is the cause of it is glorious, and in consequence has a greater right than his subjects to enjoy all that is most pleasant in life.[3]

And Louis fully practised what he preached. Apparently he was unassailable, yet he did have one weakness. His Achilles heel was his conscience. Whilst in many ways, especially in his lechery, he greatly resembled his grandfather, the debonair Henry of Navarre, in this respect he radically differed from him. Henry was brought up as a Huguenot, changed his religion twice, once to save his life after St Bartholomew's Day, once to gain the throne of France. He had as many mistresses and bastards as Louis, but no guilt feeling at all about them. Louis XIV, however, was both a French Bourbon, and, on his mother's side, a nephew of the fanatical Philip II of Spain. From childhood he was thoroughly indoctrinated with the strictest Catholic principles. Little as he, too, could resist his physical urges, from time to time his moral lapses caused him acute mental distress.

The Queen Mother died in 1666. Louis was then free from her disapproval of his amorous intrigues. Yet, however much he might have repressed them during the next eleven years, the guilt feeling she had implanted in him remained. The crucial period in this situation was invariably Lent.

Already during his liaison with Louise de la Vallière, the Queen Mother had become alarmed for her son's spiritual welfare, and at Lent 1662 she invited the Abbé Jacques-Bénigne Bossuet to preach before His Majesty. Great oratory, particularly great religious oratory, is a thing of the past in the twentieth century. It is therefore very difficult for a modern mind to appreciate the tremendous impact of Bossuet's sermons on his congregation, led by His Majesty in person. And as Bossuet boomed forth comminations against sinners with all his superlative eloquence, Louis, whilst not mending his ways, showed his appreciation of the great preacher's talents. For in spite of the prelate's condemnation of the Sun King's morals, Bossuet was appointed bishop of Condom in Gascony, and later bishop of Meaux. More important still, the King chose him as tutor to the Dauphin.

Louise de la Vallière retired to her convent in 1674. But Athénaïs de Montespan, a married woman who had borne the King four bastards, was regarded by the religious faction at Court as a far greater menace to His Majesty's spiritual welfare. Bossuet was the leader of that faction, the so-called 'Holy Conspiracy', which included the Jesuit Bourdaloue, another powerful preacher. But for a long time they had little or no success.

At the end of Lent 1675, the King was sitting in his chapel at St Germain, the Queen beside him, Mme de Montespan in the pew immediately behind them, when Bourdaloue in the pulpit, looking his royal penitent straight in the face, apostrophised him:

'How many conversions, Sire, would your own example not induce? What an encouragement would it not be for so many discouraged and desperate sinners if they might say to themselves, "Here is a man whom we have seen living in the same debauchery as ourselves, who is now converted and obedient to God!"'[4]

An even worse experience was in store for the proud mistress.

During Holy Week one of her maids went to a confessor at Notre Dame de Versailles called Lecuyer, whom she spoke so well of that Mme de Montespan decided to visit him also. To her amazed horror, when the priest heard her name, he exclaimed indignantly: 'The Madame de Montespan who is scandalizing the whole of France? Go, go, Madame, and put an end to these scandals, and then you may come back and throw yourself at the feet of the minister of Jesus Christ.'[5]

Mme de Montespan did nothing of the sort, but complained in a fury to the King of the priest's insolence, demanding that he be punished. It was the wrong moment; Louis was sufficiently concerned with his own salvation. He referred the matter to Bossuet, and that implacable bishop fully supported the priest, saying that in such circumstances a complete and absolute separation was indispensable before being admitted to the sacraments.

And Louis gave in. He requested Bossuet to convey this to Mme de Montespan, wishing not unnaturally, to avoid the painful scene which would inevitably ensue. Bossuet leapt at the chance. Moreover, he already had an ally on the spot, for Mme de Maintenon now at last saw the King's salvation, for which she had prayed for so long, in sight.

Bossuet and his colleagues never ceased to encourage her in this pious endeavour. They had already appreciated the fact that in spite of her promotion the former Mme Scarron was quite incorruptible and unimpressed by the luxury and glamour of the court. And they, like everyone else, were aware that she was exerting her growing influence over the King as well as his mistress for their spiritual good.

Here is what Mme de Maintenon told us. 'When I found myself on such terms with the King that I might speak to him frankly, one day when he was holding a reception, I had the honour to be walking with him, whilst the others were playing cards' [Mme de Montespan was a terrific gambler] 'or doing something else. When we were out of earshot I stopped and said to him, Sire, you are very devoted to your musketeers ... what would you do if Your Majesty were told that one of those musketeers whom you cherish so much had taken the wife of another man, and was actually living with her? I am sure that from that very evening he would be barred from the residence of the musketeers, and would no longer be allowed to sleep there, however late it might be.' The King thought this not at all a bad idea, and laughed a little, saying that she was quite right, but nothing more happened at that time.[6]

At that moment Louis found her sally, her daring allusion to his own adultery, quite amusing. But very shortly afterwards, when plunged into the Lenten crisis of 1675, it was no longer a laughing matter.

From Françoise's previous letters to the Abbé Gobelin describing her violent quarrels with Athénaïs de Montespan, it might have appeared that the two women hated one another implacably. This was far from the case. Throughout their lives there was a curious bond of sympathy between them. From their first meeting at the Hôtel d'Albret, each had appreciated the other's wit, gaiety and charm. After she had chosen Françoise, very wisely for their sake, to take charge of her children, Mme de Montespan continued to make a friend and even a confidant of Mme Scarron. It was only as time went on that Françoise began to realise how callous and flighty Athénaïs was, as on the occasion when her house had caught fire. And after Louis had ordered that the children should be brought to St Germain, she began to be the victim of Athénaïs's uncontrolled outbursts of temper. There were times when Athénaïs actually hated her, as Françoise had said in an earlier letter to the Abbé, yet there were others when they still got on extremely well together. It was round that period that the King had one day asked his mistress as a sacrifice not to gossip with Mme Scarron when he left her for the night, since she might find greater pleasure in her conversation than in his, wrote Mlle d'Aumale. 'When she entered Mme de Montespan's room as usual, Mme Scarron noticed this, as she did not answer her, although she was not yet asleep. "I understand," said Mme Scarron smilingly. "You've been asked not to talk to me any more, so in that case I will take advantage of your sacrifice and go to bed." Mme de Montespan was delighted by Françoise's quick wittedness; not only did she talk to her as usual, but their conversation was livelier than ever.'[7]

Having given in to the Church's demand that he should break with his mistress, Louis was able to perform his Easter duties on 14 April.

'I never wanted so much to see you as during this business,'

Françoise wrote to the Abbé Gobelin on 23 April, 'but the life we are leading gives me no hope of being able to make an appointment with you, for Mme de Montespan is out from morning till night and was only at home on one day, about which I was not told . . . You will have heard that I saw the King yesterday, but fear nothing; I think I talked to him as a Christian and a true friend of Mme de Montespan.'[8]

The last sentence in that letter has been variously interpreted. But in view of the fact that it was written to her confessor it could only mean that Françoise was also actively encouraging the King's resolve to separate from his mistress.

Had Françoise been a mischief maker, had she had personal designs to succeed Mme de Montespan, the opportunity could hardly have been a more favourable one. That was what her enemies asserted. In later years she herself described the situation frankly and not without considerable insight to the Ladies of St Cyr:

> Mme de Montespan and I were the greatest friends in the world; she was very fond of me, and I, simple as I was, returned her friendship. She was a very witty and charming woman; she spoke to me very frankly, telling me everything she was thinking. And yet we became estranged without meaning to break with one another. This was certainly not my fault, and yet if anyone had a right to complain it was she; for she could with truth have said, 'I was the cause of her advancement, for it was I who introduced her to the King and taught him to appreciate her, but then she became the favourite and I was dismissed.' On the other hand, was I wrong to have accepted the King's friendship under the *conditions* that I did accept it?

In the distress she was then suffering, Mme de Montespan turned to Françoise for comfort and it was with a perfectly clear conscience that she concentrated all her efforts on endeavouring to persuade her forlorn friend to sacrifice her worldly splendour to her spiritual salvation, and, on the face of it, not without success.

On 14 May Louis left to rejoin his army in Flanders, where

he was to remain for the next two months. The two women meanwhile, together with the children, also retired from Court. Françoise entertained Mme de Montespan for a few days at Maintenon. Far from bearing Athénaïs any malice for her previous harshness, Françoise gave her all the support and comfort she could in her seemingly sincere efforts to submit to God's law. Her ally, Bossuet, was also continuing the good work. On several occasions he discreetly visited Mme de Montespan, who then appeared to be wholly concerned with atonement for her past sins and works of charity. Nor did he fail to write several letters to Louis reminding him of the necessity of breaking with his mistress.

Both Bossuet and Françoise were showing a certain naïveté in their gratification and relief at this apparently final rupture. Neither of them was capable of appreciating the power of such sexual enchantment as Athénaïs exercised over Louis. And as the events of the following year were to prove, that power, although in decline, was by no means at an end.

Others were less optimistic and more far-seeing. As early as 16 April, Mlle de Scudéry wrote to her crony Bussy-Rabutin:

> The King and Mme de Montespan have separated, although it is said they are still madly in love with one another, their rupture being merely in deference to their religious scruples. The rumour is that when she returns to Court she will no longer be living in the castle, and will only be seeing the King at the Queen's. I very much doubt that this will be the case, for it seems to me there is more than a chance that their love will prevail.[10]

And indeed, within a very short time Mlle de Scudéry's prediction was justified.

10 *The Indispensable Madame de Maintenon*

Louis had a secondary motive in raising Françoise to a higher status. Having legitimised his children by Mme de Montespan, he was determined that they should enjoy the full privileges reserved for members of the Blood Royal. He was planning to send the Duc du Maine to a spa called Barèges, in south-west France, to seek a cure for his dermatitis, his abscesses and his limp. He would obviously travel there in the care of his foster-mother. And the young Prince could scarcely have gone there with a mere Mme Scarron.

The King had decided that the five-year-old prince who, in the event of the Dauphin's death might possibly one day succeed him, should travel in the state becoming to one of his sons, who, had he not been born on the wrong side of the blanket would have been called Monsieur, the official title of a second heir to the throne. To give him this title was impossible, but no other means of emphasising the Duc du Maine's descent was neglected. With Mme de Maintenon he travelled in the most splendid style; throughout the journey they were officially received at every stop and town on the way by the highest local dignitaries, with all the ritual, ceremony, and splendour usual on regal occasions.

Mme de Maintenon's obvious pleasure in this royal progress was apparent in all her letters, and its admission an endearing weakness. Quite obviously she had never been so happy in all her life before.

By then she was on such intimate terms with the King that throughout this journey she wrote to His Majesty personally, and received personal replies from him. Unfortunately for posterity she destroyed every one of these letters, and no record of them remains. There is, however, one significant phrase in a letter she wrote to Abbé Gobelin: on 20 May: 'those at present with us are treating us extremely well, but the same is not true of those who are absent. I am receiving no letters except from one man, and if this continues I shall be convinced that one can only rely on people whose friendship is warmer than one might wish.'[1]

This could only be an allusion to the King and his fondness for her, which she had already admitted to the Abbé at Vaugirard. Quite clearly those letters, which she destroyed, did more than flatter her. Possibly the King's absence did make her heart grow fonder of him; certainly it enabled her to bask in his friendship, however warmly expressed, without being in the dilemma she so much dreaded of having to prevent him from making love to her.

'You will gather that our prince is in perfect health; I have no news of the others, nor of Mme de Montespan. God be praised for everything!'—for she was assuming that the rupture between the King and his mistress was by then definitive, a rash assumption as matters turned out.

On 28 May she gave her brother at Belfort an almost ecstatic description of the pleasure and pride she was feeling: 'We have been received everywhere like the King, but one must admit that Guyenne is outdoing itself and that nothing could increase the demonstrations of joy we are receiving . . . At Poitiers we were nearly suffocated by affection. We were magnificently entertained at Blaye by the Duc de Saint-Simon.'[2] This was the father of the famous author of the Memoirs, who was born only six months before this visit, and who twenty

years later was to become Mme de Maintenon's bitterest deni-
grator.

She was also in touch with her cousin, M. de Villette, then
serving in the Royal Navy at Toulon, to whom she wrote from
Barèges on 23 June—'I arrived here on the 20th of this month,
having left Paris on 28 April; it took less time to go to
America . . .' and this letter contained a significant paragraph
at the end: 'I embrace Philippe [his son] and love him very
tenderly and my affection for you makes me hope to have one of
your children with me, but I do not like to be refused, and you
are so very much against it.'[3]

M. de Villette's career was hampered by the fact that unlike
Françoise he had not become a Catholic; in fact all her relatives
in the south-west, whom she took this opportunity to visit on her
return journey, were still Huguenots. Françoise showed a surprising willingness to be reconciled even with the family of
Caumont d'Addé, the brother-in-law whom her mother,
Jeanne d'Aubigné, had ruined herself fighting in the law courts.
But Mme de Maintenon's motives were not merely Christian
charity and forgiveness. She was already planning to convert the
children of these Huguenot relatives to the true Church, and
what better example of the temporal as well as spiritual benefits
of embracing the religion of the State could there be than her
own career, travelling as if she herself were almost of royal
descent? She spent three days at Mursay, where no doubt she
told her dazzled relatives how similar it was to her own property,
Maintenon, given to her by the King. And from there she took
back with her the *Histoire Universelle* by her grandfather,
Agrippa d'Aubigné, and other papers which, she wrote to her
brother, 'will prove our nobility, should this ever be necessary'.[4]
To M. de Villette she wrote that she had been consulting various
church registers to trace back her genealogy for 400 years. This,
however, was a fake, since Agrippa had tried to link his family to
a much nobler line, the d'Aubignys of Anjou, who had no wish
at all to accept him as of their descent.

There was no clue in these letters to her reason for suddenly
showing this 'infatuation' as she called it, with her ancestry,

except the tentative suggestion that one day they might regain Surimeau, Agrippa's original family seat, from the descendants of Caumont d'Addé, a plan that was never carried out. They did, however, reveal that since she had become the Marquise de Maintenon, her girlish desire to stand well in the eyes of the world had become stronger than ever. There is a marked contrast between the worldliness of their tone and her previous letters to the Abbé Gobelin, when she was constantly insisting on her longing to retire from Court and Society.

Meanwhile, however, she was to have a great disappointment. She and the little Duke did not return to Paris until the beginning of November and it was only then, after an absence of six months, that she was to learn that all the good work she had devoted to his mother's renunciation of her royal lover had been to no purpose.

On 14 April Louis had been able to perform his Easter duties with a clear conscience. On 10 May he rejoined his army. Mme de Maintenon had left Mme de Montespan at Clagny, the superlative country seat that the King had given his mistress, but which was not yet completely built. There, Mme de Sévigné wrote to her daughter on 7 June, her life was 'exemplary', but not so exemplary as all that, since she frequently visited St Cloud, where she played at *hoca*. This was the most popular gambling game of the day, at which Mme de Montespan lost or won huge sums.

Like all the *précieuses*, Mme de Sévigné invented nicknames for those eminent persons about whom she gossiped to her daughter. Mme Scarron, in her Vaugirard days, had been called the Thaw (*le Dégel*), because when she dined with her women friends she threw off the icy restraint at that time required of her by the secrecy of her charge. Mme de Montespan was referred to either as *Quantova* or *Quanto*, after the game introduced from Italy to France by Cardinal Mazarin, rather like modern roulette, the table being divided into thirty squares, and the calls being made in Italian—'*quanto va*' meaning 'how much goes?'

On 14 June, wrote Mme de Sévigné,

the Queen went to visit Mme de Montespan at Clagny . . . in her room, where she remained for half an hour; she then visited M. de Vexin [the second little prince] who was slightly ill, and afterwards took Mme de Montespan to Trianon . . . some ladies who went to Clagny found the beauty so busy with the works and delights that are being carried out there for her that it reminds me of Dido having Carthage built . . .[5] You cannot imagine how triumphant she is in the midst of her workmen—there are 1200 of them rebuilding Clagny and laying out the gardens . . . Her regular friend's wife and all the family visit her by turns; and she takes precedence over all the duchesses . . .[6]

Athénaïs de Montespan's optimism was fully justified on the King's victorious return from battle. Easter with its religious obligations was nearly another year away. As Mme de Montespan had hoped and calculated, Louis was still in love with her. On his way back to Versailles he ordered that she should be awaiting him there. Bossuet made a futile attempt to intervene; he went out with the Dauphin to meet His Majesty, but the moment the King saw him he held up his hand and said: 'Say nothing to me; I have given my orders that an apartment in the castle be prepared for Mme de Montespan.'[7]

'But,' wrote Mme de Caylus,

it was necessary that they should meet privately before Mme de Montespan appeared in public . . . and in order to give malicious gossip no opportunity it was agreed that the most respectable Court ladies should be present at this interview, and that the King should only see Mme de Montespan in their presence. The King therefore came to Mme de Montespan as arranged, but he gradually drew her into a window embrasure where they talked for a long time, wept, and told one another what is usually said on such occasions; then, with profound obeisances to those venerable matrons, they went into another room.[8]

In consequence, Mme de Caylus concluded, they in due course had two more children, Mlle de Blois and the Comte de Toulouse.

Mme de Sévigné wrote to her daughter on 31 July that 'the attachment is still very great; enough to annoy the curé [Bossuet] and everyone else, but not perhaps enough for her; for in spite of her outward triumph there is a basis of sadness.'9

This was a veiled reference to Louis's unfaithfulness to Athénaïs, for during that year he began to tire of her; although he still slept with her and gave her two more children he was having a whole series of passing liaisons with younger and more attractive women.

But Mme de Sévigné's most sensational scandal-mongering was contained in letters to her daughter during August and September:

> I'm going, my dear, to turn up a few cards that will surprise you, namely that the great friendship between Mme de Montespan and her absent friend has in fact for the past two years been a case of intense mutual aversion, bitterness, and antipathy . . . How, you may ask, did that happen? The answer is that the friend's pride cannot stomach the other one's orders. She does not like obeying them; she is quite willing to serve the father, but not the mother; she has taken this trip for love of him, not at all for love of her; she writes to him, but not to her. The friend is scolded for showing this conceited person too much affection, but this is not expected to last unless the aversion changes, or the success of the journey changes their hearts.10

By this time Mme de Montespan was also extremely jealous of the King's increasing affection for Mme de Maintenon, which he must have inadvertently betrayed to her, perhaps showing her one or two of the letters Françoise wrote him and which he found very entertaining.

As Louis's sexual interest in Athénaïs began to wane again her arrogance became greater than ever.

Possibly because she wished to remind the King that she was the mother of his favourite child, Mme de Montespan with her two sisters, the Abbess of Fontevrault and Mme de Thianges, went out to Blois, to meet the governess and her precious charge on their return early in November. Before they arrived at Versailles on the 5th they decided to give Louis a pleasant surprise.

'Nothing,' wrote Mme de Sévigné on 10 November, 'was more delightful than the King's astonishment; he was not expecting M. du Maine until next day; he saw him enter his room, simply holding Mme de Maintenon's hand. It was a transport of joy . . .'[11]

Although the little Duke's limp was not completely cured he was able to walk quite easily, almost run into his father's arms, and Louis wept with joy as he kissed the child's rosy cheeks. Blushing as usual when she felt any strong emotion, Françoise stood demurely in the doorway, not unnaturally expecting and receiving her sovereign's grateful thanks. He even sent Louvois to convey them to her officially and that evening, Mme de Sévigné continued, 'the Thaw went to supper with her old friend, Mme de Richelieu, where,' as Mme de Maintenon was now in the highest favour, 'some kissed her hand, others her dress; and if she has not changed a great deal she was laughing at them all; but they say that she has.'[12]

Yet the success of the little Duke's cure did not compensate Françoise for her failure to part the King from his mistress and his generally dissolute way of life. It was primarily to this purpose that the Abbé and the Holy Conspiracy had insisted on her remaining at Court, and by then she was becoming conscious that she was wasting her time there.

'With all my heart,' she wrote to the Abbé on 2 January 1676, 'I would wish to lead a less dissipated life than mine; I shall soon spend a good part of it at the opera [at the King's invitation, which was a command], where it seems to me shameful to be when one is nearly forty, and a Christian.' Such vestiges of her puritanical childhood constantly appeared in her character and letters. Her deepest suffering was caused by the realisation that it was not she who was winning him over to her way of life, but he, who by showing her such constant kindness and favour was binding her more closely to him every day.

Two years previously, she had sent her confessor a detailed

plan of how she would spend her life at Maintenon, had she been free to follow her own inclination:

I would like to get up at seven in summer and eight in winter; spend an hour in prayer before calling my maids, then dress, and during that time see the tradesmen, workers, or other people on business; when dressed go to church and stay there until dinner-time.

I would reckon to go out perhaps twice a week, either for my own amusement or to pay duty calls; on those days to have supper with some of my women friends, and return home at ten o'clock.

I would spend the other three days of the week visiting on one day the Hôtel Dieu (the hospital) on another, the poor or my parish, and on the third the unfortunate prisoners, and by being alone in the evenings, either working or reading.

Never to see anyone on the eve of the holy days, nor on the eve or the day of communion; never to miss the special devotions at certain times; be simply dressed, never wearing either gold or silver; give one-tenth of my income to the poor.[13]

She asked the Abbé Gobelin to suggest any further improvements on this laudatory scheme. No doubt she had specially included the last sentence, since he had reproached her for being too well dressed, to which Mme de Maintenon had replied in her own defence that she never wore anything except black, but that at Court either silver or gold lace were obligatory with it. And by the spring of 1676 she knew that this ideal scheme would never be possible.

On 15 April Louis left again for the army; the inexhaustible Mme de Sévigné wrote on the twenty-second that 'Quantova was to have gone to Bourbon, but will not do so, which suggests that her regular friend will return sooner than was expected. Her woman friend has taken her to her château, for two or three days.' For they were still on the same terms, disliking one another more and more and yet bound together by their unhappiness; Mme de Montespan knowing that her power was waning, Mme de Maintenon unable to prevent the reluctant lover from further dangerous infidelities.

During Louis's absence Athénaïs did go to Bourbon, travelling in the greatest state, in a coach-and-six, with a retinue of fifty horsemen. There she took the waters in order to reduce her weight and appear more radiantly beautiful than ever when the King returned.

Mme de Montespan left the spa at the beginning of June 'in a gilded barge lined with crimson damask, painted all over with the Royal Arms, and flying all the banners of France'[14] determined to show the whole world that in spite of Louis's transient infidelities she was still the official mistress.

'Her beauty,' wrote Mme de Sévigné, 'is marvellous. She is not half as stout as she was, and her complexion, eyes and lips are no less beautiful.'[15]

And the result was all she had hoped for. Her rivals were forgotten. On 11 July Louis arrived back at St Germain. The Queen and the Dauphin had gone to meet him. But as had happened during his previous absence, the King's desire for Mme de Montespan was more insatiable than ever.

'*Quanto's* friend arrived a quarter of an hour before *Quanto* and whilst he was talking to his family he was informed of her arrival; he immediately ran to meet her and spent a long time with her. Yesterday they went for a walk . . . but only the three of them, with *Quanto* and her woman friend [Mme de Maintenon] nobody else being allowed to join them . . . The friend's wife wept a great deal.'[16]

One would give a lot to know the thoughts of *Quanto's* woman friend on that *promenade à trois*. But her letters at that period provide a few clues. On 17 June she wrote to the Abbé that she was on the best of terms with Mme de Montespan and was trying to make it clear to her that she wished to retire, but 'she makes little response to these suggestions and we will have to wait until her return.'[17] And the strain she was feeling was giving her, as she told him in a note of six brief lines on 9 July, violent migraine.

Finally, in August she was able to spend three weeks at Maintenon. Once again Mme de Sévigné is the best day-to-day source on the complicated situation that was developing between the three friends.

7 August: I have seen some people who have come back from Court and are convinced that . . . the sovereign situation of *Quanto* has never been more firmly established. She feels herself above everyone . . .[18]

21 August: Mme de Maintenon has gone to Maintenon for three weeks. The King has sent her Le Nôtre [the famous royal landscape gardener] to arrange those lovely but neglected grounds.

26 August: It is true that she is in the highest favour and that *Quanto's* friend refers to her as his first or second best friend. He has sent her a famous man to make her house admirably lovely. It is said that Monsieur [the King's brother, the Duc d'Orléans] is going there; I think he actually went yesterday with Mme de Montespan.[19]

Yet at the same time Louis was having a series of unconcealed although transient liaisons, notably with Mme de Soubise. It was these that were causing his 'first and second best friends' such mental anguish. Perhaps it was as a gesture of compensation that Louis sent his best craftsmen to embellish Maintenon; but if this was the case he must by then have decided that of all the women so easily available to his favour, this one—the little governess then more than forty who, for all those years had never become his mistress—was the most essential to his happiness and peace of mind.

Louis was then in his late thirties, apparently dominated by his insatiable sexual urges, dutifully sleeping from time to time with his neglected Queen, giving his reigning mistress the last of their children, having a series of affairs due either to capriciousness or boredom. But in none of these relationships did he find genuine emotional satisfaction; none of these women could give him the intellectual companionship, the marital intimacy and comfort he had lacked all his life. And his passing liaisons had not the slightest bearing on his one steadfast affection, a feeling that was deepening in spite of all outward appearances into love, real and lasting love, that was making Françoise de Maintenon irrevocably and permanently indispensable to him.

In November she went to Maintenon for a few weeks, her

discouragement as deep as ever, and on her return she wrote on 20 December to the Abbé:

> I arrived back from Maintenon yesterday, where I spent a week in such peace and mental restfulness that makes me find my life here more unendurable than ever, and if I were to follow my own inclinations there would not be one moment of the day when I would not ask to retire. I cannot possibly go on leading my present life; I am taking too much on myself for body and soul to endure; let God's will be done, and whatever He decides ... and if I knew His will I would follow it, however strongly my own inclinations were against it.[20]

The obvious inference from all these half-truths and hints could only be that Françoise's own secret feelings about Louis were torturing her. She had ostensibly remained at Court in the hope of bringing him to God. In this she had failed. But she was in higher favour than ever. Why did she not take advantage of it to continue the good work? Was the answer that if she knew God's will she would follow it, however strongly her own inclinations were against it? No: God's will could never condone the King's immorality, nor the slackening of her own zeal. The true explanation was that Françoise felt herself surrendering to Louis on his own terms; that she found herself lacking the strength of will and even the inclination to leave Court, to renounce her permanent servitude to his need of her and— although this was never even so much as hinted at—her need of him. This would have been quite enough to bring her to the edge of a nervous breakdown, the migraines and general physical and mental distress of which she was complaining. Even if she was still not in love with Louis, she was realising against all her deepest resistances and repressions that the King was a man who loved her and would never give her up. He could sleep with as many mistresses as he desired; he was making no physical demands on her, yet emotionally he was asking for her complete surrender and by then she was finding it impossible to refuse it to him.

The King on the Brink of a Precipice

Mme de Soubise was soon succeeded by Mme de Ludres, whose favour lasted for nearly a year. As usual, during Louis's periods of desertion, owing to their shared unhappiness, the two friends Françoise and Athénaïs were again inseparable.

On 28 February 1677 the King left to rejoin his army. Mme de Montespan, who was then expecting her sixth child by him, spent the last three months of her pregnancy at Maintenon. Mlle de Blois was born there on 4 May. This time Athénaïs was unable to escape Françoise's renewed insistence that she should give up the King. Not only was Mme de Maintenon exhorting and remonstrating with her, but, for the first time, she positively refused to take charge of the baby.

This, however, may have been partly due to the fact that she was about to take the Duc du Maine to Barèges for a second cure, regarded as advisable, since the initial improvement in his health was showing signs of decline. The infant was smuggled away with the usual secrecy to Vaugirard, where she was looked after by Mme Louvois, the Minister's wife.

Brother Charles had found his post at Belfort intolerable, and once again using all her influence on his behalf, his loyal sister had succeeded in having him appointed governor of Cognac, where, she wrote, she was looking forward to seeing him shortly on her journey to the south-west. But the note she sent him from Maintenon on 27 May expressed no less than disgust at the sudden reversal of her hopes that Mme de Montespan's liaison with Louis might be ending.

Athénaïs had apparently not kept her dear friend informed that during her stay at Maintenon she had been having a long and affectionate correspondence with the King. He had tired of Mme de Ludres and was again longing for her.

For Athénaïs had the sexual techniques of a supreme courtesan; she knew as none of his other mistresses did every note in the repertoire required to excite and gratify his desires. And, as was to transpire a year or two later, she was possibly using more sinister means than her own unaided sex appeal to do so.

'The King arrives at Versailles on Monday,' Françoise informed her brother, 'and we are going there on Sunday, however one may have hoped to have got rid of us. You who know us, will understand that one does not discard us so easily.'[1]

'We' were herself and the little Duke. 'One' was Mme de Montespan, who had been attempting in vain to persuade Mme de Maintenon to leave for Barèges with him before the King's return. But Françoise was determined that the little boy should say good-bye to his father before their departure and possibly even more so that the Sun King's pleasure in his reunion with his mistress might be slightly clouded by her own sad and reproachful glances. If that was the case, her unspoken but clear disapproval made no impression at that time.

'Ah! my daughter,' wrote the irrepressible Mme de Sévigné on 11 June, 'what a triumph at Versailles! what a splendid establishment! . . . what a return to power! I spent an hour in her room; she was in bed, adorned, her hair dressed, resting before the *media noche*. Imagine everything an ungenerous and proud character might say in her triumph [over de Ludres] and you will have an idea of it.'[2]

·　　·　　·　　·　　·

Mme de Maintenon and her charge had left on 8 June. They first stayed at Fontevrault with Mme de Montespan's sister, the Abbess. Her letter to Charles from there on 12 June gave him full instructions for their reception at Cognac:

I will let you know the day and time of our arrival, for on no account must you fail to come to meet the prince two or three *lieues* from Cognac. The prince and I have our own beds [but M. d'Aubigné was to provide the necessary accommodation for the rest of the Duke's suite] M. Fagon [his doctor] M. le Ragois [the nephew of the Abbé Gobelin, whom she had had appointed as the Duke's tutor] an almoner, six valets, and other officers, and I have three women servants; ... the prince and I sleep in the same room.

Françoise remained in a state of depression throughout the journey. A letter to the Abbé from Barèges on 30 July pinpointed the reasons for her heartache with the greatest clarity.

When I was in disfavour at Court I was advised not to leave under those conditions, but now that I am so well-liked I do not know how to tear myself away from people who are holding me back by kindness and friendship. Those chains are more difficult for me to break than if I were forced away violently.[4]

Those 'people' who were holding her so firmly in thrall could hardly have included Mme de Montespan, who for years had made Françoise the butt of her vicious temper, with whom she had row after row, and for whose sake she had not, as Mme de Sévigné pointed out, undertaken her former trip with the Duc du Maine. No, those people were in fact only one person, His Majesty, to whom she by then knew herself bound for life, whatever his conduct. Her pride quite naturally rebelled at her own total inability to break those chains of affection, and when she continued that it would be impossible for her to sacrifice her freedom, health, and salvation for the rest of her life, she ended up half-heartedly that, 'this is not the time to make a change'.

Meanwhile she had another cause for the greatest anxiety. The second cure at Barèges was a failure; the little Duke's symptoms had all returned; he was as lame as previously and also constantly running a temperature. She took him away, to Bagnières, and from there she wrote on 7 September to the Abbé in near desperation:

> I am therefore expecting that he may die, for if he is in the state they think, it will be impossible to save him, and he is the sweetest creature on earth, whose intelligence surprises one twenty times a day. But these agitations are not the only ones I am suffering; I am being tormented by continual information from Court . . . I am dying to leave, but I would not like to do so on bad terms; it is very difficult to see how, and I spend my life in a turmoil that is destroying all pleasure for me and the peace of mind one needs to serve God.[5]

During this second trip the King and Mme de Maintenon exchanged only a few letters. In the distress she was feeling at the renewal of his liaison with Mme de Montespan and possibly knowing in her heart of hearts that her own disapproval of it was not unmixed with jealousy, she refrained from writing to him. Louis was only too well aware of her disappointment in him, but was then utterly indifferent to it.

'*Quanto* and her friend,' Mme de Sévigné wrote gleefully on 2 July, 'are together longer and more intimately than ever; the eagerness of their earlier years has returned and all restraint is lifted . . . one has never seen anyone more solidly in power.' Further evidence came from her at the end of that month: 'The other day Mme de Montespan was simply covered in diamonds; one's eyes were nearly dazzled by the brilliance of such a goddess.'

But Mme de Maintenon found an ingenious way of giving news of herself to His Majesty. The little Duke was now seven; she had taught him to write and so he was sending his father and mother, whom he addressed as 'lovely lady', a series of little notes from Barèges, which were afterwards included in a collection of his childish efforts entitled *Oeuvres d'un Enfant de sept ans*. Most of these notes were the kind that any small boy might have written; but one long letter, if it was in his own hand, was certainly copied out from a draft by his governess herself.

Françoise de Montespan in the Château de Clagny
Portrait by Gascard

Philip V, King of Spain
Portrait by Rigaud

Marie-Adélaïde de Savoie
Portrait by Gobert

It was addressed to Mme de Montespan and began by saying that he would give her all the news; a little of it concerned the other members of his suite, but mostly it was an oblique method used by Françoise to convey news of herself to the King, to whom she knew it would be shown:

> ... Mme de Maintenon spends all day spinning, and if one let her, would spend all night at it, too, or at writing. She gives me lessons every day and hopes to improve my mind; so does the *mignon* [which was how they all referred to him, their pet] who will do all he can, as he is dying to please the King and you . . . Yesterday Mme de Maintenon had a migraine and only got up for Mass . . .[6]

The travellers arrived back at Versailles at the beginning of October. This surely might have been the moment for Mme de Maintenon to retire, had she really wanted and intended to do so. Instead, she accepted the situation exactly as before, but it was taking a great deal out of her. On 25 October she wrote to Gobelin that she was looking forward to seeing him, but that she was feeling very tired: 'I rest a great deal, and I have so few plans and visits that, shutting myself up only with the King, Mme de Montespan, and the Duc du Maine, I have plenty of time to rest.' The strain on her in these odd circumstances, a situation almost like a *mariage à trois*, with the two women becoming more and more jealous of one another, and their lord determined to keep both of them for his entertainment and relaxation, must indeed have caused her acute tension. 'God knows my inner soul,' she repeated again, 'and I hope He will break my chains if that is necessary for my salvation; I beg you to ask Him to do so . . .'[7]

Why should she not herself have asked God for her freedom? There was no reason to suppose He would not have granted it to her had she really desired it. But her heart was now divided between sacred and profane love, and the profane was growing stronger every day.

There was only one more letter to the Abbé during that year; apparently he had come to see her but had been unable to make up her mind for her. The situation was beyond his control.

Did he advise her to remain, when it must have seemed to both of them highly improbable that the King would now give up Mme de Montespan? Or did he advise her to leave, when with her usual plausibility she explained to him her fear of hurting the King's feelings when he was being so kind to her? At the end of that letter of 9 December there was a curious half-admission. Referring first to the breakdown of the negotiations for her brother's marriage she wrote, 'I would like to feel as greatly indifferent to everything else in the world as I do to that situation' and, finally, 'Pray to God for me, since He does not allow you to do more.'[8]

But clearly it could not possibly continue indefinitely, and within the two following years, Mme de Montespan's reign was at last to end. At the beginning of 1678 there was as yet no sign of this. The King, taking the Queen and part of the Court with him, left on 7 February on his campaign against the Netherlands. Mme de Montespan was again pregnant with her last child, yet, at Louis's invitation spent a month with him before retiring to her splendid estate, Clagny.

Mme de Maintenon remained at St Germain with the Duke, who was again her instrument in sending oblique messages to his parents:

'My lovely lady,' the little boy wrote to his mother on 20 February, 'I am very bored by your absence; we are told that you are returning, but we think this news is false . . . It seems to me that for some days now Mme de Maintenon is sadder, I don't know why, although she does not generally hide her thoughts from me . . .'

A few days later the child wrote that he was 'persecuting Mme de Maintenon to be allowed to join the King', when this clearly did not depend on her agreement.

She, meanwhile, was writing to her brother about his marriage, which had at last taken place. Just like his father, and at almost the same age, 44, Charles became engaged to a girl of 15, a mere little bourgeoise, not at all the kind of aristocratic wife Françoise had been trying for so long to find for him. In order to discover whether she could make a lady of her she invited her to St Germain. Her efforts to improve her manners were in vain. Charles's bride was as stupid and arrogant as her husband. For the first time Françoise lost both her patience and temper with him and wrote him a very long letter, mercilessly detailing all his wife's faults. Later on, owing to her affection for their daughter, her niece, and the only direct descendant of the d'Aubigné family whom she adopted, brought up and married off brilliantly, she struck out the strongest passages.

But these remained in a copy found in the archives of St Cyr and show that when she was really angry Françoise did not mince her words:

'She is unbearably rude, the inevitable result of her low birth . . . in fact a typical little Parisian guttersnipe . . . She seems very conceited and her silly parents have made her believe that she is beautiful, which, as I have pointed out to her, is far from true!' She also gave Charles a good dressing-down for not having given up his gambling and other profligate habits in spite of his marriage:

'I will help you in everything so long as you do not live above your income, and your family will be as my own to me, but if I see you ruining yourself and making yourself ridiculous, we shall become estranged. I would rather spend my money on myself'—for years he had been sponging on her—'than see you waste it . . .'[9]

It was in this long and minatory letter that a passage occurred which later gave rise to much speculation.

'You will perhaps think it strange that a woman who has never been married gives you so much advice on marriage, but I venture to tell you that the confidence people have always had in me, and what I have myself seen, have taught me that one often makes oneself unhappy through trifles that, if they recur day by day, lead to a great aversion.'

Since there was never any question that she had been legally married to Scarron, this allusion could only mean that the marriage had never been consummated, and that if Villarceaux had not been her lover in her twenties, in her middle forties Mme de Maintenon was still a virgin. The whole tone of this letter was certainly spinsterish, and showed little of the Aubigné charm that had so endeared her to the King; the 'people' who had so much confidence in her.

Her admonitions to her brother proved as useless as usual. He and his wife settled in Paris and became increasingly burdensome to her, always dunning her for money or favours and quite unpresentable at Court from her point of view. Yet she never carried out her threat to discard him, but bore the cross he was to her with true Christian patience.

The only letter Mme de Maintenon wrote to the Abbé Gobelin during that year was a very short one, dealing with ecclesiastical appointments he had requested her to ask the King to make, almost a business letter. Not a word about her own difficulties and perplexities, which were increasingly giving her violent migraines, only a mild reproach at the end because he had not written to her on her Saint's Day—St Francis's. As always at a time of crisis Françoise shut up like an oyster. Not until six months later, in March 1679, did she send him a desperate appeal:

'You know how much I need to have prayers said for me; I ask you to do so again, and to pray and have prayers said for the King, who is on the brink of a great precipice.'[10]

Mme de Montespan's last child, the Comte de Toulouse, was born on 6 June 1678. Like his sister, Mlle de Blois, he was secretly taken to Vaugirard, where the two babies were in charge of Mme Le Tellier, the wife of a Court official.

But *Quanto* was to make no dazzling come-back; her reign of twelve years was definitely over.

The Sun King was at the zenith of his power and success. The fairy-tale palace of Versailles was finished, all his policies and wars had been a succession of triumphs. And as if dazzled by his own brilliance, Louis was about to commit the last of his amorous follies.

A fascinated and sharp observer at the French Court, an Italian envoy called Primi Visconti, reported:

The King is not handsome, but he has regular features, his face is pockmarked; his eyes are in turn majestic, lively, mischievous, voluptuous, tender, and large; he has a presence, and as is said, a genuinely regal air; had he been only a courtier he would have stood out from among the others. Apart from these qualities, women are born with the ambition to become the King's favourites. Mlle de Fontanges appeared at Court with this idea in her head. She was tall, with a good figure, and very pretty, but as she was very fair, those who were jealous of her said that she was a redhead, because in France there is a prejudice against redhaired women, according to which they are all bad-tempered and smell nasty . . .[11]

Mlle de Fontanges was neither, but she was over-ambitious and very stupid. Her beauty, however, was unassailable. She had been chosen as a lady-in-waiting by Madame, the second Duchesse d'Orléans, Louis's sister-in-law, the German Elisabeth Charlotte, Princesse Palatine who was herself a woman of exceptional intelligence and also exceptional ugliness. Almost immediately Mlle de Fontanges met the King she fell violently in love with him. She was soon to become Mme de Maintenon's bitterest enemy, hating her with unquenchable spite and envy. Meanwhile, however, Madame had invited Mlle de Fontanges to serve her because, wrote Visconti, 'she chose the loveliest ladies-in-waiting to attract the King to visit her'.

Mlle de Fontanges's career was meteoric and tragic. At nineteen she ousted Mme de Montespan, the supreme mistress of twelve years' standing; at twenty-one she was dead.

Visconti told how

one evening Mme de Montespan, who was with the King, lost three millions, which she won back by making the courtiers continue playing with her until dawn. . . .

The King could not bear these losses, because he did not want it said that he was wasting money on ballets and gambling, when so much was needed to carry on the war [against the Netherlands] and the people were bowed down by taxation, for he wished them to believe he was asking these sacrifices from them not for his own pleasure, but for the needs of the State. Yet he allowed Mme de Montespan to continue in order to pull the wool over her eyes with regard to Mlle de Fontanges.[12]

But not for long. On 15 March 1679, after a furious quarrel, Mme de Montespan swept out from Court in a livid rage, literally bag and baggage, taking all her possessions and her entire retinue with her.

In April Louis officially appointed her superintendent of the Queen's household, the highest post a woman could hold at Court, and created her a duchess, giving her the right to be seated on a *tabouret*, a small stool, in the royal presence, so she was compelled to return. But this only confirmed her fall, since such a post could never be held by the reigning mistress. She was said to have shed bitter tears, especially after her interviews with the King, and after being obliged to meet her successful rival, who was giving herself insufferable airs. Where even Mme de Montespan only had a coach-and-six, Mlle de Fontanges had one, all upholstered in pearl grey, with an eight-horse team.

The final sensation occurred on New Year's Day, 1680, when Mlle de Fontanges 'appeared at the King's Mass loaded with jewellery, and wearing a gown of the same material as His Majesty's, and like him bearing the blue riband of the Order of the Holy Spirit'.[13]

Visconti commented:

> The King lived with his favourites . . . as if they were his legitimate family; the Queen received their visits and those of his natural children as if it were her duty, since . . . everything had to be done according to the King's will. When they went to Mass at St Germain they seated themselves under the King's gaze, Mme de Montespan and her children on the left-hand rostrum, facing everybody, and the other one on the right, whilst at Versailles Mme de Montespan was on the side of the Gospels and Mlle de Fontanges on the side of the Epistles. With their rosaries or missals in their hands, they prayed with eyes raised to heaven, like saints. Well, Court life is the most amusing comedy in the world.[14]

The one person who did not find it so was Mme de Maintenon. No wonder that her conscience was torturing her; no wonder that she prayed with all her fervour for the King's rescue from the abyss into which he was falling. And her prayers were answered sooner than she might have dared to hope.

In April 1680 Mlle de Fontanges was also made a duchess, with a stipend of 20,000 *écus*. The King went openly to visit her. 'Mme de Montespan', wrote our chronicler Mme de Sévigné,

> is furious; she cried a great deal yesterday; you will appreciate the martyrdom her pride is enduring, even more outraged by the high favour shown to Mme de Maintenon. His Majesty often spends two hours in the afternoon in her room, chatting to her with such friendliness and intimacy that her position is the most enviable in the world.[15]

Mme de Maintenon's earlier prayers were answered. At last the King had made the final break with Mme de Montespan, and it seemed that his passion for her successor was already waning.

Whilst at that stage Françoise was unable to persuade him to break this liaison off completely, in fact he was tiring of it. Mlle de Fontanges, silly little thing, had overplayed her hand. Louis was already relying so much on Françoise's discretion and persuasiveness that he asked her to visit Marie-Angélique and try to persuade her to moderate her arrogance. However much Mme de Maintenon might have wished that the liaison should be finally broken off and inwardly resented Louis's request for her assistance in keeping it on a more decorous keel, it was impossible for her to refuse this request from her Royal Master. So she spent several hours with Mlle de Fontanges and possibly following her own bent rather than her instruction did endeavour to persuade her to end the affair. Once again Françoise was unable to appreciate the power over Louis's sensuality of a pretty face and figure. And from Marie-Angélique's reply to her it would appear that Mlle de Fontanges was well aware of the fact.

'You talk,' she said indignantly, 'as if it were as simple to throw off a passion as it might be to change one's chemise.'

But Mme de Maintenon did not have to wait another twelve years for Louis to discard this mistress. Very shortly afterwards Mme de Sévigné was writing that Mlle de Fontanges was looking pale and wan, miserably unhappy, and finding the fact that she had been created a duchess and had been given a large

income no compensation, as she realised that Louis's passion for
her had already ceased to exist.

In January 1681 she had a still-born baby and owing to the
resultant haemorrhages went into an anaemic decline. Louis
could not bear the sight of ailing, weeping women; the moment
his short-term mistresses lost their initial bloom, beauty and
gaiety, he fled from them. Mme de Montespan's tremendous
vitality was certainly one of the main factors that had bound
him to her for so long.

On 22 March 1681 the English *chargé d'affaires* reported that
'On Sunday the Duchesse de Fontanges was taken to a convent
[Port Royal] to die there, her confessor having convinced her
that the Court was not a suitable place to do so; the doctors hold
out no hope for her recovery, nor even for her lasting until
Easter . . .'[16]

She died a week later. Louis did finally visit her, very
reluctantly, it was said, on her deathbed, when her famous last
words were spoken: 'I die happy, since I have seen my King
weep.'

The autopsy made it quite clear that the poor girl had died of
natural causes, pleurisy and pneumonia. But there was a
sinister undercurrent to her death. Rumours spread that she
had been poisoned by her deposed rival, Mme de Montespan.

All Mme de Maintenon's hagiographers maintained that it was entirely due to her influence that after Mlle de Fontanges Louis never had another mistress-in-chief. Had they been able to do so they would no doubt have ascribed Mme de Montespan's disfavour solely to Françoise's unremitting efforts during all those years to bring it about. Some of them fell back on the suggestion that in his early forties, the Sun King satiated by the hectic sexual activities of his previous years, had become impotent, as it turned out a demonstrably inaccurate form of wishful thinking. Yet something did happen to make him change his whole way of life; no physical condition, but a tremendous psychological trauma, or shock. This was due to the so-called Affair of the Poisons, a series of arrests and trials under torture that continued from 1679 to 1682, ending in several deaths at the stake, the course of which was reported to the King personally and privately, sometimes daily, sometimes monthly, but always most secretly and confidentially, over those years.

In these trials Mme de Montespan was accused of the vilest practices.

Ever since he became King, Louis XIV showed an increasing suspiciousness of those who served him. This developed steadily over the years and was reinforced by the Fouquet affair, when he discovered that that minister had been robbing his treasury of millions. As a result of this general mistrust, Louis founded an exceptionally widespread and efficient secret service, the members of which were under the direction of one of his chief ministers, at this stage Louvois, who regularly presented summaries of their reports to His Majesty.

The Affair of the Poisons, as it came to be known, was preceded by the extraordinary case of the Marquise de Brinvilliers. From 29 April until 16 July 1676 the whole of Paris was agog with excitement over the trial, torture, and beheading of this gentle little blue-eyed lady of excellent birth who had murdered her own father, two brothers, and other victims with arsenic. In March 1663 her father, a Parisian magistrate, had her lover, Sainte-Croix, arrested and sent for two months to the Bastille. His daughter thereupon experimented on the unfortunate inmates of hospitals, to whom she charitably brought poisoned sweets, and when she found these effective, gave her father more than thirty carefully measured doses of arsenic, never leaving his sickbed, and unblinkingly watching his awful sufferings until he died. In order to inherit his fortune, through a scoundrelly valet in her pay called La Chaussée, Mme de Brinvilliers then poisoned both her brothers. Her crimes were discovered on the death of Sainte-Croix, who had been blackmailing her, and kept hidden in his apartment a box containing her phials, letters, and other incriminating evidence.

Mme de Brinvilliers fled first to England, then to Holland, and finally to Belgium, where she was arrested on 25 March 1676.

The Court ordered that she should be beheaded—a form of execution reserved for members of the nobility only—on the Place de Grève, her body burnt—in a Catholic country the worst possible punishment, since it would be incapable of resurrection on the Day of Judgment—and her ashes scattered to the winds.

The execution attracted to the windows of the houses on the Place de Grève every fine lady who could possibly obtain a seat to witness it, and this is what they saw:

Dressed in the usual white shroud for those about to be beheaded, she knelt down, whilst the executioner cut off her hair at the back and both sides . . . rather roughly. This lasted for a good half-hour . . . He then tore off the top of the chemise he had put over her cloak when she left the Conciergerie, to bare her shoulders . . . Her eyes were blindfolded as she said her last prayers with the Abbé Pirot, her confessor, who had brought about her repentance. The executioner then severed her head with one blow of his axe.

'Monsieur,' he exclaimed to the Abbé Pirot, 'wasn't that a nice clean stroke?' And he drank a large draught of wine.[1]

The horror felt by the aristocracy at the case of Mme de Brinvilliers was almost entirely due to her membership of their class. But there were plenty of other poisoners and equally unsavoury criminals in Paris at that time. Unfortunately for them, there was also a most remarkable head of police in the city's service, almost the first of the great detectives, who was determined to winkle them all out and destroy them utterly. His name was La Reynie. This devoted and scrupulously honest policeman was directly responsible to Louvois.

La Reynie had arrested a gang of criminals of whom the most notorious were a woman, Catherine La Voisin, and her lover Lesage, already known to the police. On the face of it, La Voisin was no worse than an ordinary fortune-teller, of whom there were crowds at that time, visited by ladies of the highest society. But her fortune-telling was a mere blind for the most sinister activities, the sale of love-potions and poisons, the practice of abortion, and most hideous of all, the celebration of Black Masses which she arranged to have performed by a renegade priest, Mariette, and another frightful character, a certain Abbé Guibourg.

As soon as La Voisin and her accomplices were put to the torture they began to name and involve in their crimes persons of high station. It appeared to Louvois, and even more to his master, the King, that to allow such evidence to be heard in open court would create an appalling scandal. On 8 March 1679 Louvois informed La Reynie that His Majesty had ordered a special Commission to be appointed to hear this evidence in secret. This was officially known as the Commission of the Arsenal, but unofficially, to the Parisians, as the *Chambre ardente*, or Torture Chamber.

Under interrogation and torture, and confronted with one another, the criminals were soon claiming that their clients included some of the greatest ladies at Court, all of whom were apparently attempting to buy poisons in order to rid themselves of their husbands. On 25 January 1680, to the utmost consternation of all their friends, the Commission issued warrants for the arrest of Mme de Soissons, one of Mazarin's three beautiful nieces, Mme d'Alluye, and Mme de Polignac. To make matters worse, these highly born women fled from Paris rather than face the awful publicity an attempt to clear themselves would have produced.

La Voisin further claimed that various women of lower birth had employed her to obtain situations for them in Mme de Montespan's household, although she admitted never having met that great lady. But Mme de Vivonne, Athénaïs's sister-in-law, had also allegedly been one of La Voisin's clients. La Voisin's questioning under torture took place from the 19th to the 21st of February; she was burnt at the stake in the Place de Grève on 22 February. It was not she, however, but her daughter who brought the gravest accusations against Mme de Montespan when in her turn she was questioned during July. The royal favourite was stated to have bought love-philtres and aphrodisiacs from her mother to give the King secretly, and after Mlle de Fontanges had won him away from her, poisons with which to destroy them both. But this was not regarded as sufficiently powerful magic to achieve her ends. In addition the younger La Voisin stated, Mme de Montespan had also had Black Masses to the devil said over her naked body by the abominable Abbé Guibourg. Similar evidence was given by Lesage. La Reynie sent verbatim reports of these interrogations to Louvois, who in turn forwarded them to His Majesty, who seeing the way things were going immediately gave orders that not even the Royal Commission of the Arsenal was to be informed of these accusations.

On 20 August, La Voisin's daughter claimed, she had witnessed two Black Masses celebrated by Guibourg in her mother's room.

'The lady was placed stark naked on the mattress, her head hanging down, supported by a pillow on an upturned chair, her legs dangling, with a napkin on her stomach on which a cross was laid, with the chalice. About three years previously Mme de Montespan had had one of such Masses said by Guibourg at La Voisin's between ten o'clock and midnight.' On 9 October she gave further details which Guibourg confirmed on the following day:

In the name of Mme de Montespan he had appealed to 'Astaroth, Asmodeus [in fact the Devil] to accept the sacrifice of this child for the things I am asking of you [the King's favour]. He had bought for one *écu* a new-born baby that was sacrificed at that Mass . . . and having drawn its blood by slitting its throat with a pen-knife, he poured it into the chalice; then the baby was taken into another room, whence he was brought its heart and entrails for a second Mass, and to make powders for (the King) and Mme de (Montespan) . . .'[2]

The motives of the accused for giving these details were said to be that by inculpating the King's mistress in such blasphemous practices and other crimes, poisoning, *lèse-majesté*, and the rest, they would save their own skins from the stake. In this they were successful; they were merely left to rot in various prisons, chained, until released by lingering deaths.

For it was simply unthinkable that the publicity of any sort of trial should be given to them, that Mme de Montespan might be called as a witness before any Court in the Kingdom, or that the Sun King's own dazzling reputation should be darkened or possibly even eclipsed by such black revelations. The whole affair was hushed up by Royal Command; the papers containing the evidence were delivered to the King in person. Many years later, in his old age, he burned them. The evidence only remained in the form of La Reynie's personal notes for his reports, which were in due course deposited in the State Libraries.

Nevertheless Mme de Montespan's reputation was lastingly besmirched by these foul accusations. But only in the eyes of posterity. In spite of his many infidelities Louis had loved her for twelve years; and had returned to her again and again. He had legitimised their children, whom he also loved dearly. For their sake he could never allow such a disgrace to befall her. When Mlle de Fontanges ousted her, he appointed her to the highest post a woman could hold at Court, superintendent of the Queen's Household. Mme de Montespan remained so for a further three years. Even after the Queen's death she retained her superb apartment at Versailles for four years longer, where the King and their children visited her every day. After leaving Court she continued to live in great pomp until her death in 1707, spending the last years of her life in edifying good works and prayer.

At the very moment when in the torture chamber the most revolting details of her alleged addiction to black magic were being dragged out of her accusers, the King presented Mme de Montespan with 50,000 *livres*. This was interpreted as meaning that never for a moment did Louis believe in her guilt. The strongest evidence of her innocence was of course that neither His Majesty nor any of those rivals whom she was said to have been trying to remove by poison did die unnatural deaths; neither Mlle de la Vallière, still peacefully living in her convent, nor Mlle de Fontanges, who died of pneumonia, as her autopsy proved.

Yet when reading through those unsavoury details so scrupulously reported by La Reynie, the Sun King must have felt profoundly perturbed. It was generally known that ladies of the highest degree did visit fortune-tellers, from whom they bought aphrodisiacs compounded of cantharides, so-called 'Spanish Fly', nail-clippings, urine, human semen, menstrual blood, and powders made from bats, snakes or prawns.[3]

Mme de Montespan might well have done so. The King

remembered his recurring bouts of passion for her, which she knew so well how to arouse; was it altogether inconceivable that she might have been using some such horrible ingredients in the dishes she prepared for him with her pretty little white hands? Had his doctors not warned him against the sexual excesses that occasionally caused him to suffer from headaches, exceptional weariness and exhaustion? Even if she had been innocent of any sinister intentions, the whole story left a very, very unpleasant taste behind. Really, one could never trust a woman—'*fol est qui s'y fie*'—or could one?

No reference to this violent underground perturbation is found in Mme de Maintenon's earlier biographies, as if this impeccable lady had been in total and sole ignorance of the main subject of conversation—or rather horrified whispering—that was going on all around her. Even Cordelier, her most recent French biographer, dismissed the matter in a few paragraphs, as having nothing in particular to do with her.

One had, however, only to refer to a letter written by Françoise which shows quite clearly that she was well aware of all the rumours at Court concerning Mme de Montespan. Athénaïs had apparently invited her again to Clagny, and referring to this Mme de Maintenon wrote jokingly 'Nanon thinks it very dangerous'. Nanon Balbien was as ever Mme de Maintenon's closest confidant and by referring to her maid's fears, Françoise was showing both her awareness for the reason for them and her own conviction that they were quite ground-less.

We also know from Mme de Sévigné, that at the height of these horrible sensational events, the King visited Mme de Maintenon for at least two hours every afternoon. And whilst even that inveterate and impassioned gossip was unable to overhear their intimate conversations it seems almost inconceivable that they never touched on the subject.

On the contrary it might well have been with these very problems weighing on his mind that Louis was making his way to his cosy afternoon chat with the one human being in the world whom he felt he could trust completely, the woman whose warnings and pleadings he had so foolishly ignored. Now he knew that she had been right. Whether or not Mme de Montespan was cruelly slandered, she was in her way a sorceress, a beautiful Circe. Basically his feelings for her had been no more than lust and lechery; they had caused him to commit sins of adultery that might have imperilled his salvation and just possibly, if her accusers had told even a shred of truth, brought his immortal soul into peril from satanic influences. He was definitely resolved to avoid all such sex traps in future. But he was still only forty-two. Mme de Maintenon was forty-five. At first he had disliked her as a pretentious *précieuse*, but as the years went by she had become more and more indispensable to him. And by 1677 in spite of her undisguised disapproval of his debaucheries, Louis had succeeded in attaching Françoise to him on his own terms; three years later he was ready to surrender to her.

But did Françoise surrender to him, body as well as soul? Did she become not only the King's best friend but his mistress, the successor to the embittered Mme de Montespan, almost dumbfounded to find that Louis was, apparently, physically as well as mentally attracted to this middle-aged governess, the very opposite of the siren she herself had been?

'*Quanto* and *l'enrhumée* [the one with the cold, Mme de Maintenon]', Mme de Sévigné wrote, 'are on very bad terms, but the latter is on the very best with *the centre of all things* [the Sun King] which is the cause of the other's fury'.

The event that occurred in the month of December, altered Mme de Maintenon's status for all time and set the whole Court in a ferment of speculation.

Until the end of 1679 her humble position was that of governess to Louis's illegitimate children, those born as the phrase goes, 'on the wrong side of the blanket'. Now, however, Louis had resolved to bring her into the highest circles, in the closest proximity to Her Majesty the Queen and his legitimate family.

The Dauphin was of age, 18, and shortly to be married to

a German princess, Marianne, daughter of the Elector of Bavaria.

The Duchesse de Richelieu, the Queen's former lady-in-waiting, became the Dauphine's; the first *dame d'atour*, or lady-of-the-bedchamber, was Mme de Rochefort. And creating a precedent, as well as an entirely new post, His Majesty, by royal command published on 8 January 1680, signed 'Louis' and countersigned by his Minister, Colbert, appointed as second *dame d'atour* 'the lady Françoise d'Aubigné, Marquise de Maintenon, whose good conduct and other qualities are well-known.'[4]

Early in February the officers of the future Dauphine's household set out to meet her; they included Mme de Maintenon, who reported to the King on his new daughter-in-law's appearance and personality. The bride was brought to meet His Majesty and the Dauphin near Vitry, and after the usual greetings and embraces 'they entered his coach together' the *Gazette* reported. 'The King placed the Dauphine in the rear seat, next to himself, the Dauphin was seated beside her by the door. Monsieur sat in front with the Duchesse de Richelieu and Mme de Rochefort, and the Marquise de Maintenon was placed by the door next to the King.'[5]

Is it conceivable that at the same time he made her his mistress?

Françoise herself wrote to the Abbé Gobelin on the same day as the decree of her appointment was published:

As for my dresses [those she would in future be wearing] I shall change them for those similar to Mme de Richelieu's. My indifference in this respect relieves me of all scruples. When I spent my days in sharing the King's and his mistress's entertainment I wore gold and now I shall belong to a princess I shall always wear black . . . all these changes cause me no distress.[6]

There then followed, as if to justify her obvious pride in her new station, but not in the vanities it entailed, a curious examination of her conscience. After a list of her devotional exercises—

I have a code of morals and good intentions which prevent me from doing wrong; I have a desire to give pleasure and to be liked which puts me on guard against my passions, and I therefore almost never have to reproach myself for anything I have done, but simply for very human weaknesses such as great vanity, a great deal of frivolity and waste of time, great freedom in my thoughts and opinions and a restraint in speaking which is merely founded on common prudence . . .[7]

This letter was remarkable for two reasons. The first was the utterly unusual and almost sneering reference to her former friend and benefactress Mme de Montespan, whom she openly and insultingly referred to simply as the King's mistress. Would she at that moment have been willing to follow her in that contemptible role? The second was the admission that she had 'passions' against which she had to remain on guard.

As soon as her appointment was unofficially spoken of, her brother began to plague Françoise to obtain some equally distinguished post for himself. She replied to him very sharply:

'You are unreasonable to expect me to ask such a thing of the King at a time when he is overwhelming me with favour, honours, and all sorts of kindnesses. I shall never ask him for anything, I think only of serving him by serving my mistress [the Dauphine] with all the zeal, loyalty and devotion that will prove my gratitude to him.'[8]

The attentions Louis was paying her, the talk of the Court, were certainly enough to have caused her great vanity, even to turn her head. Had Louis at that moment made love to her in the literal and physical sense, would she, who felt so deeply indebted and grateful to him, who had worshipped him as King for so many years, have been able to resist his advances as a man, in spite of her loathing of sex? It cannot be said with certainty that she would have refused him. But the period was crucial. The King's increasing devotion to Mme de Maintenon was occurring at a time when the horrors of the Poison trials confessions were most vividly in his consciousness, so much so that he himself might well have been temporarily disgusted with sex, seeking no more than the comfort of an intimate platonic love based on the deepest mutual trust and respect. Louis had always respected Françoise, who was the only woman who ever aroused such an unusual feeling in him. Mlle d'Aumale reported that 'the King, when he was still young, was amusing himself one day by tipping over the chairs in which ladies were seated, almost to the ground [revealing their legs and petticoats] but when he came to Mme de Maintenon he went straight past her saying, "Oh, with that one I would never dare to do it."'[9]

Although he was her King and hero, a despot whose royal command was law, whose word might never be disobeyed, in their particular relationship there was a stronger moral power than his—hers. Throughout the following thirty-two years it was she who dominated him, emotionally and spiritually; eyewitnesses reported again and again that he could hardly bear her out of his sight. Louis loved Françoise heart and soul, and although that love was consummated in due course, nevertheless on both sides it was never based merely on sexual desire.

'I am told,' wrote Mme de Sévigné

that the conversations of His Majesty with Mme de Maintenon continue to increase and flourish; that they last from six until ten o'clock; that his daughter-in-law occasionally joins them for a very short visit, that each of them is seated in a large chair and when the visit ends they continue their discussions. My friend [Mme de Coulanges] tells me that no one dare approach the lady without fear and respect, and that the Ministers pay her the court that others pay them.[10]

Having neglected the Queen almost completely for twenty years, the King suddenly began to pay her some attention.

If one might imagine oneself eavesdropping on one of those intimate talks—'My dear,' Louis might well have said, 'you were of course quite right. Those mistresses, those frivolous creatures, never loved me nor understood me but only exploited me. When I think of the millions the Montespan gambled away, and what else she cost me, Clagny and the rest! As for Fontanges, well, I always did think her the stupidest creature on earth. But I'm still only forty-two and surely you cannot expect me to remain chaste for the rest of my life?'

'Of course not, Sire; but has it not occurred to Your Majesty that you have a wife, a Queen, who loves you dearly?'

'Does she, now?' he answered rather irritably, 'then why, whenever I want her company, is she always in chapel or at Mass?'

'Because, Sire, she is praying that God may send you back to her. I know that she longs for your affection; why don't you try to be a little kinder to her?'

'Well,' Louis shrugged his shoulders with a smile, 'if you say so, Madame La Raison, I'll have a try.'

This conversation is entirely apocryphal, but founded on incontrovertible fact.

'The King at that time,' wrote Mlle d'Aumale, 'showed his wife attentions and affections to which she had not been used, and which made her happier than she had ever been; she was touched to tears, and said in a kind of transport of delight "God created Mme de Maintenon in order to give me back the King's heart".'[11]

That was not entirely true; his heart belonged to Françoise, but he himself obviously derived great satisfaction and peace of mind from taking her advice.

The courtiers were completely mystified by the Sun King's devotion to Mme de Maintenon. One wit dubbed her 'Madame de Maintenant', the present favourite. But Mme de Sévigné came nearer the truth when she said that Françoise had revealed to Louis 'an entirely new prospect, friendship without constraint or nagging', the country referred to by Mlle de Scudéry in her famous novel as *Pays du Tendre*, the land of platonic love and tenderness.

Those of Mme de Maintenon's biographers who assumed that her obvious happiness and joy in life during the next three years were due to the fact that at last she had become the royal mistress, were making the same coarse assumptions as the courtiers. Yet Françoise did have every reason to be happy; she had at last achieved the triumph for which she had been working during all those past years. The King loved her with a love beyond her dreams, a love she had never dared hope for, a love that did not demand the surrender of her body to sex that she so dreaded. He could find the physical satisfaction he needed in his royal marriage-bed, according to the highest Christian principles, whilst she herself gave him all those other delights of marital love, tenderness and complete mutual trust. She knew that he would be faithful to their love, and that at last she had achieved her ideal relationship with him.

13   *Ruthless Conversions*

When Louis appointed Françoise as *dame d'atour* to the Dauphine her whole career took on an abrupt and radical change. As Mme de Sévigné and the Court noticed, her status was as different as possible from that of governess to the royal bastards. Much as she still loved those children and especially little Louis-Auguste, she was no longer responsible for their care and education. Her last words on the subject were contained in several long letters of instruction to M. de Montchevreuil, her oldest and most devoted friend, who had become the Duke's tutor.

> . . . He must have at least nine hours in bed, which is not too much for such a lively and passionate nature as his. Do not compel him to eat in the morning, when he is not hungry, although it may seem odd to keep a child without food until two in the afternoon, but he has supper so late that he would not have digested it by the morning and it is better that he waits until dinner-time . . . You will find him used to eating several kinds of soup . . . it is a habit they all have from the King, but which is better than eating a lot of meat without bread . . . If you can, give him fresh fruit when he can eat it . . . Fresh air out of doors has never done him any harm, but draughts immediately give him a cold.[1]

After further detailed instructions on the Duke's health and diet there followed advice regarding his character, with a warning to 'always be on your guard with him, as he is keenly discerning, a trait he has from the King, but also as sharp-witted and denigrating as all the Mortemarts. I should be more afraid of doing anything foolish in front of him than of anyone else in the world.'

In her letters to her confessor at this time, Françoise constantly underlined the fact that her new and highly distinguished post would have no effect either on her way of life, her mode of dressing, nor on her religious devotion. Undoubtedly she meant this. Yet the tone of the letters might make one wonder whether in her protestations to the Abbé Gobelin she was not attempting to convince herself that this would be the case. And indeed it would have been surprising had this sudden change in her career had no effect at all on her character. Until that date Françoise had won all her successes by gentleness, tactfulness and persuasion. Only when goaded by Mme de Montespan's attacks into defending herself, did she occasionally lose that self-control, that charming complaisance which had won her so many friends and admirers. It had now brought her the greatest prize of all, the King's love. And with that love such power and influence as she could never previously have dreamed of.

Unlike Louis's mistresses and even the legitimate female members of his family, Françoise was never attracted by life at Court, nor, specially, by its frivolous side; she neither danced, nor gambled, never touched alcohol, continued to wear black with only the regulation gold or silver lace on her collar and sleeves, and spent every spare minute she could organizing and supervising her establishments at Rueil, and later St Cyr, driving there whenever she was able, her coach filled with provisions, clothes, presents and prizes for her protegées. It was only with the greatest reluctance that she returned to St Germain or Versailles and especially to Fontainebleau, which she detested and which always gave her migraines, to a position which every other woman there and also in Paris envied her heart and soul.

Yet, like every true Frenchwoman, in the midst of her own advancement, she never forgot the well-being of her relatives.

Although, to his constant annoyance, she refused to allow her impossible brother to join her at Court, she obtained favour after favour for him, including an income of thirty thousand *livres*. But at that time her real interest was centred on her other relations and their children, particularly the descendants of that beloved aunt, Mme de Villette. During her trip to Barèges with the Duc du Maine in 1675, she had visited them on her return to Paris. Her cousin, M. de Villette, had two young sons and a little daughter. She had managed to secure him a captaincy in the Royal Navy, and in the battle of Messina he had shown considerable courage and seamanship, but, as she repeatedly wrote to him, her efforts to further his career were hampered by his obstinate refusal to renounce his Huguenoterie. The plan she set into operation in 1680, to help him and his family in spite of himself, was as bold as it was unscrupulous. If M. de Villette was pig-headed enough to refuse the conversion she considered essential to his advancement as well as to his salvation, his three young children should become Catholics in spite of and in actual defiance of their father's will. No doubt Françoise was convinced—as all her Catholic contemporaries were—that the end justified the means. Yet the way she set about achieving it was morally indefensible. She was aware of the fact, but still had no scruples in carrying out her carefully laid plan.

First of all she arranged for M. de Seignelay, the Secretary of the Navy, to send M. de Villette to sea with his younger son as his midshipman. The elder boy was attached to the squadron of M. de Château-Renaud, who, immediately after his father's departure was requested to send the lad to Versailles, where he arrived in November 1680. Françoise then wrote to the Abbé Gobelin:[2]

'I have a young relative of mine here, a Huguenot, whom I am anxious to convert . . . he is only fourteen and . . . I therefore pray you to come here on Monday or Tuesday to begin this task.' But as the Abbé was unable to do so, she sent the boy to him in Paris on 22 November with another short note, repeating her request. Young Villette proved a docile convert. Her main interest, however, was in M. de Villette's little daughter, Marthe-Marguerite de Mursay, who was then only nine years old. Françoise, to put it quite bluntly, had not the slightest scruples in kidnapping this child during her father's absence. She was to live with her for many years; in due course Mme de Maintenon arranged a match for her with a M. de Caylus, and it was as Mme de Caylus that many years later she retold the story in her Memoirs:

> No sooner had my father embarked on this voyage of long duration . . . than one of my aunts [Mme de Fontmort, his sister] by arrangement with Mme de Maintenon, asked my mother to visit her at Niort, bringing me with her. My mother was intending to return home the same day, as we lived near the town, but when she was leaving my aunt begged her so insistently to let me stay with her at least until the next day, that she at last reluctantly agreed, for although she herself was a Catholic she was not in the secret of the plans they had made for me because they wished to spare her my father's reproofs. As soon as my mother left Niort, my aunt departed for Paris, taking me with her. On the way we met M. de Sainte-Hermine with one of his sisters, and Mlle de Caumont [other cousins who were also leaving according to Mme de Maintenon's similar plans for their conversion] all of them as astonished as they were grieved to see me, having a pretty good idea of what was going to be done with me. I myself knew nothing of it, and was quite happy to go along with them, without knowing where I was being taken . . . We arrived together in Paris, where Mme de Maintenon immediately came to fetch me [this was in the last week in December] and took me back with her to St Germain, where the Court then was. At first I cried a great deal, but next day I thought the King's Mass was so beautiful that I agreed to become a Catholic, on condition that I would hear it every day and that I would not be whipped.[3]

Mme de Maintenon, having attained her end, immediately wrote the most affectionate and contrite letters to the child's mother explaining how and why she had been obliged, of course for the child's own good, to take this drastic step; she hoped that

M. de Villette would not take the abduction of Mlle de Mursay 'too seriously', and that he would allow his daughter to continue to live with her. She assured his wife that on his return in March of the following year she would be able to deal with him. And in her usual indomitable way she did so. At first Philippe de Villette was naturally furious at the trick she had played on him, and wrote her several extremely angry and reproachful letters. She replied to him at very great length, with sweet reasonableness. And as she had predicted, in due course he not only decided to accept the *fait accompli*, but in fact sent her his younger son to be converted as well. The final touch of irony was M. de Villette's own surrender, in 1685, when on returning from another tour of naval duty he himself abjured the creed of the redoubtable founder of the family, Agrippa d'Aubigné, and became a Catholic, for by then he was more interested in his naval career than in religion. As Raunie, the editor of Mme de Caylus's memoirs, dryly remarked, although his conversion was not merely for advancement's sake, and he told the King that '"it was the only occasion in his life when his aim had not been solely to please His Majesty," he was in due course appointed to the command of a squadron, and later, Lieutenant-General of the Navy.'[4]

Françoise however was determined that all her young Huguenot relatives should become Catholics. Having satisfactorily solved the problem of the Villette children she next proceeded to turn her attentions to her other cousins, the Sainte-Hermine and Caumont d'Addé descendants. In the instance of the little Sainte-Hermine girl, Minette, she was sailing very close to the wind indeed.

D'Aubigné was then Governor of Cognac, and in a letter dated 19 December 1680, she gave him the following instructions:

... I love Minette and if you could send her to me it would give me very great pleasure; no other method than violence is possible since the family will be very upset on hearing of the conversion of the Mursay children. It will therefore be necessary for you to get her to write to me that she wishes to become a Catholic. You will send me her letter, and I will then send you a *lettre de cachet* [a royal command that could not be disobeyed] with which you will take Minette to live with you until you find an occasion to send her to me.

She assured her brother that she would make arrangements for the child's safe journey, and insistently asked him to 'work at this affair, as I have an affection for this little girl and you would be obliging me as well as doing a good deed'.[5]

Nothing but good, in the worldly sense, came to Mme de Maintenon's young relatives—male and female—as a result of her intentions and actions, regarding their religious adherence. Only her interest in them raised them from dull and boring provincial existences to lives of such brilliance and success as they would never otherwise have known. And in taking the steps she did to bring this about, that was Françoise's principal motive. Nevertheless, as her letter to her brother proved, she was quite aware of the fact that even if the end did justify the means, those means themselves—kidnapping, violence, abduction, a *lettre de cachet*—were morally reprehensible. Yet looking back on her own childhood of which throughout her life she retained such keen memories, she probably considered that she was doing no worse by Marthe-Marguérite de Mursay and Minette than had been done by her. These two little girls were docile converts, but Françoise at their age had been stubborn and obdurate. Only after years of effort by her mother, her rich aunt and the kind nun who at last worked successfully on her conscience, did she herself become a Catholic. When she did give in and was converted, she laid the foundations for her whole future career. Her determination that her little cousins should have similar opportunities outweighed any scruples she might have felt in so forcibly providing them.

Moreover, these conversions were mere straws in the wind that was then beginning to sweep France, the bitter wind that was blowing from the Sun King's orbit over his Huguenot subjects and that was to culminate five years later in the notorious Revocation of the Edict of Nantes.

14 *Morganatic Marriage*

The young Dauphine was a very plain girl, whose health was far from good, painfully conscious of her lack of beauty, vivacity, and any qualities necessary to shine at the Sun King's Court. Her best physical asset was her hair, which was thick and long. Because Mme de Maintenon had an exceptionally gentle touch she was at first in high favour with her new young mistress, who would allow no one else to comb and brush it. But the Duchesse de Richelieu was bitterly resentful of Françoise's promotion as second lady-in-waiting and began to poison the princess's mind against her. In view of the evidence this was not difficult, for whenever His Majesty visited his daughter-in-law, she herself was the first to notice that he spent most of his time in conversation with her second *dame d'atour*.[1]

And Mme de Maintenon was more often in their Majesties' coach than her official position necessitated. These trips—especially those on which the ladies accompanied the King on his sorties to distant cities, as part of his military voyages, were a most strenuous experience. 'He always travelled,' wrote Saint-Simon, 'with his carriage full of women: his mistresses, later his bastard daughters, his daughters-in-law, sometimes Madame [his sister-in-law, the Duchesse d'Orléans.'] They were obliged to wear full Court dress and needed to be prepared for certain unpleasant ordeals. For,

> on these journeys the coach was always full of food; meat, pastry, fruit . . . The King never ate anything between meals, not even fruit, but it amused him to see people eat, and eat until they burst. They had to appear hungry, gay, eating with good appetite and spirits, otherwise he would be displeased, and showed it . . . As for the needs of nature, they were unmentionable, apart from the fact that for the women to relieve themselves would have been highly embarrassing, with the King's cavalry escort both in front of and behind his coach . . . covering everything inside with clouds of dust. The King, who liked fresh air, insisted on having all the windows down and would have thought it very bad if any lady had drawn a curtain against the sun, wind, or cold . . . the King always drove very fast and to have shown the least signs of feeling unwell, would have been unpardonable . . .[2]

In 1680 Louis went on an extended trip to inspect the fortifications of France on the Flanders frontier. The journey lasted from 13 July until 30 August. He took with him the Queen, the Dauphine, and of course, Mme de Maintenon in attendance. No one was more delighted than she to note the attention the Sun King paid to his Queen; he made a point of taking her on several tours of inspection, and she, poor woman, plain, dumpy and unintelligent little Infanta though she still was in her early forties, blossomed like a girl under this long prayed for kindness.

And this new and delightful mutual affection between the Royal spouses lasted for the next three years. In 1681 the Sun King's greatest monument, the superlative Palace of Versailles, became his principal residence, where Her Majesty was housed in great splendid apartments of marble and gold, facing southwards. On 2 May Mme de Maintenon wrote from there to M. de Montchevreuil, then at Bagnières with the Duc du Maine, that 'Versailles is of astonishing beauty and I am enchanted to be here; we shall be entertained by all kinds of pleasures; frequent balls given by the King, plays at Monsieur's, walks everywhere . . . for the King wants us all to enjoy ourselves.'[3]

But Queen Marie-Thérèse was unlucky and lived less than two years longer to bask in her belated happiness. In the summer of 1683, on returning from another very tiring trip to the fortifications of the Franche-Comté and Alsace, she developed an abscess under her arm. She was attended by Fagon, a doctor whom years before, on her first journey with the Duc du Maine, Mme de Maintenon had discovered at Bagnières, and brought back to Court, where he was in the highest favour. Unfortunately, his treatment of the abscess was fatal, for 'instead of making it burst [he] had his patient bled; this drove in the abscess, and after four days of almost unendurable suffering on 31 July the Queen died of blood poisoning. She was forty-five; she had been married to Louis for twenty-three years, during only the first and last of which he had been a good husband to her.

He grieved for his late Queen decorously rather than deeply. Nevertheless he carried out all the usual ceremonial connected with such an occasion, with his habitual thoroughness and sense of kingship. His main problem, however, was to decide what new responsibilities to his House and nation his new widowerhood laid upon him.

As he was still only forty-five, the obvious solution would have been for him to marry a second princess of equal rank to his former wife's. Subsequent events were to reveal his personal motives for rejecting this course. Yet Louis the man never for a moment forgot the obligations of Louis the King. Despite the fact he had already decided on the daring plan he was shortly to carry out, he still, with apparent candour and sincerity, went through the motions of gravely considering a second royal marriage. He even took his ministers and Parlement partly into his confidence, and whether it was he or one of those agile politicians, who provided the conclusive argument against it, sufficient reasons were found to dismiss the project.

Louis already had two apparent heirs and successors. The Dauphin and the Dauphine had a baby son, the Duc de Bourgogne; another child was on the way, and in the normal course of events there would have been no reason for anxiety about the Bourbon succession. A second royal marriage might produce offspring that would later cause considerable political troubles to the first, and even possibly civil war.

According to Dangeau, at supper on 13 August, Louis informed the Court that the Council had decided second royal marriages were unfortunate, thereby quite clearly indicating his intention not to make one.

In retrospect the King's decision seems not to have been based on a very strong case. Even had he thought otherwise, it is doubtful whether at that stage his sense of duty would have prevailed over his personal, secret and very definite intentions. At forty-five Louis also knew that he no longer desired a glamorous, extravagant, cantankerous mistress. He needed and intended to have a devoted, discreet, charming, intelligent, reliable legitimate wife.

Throughout his childhood and adolescence Louis was dominated by his mother, Anne of Austria. Sun King he might be, yet even after her death the shadow of her influence lay over his subconsciousness. Although it might be an exaggeration to suggest that his passion for *gloire* was due to a repressed inferiority complex, Louis XIV was frequently unsure of himself. After Anne's death he may well have been seeking a mother surrogate, and unquestionably Françoise's love for him was predominantly maternal.

She was three years older than he, forty-eight, and there was therefore no risk that they would have a family that might one day compete for the throne with the Princes of the Blood.

Yet he was well aware of the tremendous opposition he would arouse if even he, the arch despot, were to raise Françoise de Maintenon to the throne. Queen she might never be. The legitimate members of the Royal Family, the princes and princesses, already found the King's preference for the former Mme Scarron scandalous. The higher aristocracy, including the proud Lorraine princes and the dukes would have been horrified by the raising of a woman of such dim social antecedents to the highest position in the land. No one was more clearly aware of this than the King; in addition to the Royal Family and the aristocracy, his clergy and ministers would have been more than reluctant to accept such a fantastic reversal of the code by which he governed them, and which even he could not defy.

There was, however, one course he could pursue. This was to marry Françoise de Maintenon morganatically. A morganatic marriage was one in which a man of royal rank could take as his lawful wife a woman of inferior birth. By marrying Françoise according to this convention, Louis might enjoy her carnally without offence either to God or the clergy, whilst she herself would continue to live with him on their previous terms of affection without having to commit fornication. Apparently he decided to do so as early as the first week of August 1683, at Fontainebleau. Thereupon he proceeded to take his principal minister Louvois and the archbishop of Paris into his confidence, when it was agreed that the marriage would be solemnized in the greatest secrecy.

According to Mme de Caylus immediately on the death of the Queen Mme de Maintenon was about to return to her own apartment. But before she could do so, the Duc de La Roche-foucault firmly took her by the arm, saying to her: 'This is not the moment to leave the King, for he needs you.' So Mme de Maintenon did as he asked, but spent only a few minutes in the King's company.[4]

Shortly after the Queen's death Louis left for St Cloud and then went on to Fontainebleau. There he was joined by his daughter-in-law, with Mme de Maintenon in attendance. 'She appeared before the King in such deep mourning, with such an air of affliction, that he, whose sorrow was over, could not help teasing her about it.'[5]

Probably Mme de Maintenon did sincerely grieve for the Queen, of whom, in a secretly rather patronising way, she had been genuinely fond. But if Louis's sorrow was so short-lived there was good reason for it. Françoise knew this very clearly indeed and the fact that at Fontainebleau she was in a quite unusual state of agitation was not in the circumstances surpris-

The Château de Maintenon

Françoise de Maintenon as Saint Francesca Romana
Portrait by Mignard

ing. For with the Queen's death her own relationship with the King reached its climax.

'During this journey,' wrote Mlle d'Aumale, 'Mme de Maintenon's favour became even greater. The King could not do without her and installed her in the Queen's apartments; the councils were held in her room, and the King conducted the greater part of his business there, frequently consulting her.' During this crucial period she spent more time than ever at her devotions, 'praying for guidance, in order better to serve the King's salvation, for she was convinced that it was for this that God had arranged matters as they stood.'[6]

Mme de Caylus wrote:

> I saw her in such an agitated state that I have since thought that it was due to a condition of violent uncertainty regarding her position, her thoughts, fears and hopes; in a word, her heart was not free and her mind very upset. In order to conceal these various emotions, and to explain away the tears we saw her shedding, she complained of the vapours, and went, she said, to breathe some fresh air in the forest of Fontaine-bleau, accompanied only by Mme de Montchevreuil ... The vapours finally disappeared and her agitation gave way to calm.

From Mme de Maintenon's point of view the last three years had been almost perfect; perhaps the happiest of her life. She had been enjoying power without responsibility, love without sex. The Court, the clergy, everyone knew that it was she who had reformed and rescued Louis from his life of dissipation; even the Pope was aware of it, and sent her several presents, including reliquaries, as a mark of his gratification. She could ask for nothing more.

But the Queen's death radically changed the position. Until Louis made his will clear to her, Françoise could not see how her future would turn out. Now that he was a widower, would he marry another Royal princess? Would he then still find her as indispensable as she had become to him? Would he make another attempt to persuade her to become his mistress? Since she was resolved not to do so, this might mean that she would have to find some way of obtaining his permission to retire from Court. If his intentions were honourable, how could they be carried out?

Françoise's agitations lasted only a short while, from the Queen's death at the end of July until little more than a week later. Presumably Louis had made it clear to her at Fontainebleau that he intended to marry her, and it was to this determination on his part that her happiness was due.

The King would not, of course, have 'proposed' to Françoise; it was sufficient for him to inform her that he intended to bestow this supreme honour on her.

It has never been definitely established when this most famous of morganatic marriages took place. But Mme de Maintenon's letters during August and September proved her proud acceptance of her new position. As in no circumstances she ever wrote anything factual about her relationship with His Majesty, these letters of the late summer and autumn of 1683 contain only hints, but fairly definite ones to those who can read between the lines. Louis had obviously made his intention clear to his beloved as early after the Queen's death as he could decently do; already he had installed her in the royal apartments at Fontainebleau.

Mme de Caylus wrote that after Mme de Maintenon's death she herself had read the letters Françoise wrote to the Abbé Gobelin; the earlier ones, 'reveal a woman disgusted by Court life, who was only seeking an honest excuse for retiring from it; but in those written after the Queen's death, that same woman no longer hesitates, her duty is clear and inevitable to her—she has to remain there'.[7]

But that seems putting it on a rather low, prosaic basis. Françoise herself expressed it differently in her letter to her brother from Fontainebleau on 7 August. For the obvious reason that the King had already spoken to her, the time had arrived to make it quite clear to Aubigné that on no account would she receive him if he insisted on coming to Paris:

'The reason that prevents me from seeing you is so beneficial and so glorious that you should only feel joyful at it.'[8]

A week later she wrote to her cousin, M. de Villette, that 'the news you send me [gossip and rumour he had passed on to her] is false; the King has no love affairs; you can state this without fearing to appear misinformed.'9

This was surely an obvious indication that Françoise was aware of the allegations that Louis had made her, or was intending to make her his mistress; allegations which the King himself might well have encouraged to circulate in order to conceal from the public his true intentions towards her. Françoise, however, was not prepared to allow these rumours to gain credence.

On 22 August, in a letter to her friend Mme de Brinon she returned to the subject:

'I am so glorified in this world by certain good intentions that are by God's will, that I have reason to fear being humiliated and confounded in the next. There is nothing to answer with regard to *Louis et Françoise*, this is mere folly. I would, however, like to know why she would not be willing? I could never believe that difficulties in this matter would come from her side.'10 This may have been in reply to an inquiry from Mme de Brinon, in which case rumours and gossip of an impending marriage between them were then already circulating in Paris.

And finally there is the only letter she wrote in that year to the Abbé Gobelin dated 20 September. From this it is clear that he had been visiting her, no doubt at her own urgent request, during the previous period when she had been suffering from the vapours and the anxieties that brought them on. He had written to inquire after her health, and now Françoise assured him that her indisposition had been very slight and that she greatly regretted her temporary distress during his recent visit.

'That time was badly spent and let you partly perceive the agitation I was suffering; this has now calmed down and I am in a peaceful condition which I would far rather have you know of than the troubles of which we informed you.' The plural noun no doubt included her confidante at that period, Mme de Montchevreuil. And this letter ended: 'Adieu, Monsieur; do not forget me before God, for I have great need of strength to make good use of my happiness.'11

With reference to the suggestion that Françoise's happiness at that period was caused by Louis having made her his mistress, the names of those to whom these letters were addressed appear integral. M. de Villette was her first cousin, and her desire to stand well in the eyes of her family was as steadfast as ever. Would she therefore have boasted to him that she had succeeded Athénaïs de Montespan?

Mme de Brinon was at that time the head of the small foundation supported by Françoise for the secular and religious education of poor village girls, and was later to become the first headmistress of St Cyr. Was it likely that Françoise would have boasted to her that she had formed a liaison with Louis?

Finally, all her correspondence over the years with her confessor demonstrates how unremittingly she and the Church had been working to detach Louis from his immoral intercourse with other women. Would she have written to the Abbé with such impudence and hypocrisy at this stage assuring him that her new peace of mind was due to both sin and moral turpitude?

Since the actual date of the marriage was never divulged, it was natural for everyone both at the time and later, to produce their own guesses. Madame, the German Duchesse d'Orléans, and Mme de Maintenon's bitter although impotent enemy, wrote in 1686 that 'as long as there is no declaration of it [the marriage] I find it difficult to believe'; in 1687 she was still vainly trying to ferret out the truth, yet 'I have not been able to discover', she was compelled to admit, 'whether or not the King has married Mme de Maintenon . . . What is certain is that the King has never had, for any of his mistresses, the passion that he feels for her; it is really curious to see them together. If she happens to be in the same place he cannot remain a quarter of an hour without whispering something to her or speaking to her in secret, although he has spent the whole day with her.'[12]

From that day to this, such speculation has never ceased, from Voltaire's to Louis Hastier's, who in 1957 wrote a whole book on the subject. Hastier's guess was as late as 1697, which seems highly improbable. Lavallée suggested that the marriage took place in the spring of 1684. The most reasonable date suggested appears to be Langlois's, who placed it in October 1683, only three months after the Queen's death. From Mme de Maintenon's own letters we know that by the beginning of August she was already hinting that she had unusual cause for happiness. Nor was there any reason why, once Louis had decided to marry her, he should not have proceeded to do so at his own pleasure, which obviously would have been at the earliest moment compatible with the minimum of decorum.

Whatever the year or the date, on a certain night seven people did gather in the greatest secrecy in the King's private chapel, where the altar was dressed by Bontemps, His Majesty's personal valet and confidential servant, who also served the Nuptial Mass. This was celebrated by Father La Chaise, the King's Jesuit confessor, and the blessing was given by Harlay de Champvallon, Archbishop of Paris. The two witnesses were Louvois, the powerful Minister for War, who had known the bride for many years, and her old friend, M. de Montchevreuil.

On that night Françoise d'Aubigné, the poor little Huguenot girl nobody wanted, Françoise Scarron, the girl who had married a helpless cripple rather than become a nun, the widow Scarron, governess to the royal bastards, and finally Mme de Maintenon, a very lowly member of the aristocracy, became, and remained until the death of her husband, the Sun King, more than thirty years later, the uncrowned queen of France.

Part Two

On 15 April 1684 Françoise heard of the birth of d'Aubigné's daughter and only child who was named after her. She provided the baby's layette and a spate of advice on her nursing and up-bringing, for it was understood that as soon as the little girl was old enough she would adopt her. Meanwhile, however, she was staving off d'Aubigné's importunities with a new and implacable firmness:

> I advised you not to settle in Paris because it seems to me that it would be regarded as bizarre that you should be so near me, and yet not be in touch with me. I cannot forbid you to do so, and I should be sorry to place you under the least restraint. Let that be clear once and for all, and also that I desire your happiness more deeply than my own. [But] Our situations are different; mine is brilliant, whilst yours is in-conspicuous . . . God has placed me where I am; I have to manage as best I may; He knows that I did not seek it; I will never be raised any higher and I am far too highly placed already.[1]

D'Aubigné complained again and the wrangle continued for the following months. He must by then have been informed of her marriage, for he had written with bitter sarcasm that 'it was no doubt a personal adventure, which was not to be shared', a clear reference to Françoise's position, to which she replied, as reasonably as possible, yet throwing his own words in his teeth— 'Remember your past and be happy to have an income of thirty thousand *livres*. Do not let my present position poison yours, since mine is a *personal adventure* which, as you very rightly say, *is not to be shared*'.

But Françoise was still not freed from Charles's absurd pretensions. He had, apparently, conceived the fantastic notion that as His Majesty's brother-in-law he was entitled to some unusual honour, and seriously suggested that the King should appoint him Lord High Constable of France. She had been unable to prevent him from coming to Paris, but at the time the Court was at Chambord, from where she wrote him on 27 September quite categorically:

> Even if I wished to do so I could not have you appointed Constable, as I am quite incapable of asking anything unreasonable from him to whom I owe everything . . . Perhaps you may feel hurt at this, but perhaps also, if I had not the sense of honour to feel like this, I would not be where I am.[2]

There is a note of unusual contentment and even of gaiety in Mme de Maintenon's letters from Chambord. She was beginning to put on some weight, but, she wrote gaily, a little plumpness was more becoming in old age than scragginess.

What did Françoise look like, in early middle age, when Louis was so deeply in love with her? There is no portrait of her at that precise date. The nearest impression of her personality then is conveyed by the painting by the artist Ferdinand Elle made of Mme de Maintenon and her niece, a few years later, when Françoise must have turned fifty. Her hair is covered by a black mantilla, but what can be seen is also black and slightly coquettishly pulled forward over either temple. There is an unmistakable double chin, but a high, well-moulded forehead. The face is as unlined as that of the child at her knees, but this no doubt was partly due to artistic flattery. The mouth is smallish and quite pretty, with a slight pout, that one feels might deepen into a less pleasant fold when its owner was annoyed. By no stretch of the imagination could one call this either a beautiful or a glamorous face. Françoise's eyes, however, had always been admired for their brilliance and sparkle, and in this portrait those of the beholder are immediately attracted and held by them. They seem to express everything their owner was so carefully refraining from saying or writing. Happiness, a glint of the consciousness of her success and the position of secret power, considerable pride and almost defiance. The impression is of a woman supremely in command of herself and her circumstances. It is not difficult to imagine that when those eyes smiled up at her husband, he found their expression of marital devotion very attractive.

Françoise continued her letter by informing her brother that the weather was lovely and the Court 'very gay'.

The King hunted every day and each evening there was some entertainment, a ball or a play. The Dauphine was 'marvellous' and everyone else was happy. 'We always dine with the King, in a very agreeable family atmosphere.'

The Duchesse de Richelieu, who had prejudiced the young Dauphine against her second *dame d'atour*, had recently died and the princess, possibly prompted by her father-in-law, became devoted to Mme de Maintenon, offering her the honour of becoming her first lady-in-waiting. Louis would have liked Françoise to accept it, since it would have provided them with a welcome alibi for her constant presence in the royal family circle. She dared, however, to refuse it and 'people' wrote Mme de Caylus, 'saw in this more pride than modesty'.

Her pride at being accepted as His Majesty's legitimate wife by 'his royal relatives did not, however, turn her head'. The suggestion made by certain of her biographers that at that time she had higher ambitions, no less than to persuade Louis to have her proclaimed Queen, is refuted by Saint-Simon's description of her public appearances. Although in the privacy of the royal family she sat in an armchair similar to the King's, an honour only permitted to his wife, in public her demeanour was as modest and as simple as in the past . . .

dining with him and the ladies . . . invariably ceding precedence to persons of higher quality, and in every way polite,
affable, speaking like a person of no pretensions nor revealing
anything, but making a great impression nevertheless . . .
Always very well dressed, nobly, suitably and in good taste,
but very modestly and in the style of an older woman than
she actually was.[3]

Yet there is some truth in the view that she was equally
anxious that her position should not be thought to be an
irregular one.

'Although,' wrote Mme du Perou, author of the *Memoirs of
the Ladies of St Cyr*, with whom Mme de Maintenon spent much
time in her later years, 'on that subject her secrecy was inviolable, one day when I had the honour of being with her, she
said, speaking of Mme de Montespan and the King's other
mistresses, that there was a great difference between his
affection for her and his feelings for those ladies, for the former
was a *sacred bond*.'[4]

Moreover, the King bestowed on her all the prerogatives to
which only his wife was entitled, never calling her anything but
Madame, with neither prefix nor title, treating her with deference
little short of submission. The Dauphin and all the princes of the
royal family always spoke and wrote to her with respectful
affection, consulting her in everything, addressing her and the
King as the *heads of the family*.

But neither then nor later did Françoise change her personal
household arrangements. She was able to inspire in those who
served her unstinting and lasting devotion. With her unusual
flair for character she surrounded herself with men and women on
whose complete discretion she could count as well. In describing
her household, Saint-Simon, that incorrigible snooper, showed
an irritated sense of frustration:

'Mme de Maintenon's servants,' he wrote, 'were very few,
uncommunicative, modest, respectful, humble and silent. In the
course of time they acquired small fortunes . . . all remaining
more or less comfortably in the background . . . The King knew
them all; he was on friendly terms and often chatted with them

if he happened to call on her before her return.' And with his relish for small but dramatic detail the Duke drew an unforgettable portrait of the most important of them all, of Nanon Balbien, the faithful maid who had entered the young widow Scarron's employment in her days of direst poverty; who probably dressed her mistress on her second wedding night, and who in their old age became almost as powerful a figure behind the scenes as Mme de Maintenon; 'even the royal family, legitimate and bastards, the princes of the Blood and the ministers, feared and respected her.'[5]

Mme de Maintenon's confidential man-servant, Manceau, had been in her service ever since Louis had conferred her title and estate on her. On a higher social plane the King's and her most trusted official was the controller of her household, the Marquis de Dangeau, who from 1 April 1684 also kept a diary of Louis's daily life and who was one of Mme de Maintenon's most fervent admirers. Dangeau, a widower, married the Countess of Loevenstein, a very attractive young woman who was a maid-of-honour to the Dauphine, and who became one of Mme de Maintenon's most intimate friends and companions.

It was not to be expected that Louis would be an easy husband to live with. He had an exceptionally robust constitution for a man of his age and period. Almost none of his countrymen—but a great number of the rude islanders across the Channel—shared his passion for fresh air. The huge palace of Versailles was freezingly cold in winter, yet the master insisted at all times that in his presence the windows should be kept wide open. Mme de Maintenon was no weakling. But like all her female compatriots she had a horror of draughts, which since her marriage she was compelled constantly to endure. As she grew older she became increasingly rheumatic, but Louis allowed no physical weaknesses in his female companions, whether mistresses or wives. In later years the former Madame Scarron boxed herself in against the draughts, like her crippled first husband. She had a kind of padded wicker chair constructed, in which she found some protection from those *mauvais courants d'air*.

If, according to Saint-Simon, His Majesty was in a bad mood, he did not spare even Françoise, and from time to time would make a terrible scene, reducing her to tears, and leaving her on tenterhooks. She herself repeatedly told her confidantes in later years that 'the King had no conversation' and that it was necessary to keep him perpetually entertained. On such occasions she would suggest that they send for the young Princesse de Conti, who frequently drove out with them. In June 1685 she wrote to her brother that 'this young Princess is turning out very well', but both His Majesty and Mme de Maintenon were to change their minds about her very soon afterwards.

The Princesse de Conti was Louis's daughter by the gentle and modest Louise de La Vallière, who had become a nun. According to Mme de Caylus, this girl was 'as beautiful as Mlle de Fontanges, as delightful as her mother, with the figure and air of her father'. She also had almost as sharp a tongue as the Montespan and although she was not a member of the brilliantly witty Mortemart family, her audacious sallies amused her father. He had legitimised her and married her brilliantly, to the Prince de Conti, a Prince of the Blood and descendant of the great Condé. The Conti princes, tired of the monotony of Court life, had defied Louis's orders and left, followed by several other members of the aristocracy, to fight in the Hungarian war.

In consequence of this insubordination one of the Prince's couriers was intercepted, and the correspondence he carried submitted to the King. To his justified fury, Louis found among these letters several from the ungrateful Princess to her husband, in which she told him of the boredom she had to endure when obliged to accompany His Majesty and Mme de Maintenon on their outings. It was to Françoise that the King assigned the perhaps not altogether unpleasant task of disciplining the indiscreet girl:

Mme de Caylus wrote:

> The Princesse de Conti was let off with her fear and shame to have to appear every day before her justly irritated King and father and, in order to be forgiven, to have to appeal to a

woman whom she had insulted. Mme de Maintenon spoke to
her very severely indeed . . . telling her several home-truths
. . . . but did not fail to soften the King's anger, and as he was
naturally kindhearted and loved his daughter tenderly, he
forgave her.[6]

Only in Mme de Maintenon's company was Louis able to be
himself and wholly at ease, as she herself told the ladies of St
Cyr in later years:

When the King returns from hunting he comes to my room,
the door is shut and no one else is admitted. Now I am alone
with him. I have to listen to his worries, if he has any, to his
melancholy, his vapours. Sometimes he has a fit of weeping,
which he cannot control, or else he is ill. One of his Ministers
arrives, often with bad news. The King works. If they want
me in their councils they call me, if not I withdraw a little
further off and it is then that I sometimes say my afternoon
prayers.[7]

16 The Revocation of the Edict of Nantes

According to Saint-Simon Mme de Maintenon sat in the centre of the great golden palace of Versailles like some sinister black spider in its glittering web, ruling the King, the Ministers, and the country.

Yet until the war of the Spanish Succession, some fifteen years later, Louis did not consult Françoise with regard to his military campaigns. But he almost certainly did do so concerning the political and religious decisions he made affecting France.

The most important of these was the Revocation of the Edict of Nantes, on 18 October 1685.

'No other method than violence is possible,' Françoise had written to her brother when ordering him to abduct and send her Minette, the little Sainte-Hermine girl from Cognac. These words alone, her enemies never ceased pointing out, proved her complicity in the renewed persecution of the Huguenots.

During the previous century, under the Valois dynasty, France had been bled almost to death by the terrible Wars of Religion between Catholics and Huguenots. These were at the same time political wars in which foreign mercenaries, mostly Germans, savagely decimated many French regions; their culmination, although not their end, was St Bartholomew's massacre in 1572. At that time, Henry, the young Huguenot King of Navarre, only saved his life by accepting Catholicism. On escaping from his imprisonment in the Louvre, Henry immediately reverted to the Reformed religion. On the death of Henri III, the last Valois king, Henry was obliged to recapture the kingdom he had inherited by another series of battles. The majority of the people were staunchly Catholic and in order to ascend the throne, the Bourbon monarch for the second time and finally reverted to Catholicism and was crowned in Rheims Cathedral as Henry IV.

Henry was an enlightened ruler and in 1598 issued the Edict of Nantes, guaranteeing to the Huguenots, his former co-religionists, liberty of conscience and the right to practise their creed without persecution. Under his successor, Louis XIII, there were further religious wars from 1621 to 1624. But whilst the Huguenots were in status second-class citizens, they still enjoyed the benefits conferred on them by the Edict of Nantes.

Louis XIV had succeeded his father when he was a child of five. From his childhood onwards he was a strict and sincere Catholic. And whilst under his despotic rule neither the Pope nor the French clergy wholly dominated him or his policies, apart from war, religion was his most real concern. Had this not been so, the Catholic faction at Court would never have achieved such ascendancy over him, even at the time of his wildest dissipations. His creed was essentially simple. God was the Heavenly Father of all his children on earth; the Most Christian King was His secular representative in France. And just as all Christian souls were pledged to obey the Almighty so all Frenchmen were their King's children, under oath of obedience to him. It therefore followed that the King's religion was theirs, and in this simple paternalistic light Louis saw no reason for any exceptions or exemptions to this rule. It was the spirit of unity that Louis was so anxious to establish throughout his realm; religious unity that would keep pace with the other unities in the social structure, the administration and the arts. And in religion as in secular life deviationism was not merely displeasing. It bore undertones of incipient radicalism and even rebellion. During the previous century it was impossible to draw the line between the Wars of Religion and revolt; in Louis's opinion, the time had come to nip in the bud any such recurrence.

Of his twenty million subjects only one million still adhered to the Reformed religion. And it did not appear an insuperable task, either to the King or the Catholic leaders, to persuade them to abjure their faith. Preaching and persuasion were to be the instruments of their conversion.

'The King,' Françoise wrote to her confessor on 27 September, 'is very well, praise God, and rejoicing. The couriers bring us news of thousands of conversions.' Dangeau wrote on 2 September that the entire Huguenot population of Montauban decided to become converts; on 6 September more than 50,000 at Bordeaux; on 5 October the whole diocese of Montpellier, and the same was the case for Nîmes, Uzes, Lyons and many other cities. Nevertheless, such pacific methods proved insufficient to bring the hard core of Huguenots to heel.

Commanded by one of Louvois's most brutal intendants, Marsillac, companies of dragoons were billeted on all the leading Huguenot households in the Protestant strongholds, such as Poitou. Under this violent pressure, compulsory conversions of the majority of the Huguenots took place in tens of thousands; but a quarter of a million, including the most intelligent and highly skilled, emigrated to Germany, Holland and England. It was then that Louis ordered the Revocation of the Edict promulgated by his grandfather abolishing all the rights previously conceded to those who still remained.

Indignation at these ruthless measures of salvation was not confined to the Huguenots and the Protestant countries that had given the refugees asylum. It inspired Saint-Simon, a devout Catholic, to a passage of splendid invective:

The Revocation of the Edict of Nantes . . . was the outcome of that appalling plot which decimated a quarter of the kingdom; ruined its commerce and weakened it everywhere, exposing it to admitted and public looting by the dragoons, authorising the torments and tortures by which thousands of the innocent of both sexes died, tore apart whole families, kinsmen against kinsmen, in order to seize their property and let them die of hunger; handing over our industries to the foreigners so that their States flourished at the expense of ours; revealing to them such outstanding people proscribed, naked, fugitives, innocent exiles seeking refuge far from their own country . . . and to crown all these horrors filled every province of the realm with perjurers and sacrilegers . . . dragging them to adore what they did not believe in, receiving the Holy Sacrament . . . whilst convinced that they were only eating bread . . .[1]

Louis was said to have been largely ignorant of the more brutal aspects of this renewed War of Religion; the blame was placed chiefly on Louvois and Marsillac, and the King was allegedly highly displeased when he learned to what extremes they had gone. Père La Chaise, his own confessor, was a Jesuit, as was Bourdaloue, the most fashionable preacher at Court, yet it was no Jesuit sophistry but supported by the entire Catholic clergy that in this case the end justified the means, and that His Majesty's Act was inspired by and pleasing to divine Providence.

The view that it was, in fact, inspired by his morganatic wife was so long and so strongly held—not only by the Huguenots themselves—that her panegyrists went out of their way to deny that she was, as Saint-Simon maintained, in any way personally responsible for it. Mme de Maintenon referred in none of her correspondence to the Revocation of the Edict of Nantes. Her editor and admirer, Lavallée, however, found it incumbent to quote a passage on this subject from the *Notes des Dames de Saint-Cyr* to prove her utter lack of complicity.[2]

'At that time,' they wrote,

the King thought that to crown his glory it was necessary to uproot a heresy which had so deeply ravaged his realm. The methods employed were somewhat rigorous, but although the Huguenots imagined the contrary, Mme de Maintenon had no part in them; she longed with all her heart for their reunion with the Church, but would have preferred this to have happened rather by persuasion and kindness than by severity; she told us that the King, who was very zealous, thought that she should show more enthusiasm than she did and therefore said to her, 'I fear, Madam, that your wish that the Huguenots should be treated gently stems from your slight inclination for your former religion.'

The King was also naturally inclined to kindness, but he had been led to believe, probably by Louvois, that only violence would extirpate this heresy, and that if, after all, such violence did not create good Catholics, at least the children of those on whom it was inflicted by force would become so in good faith.

Yet in spite of the Ladies of St Cyr's efforts to exonerate her from any blame in the matter, the difference between Françoise's and Louis's procedure, was a quantitative and not a qualitative one. When she had decided that her six young relatives, the three La Villette children and the three Saint-Hermine cousins should become Catholics whether or not their parents approved, she had shown no scruples at all in the methods she employed because the end justified the means. Undoubtedly when writing to Charles on 19 December 1680 with regard to little Minette that violence was the only method, and by taking advantage of her position to obtain a *lettre de cachet*, a royal command ordering the child to be brought to Paris, she knew perfectly well the moral impropriety of the step she was taking. Yet in spite of her tactful and sympathetic letters to these children's parents, it might well have been to her that Saint-Simon was referring when describing the tearing apart of whole families. These events occurred only a few years before the final suppression of the Huguenots, and to say, as the Ladies of St Cyr claimed, that Mme de Maintenon might have baulked at stronger measures than mere persuasion, appears in retrospect mere hair-splitting.

It is improbable that as early as 1685 Mme de Maintenon's influence over her husband was already so strong that she could be held entirely responsible for such a far-reaching act of statecraft, yet there can be no doubt that, if not having actively caused it, she was wholly in agreement with it.

On 5 February 1686 the King's doctors were alarmed to discover that he was suffering from a very painful abscess of the rectum. Louis's favourite playwright, Molière, in several of his comedies ridiculed the medical practitioners of the day, little more skilled than barbers, whose common remedies for most human ills were bleeding, purging or both, which killed as often as they cured. After three weeks the abscess had not yielded to these and similar treatments. Fortunately, however, among the quacks consulted was an able surgeon, Felix de Tassy, who on 23 February opened it up with a pair of scissors and immediately diagnosed the cause of the inflammation, which was a fistula that could only be removed by a radical operation. In spite of his exceptional physical courage Louis flinched from this ordeal, known and dreaded as *la grande opération*, and decided to try every suggested remedy before undergoing it, in the hope that his condition would yield to less drastic measures. Felix, meanwhile, convinced that it would not do so, visited the Paris hospitals, where for the following eight months he practised this operation on patients with a similar condition. Month by month Mme de Maintenon's letters reflect her acute anxiety.

'I do not know where I am, my dear,' she wrote to Mme de Brinon on 27 February, 'they keep telling us that the King is getting better, yet threaten us with another snip of the scissors. Whenever I think of it I feel the pain of it.'[1]

During the following months, Louis's condition alternated between apparent recovery and relapses. On 18 November he finally decided to submit to the dreaded operation. On the previous evening, although he was in such pain that drops of perspiration were covering his brow, he nevertheless received the foreign ambassadors. 'We are not,' he stated, 'like private individuals; we owe ourselves to the public,' and he endured his ordeal with truly regal courage.

The operation took place in the greatest secrecy, the only non-medical witnesses being Mme de Maintenon, Louvois and Perè La Chaise. Louis stood it admirably, but the inevitable reaction set in three weeks later. On 11 December Françoise wrote to Mme de Brinon that 'during seven hours he suffered such pain as if he had been broken on the wheel', yet thanks to his superb constitution, on Christmas Day he was able to write that he was cured and everyone was enraptured to see him in public again. The skilful Felix was rewarded with a peerage, a country seat and £15,000.[2]

Mme de Maintenon was undoubtedly a most devoted wife and during this painful year gave her royal husband all the comfort and consolation she could provide. Nevertheless, however much his sufferings distressed her—as they undoubtedly did—her letters prove that they had little effect on her main interest in life at that period, the completion and opening on 29 July of St Cyr.

When in January 1680, Mme de Maintenon ceased to be the professional governess of the royal bastards, she did not for one moment lose her love of children or her interest in their welfare. Her former profession became, and for the rest of her life remained, her hobby and chief interest.

She had met at the Montchevreuils' country house, where she frequently stayed, an Ursuline nun, Mme de Brinon, whose convent had been closed owing to poverty. Mme de Maintenon took an immediate fancy to this lady, seeing in her the perfect instrument for carrying out a plan she had by then only partly developed—the upbringing and useful employment of several poor girls from Maintenon, who were to be taught religion, their letters, weaving and spinning. She therefore established Mme de Brinon and three similar instructresses in what was at first little more than a barn at Rueil, near enough for her to pay them frequent visits and supervise their wellbeing. In this humble framework Mme de Maintenon laid the basis for her life's great work, the foundation of St Cyr, the school for impoverished daughters of the minor aristocracy, in similar circumstances to those of her own unhappy youth, which was to become the model for the education of young French women. The passion with which she undertook this work of pure charity was no less characteristic than the talent for organisation she showed in carrying it out. For years she wrote regular and long letters of instruction to Mme de Brinon, which went into the minutest details.

In February 1684, shortly after her marriage to Louis, the original school at Reuil was transferred to Noisy, a country house with large rooms and gardens laid out by the royal landscape gardener Le Nôtre, which the King had given his wife for the purpose, and possibly as a wedding present. Louis's vivid sense of the dramatic may well have appreciated the immense difference between the personal ambitions of his former mistress and his second wife. Mme de Montespan had unhesitatingly extracted millions from him, which she spent on her superlative country residence, Clagny, on jewels and especially on frenzied gambling. Mme de Maintenon, almost from the day of their marriage, living in semi-retirement at Versailles or wherever else the Court resided, actually saved and scrimped on her own personal expenditure in order to realise her one and only ambition—the education of girls of her own class and station. Nowhere in her correspondence is there such serenity, such pure joy, such a cry of triumphant elation at ambition fulfilled, as the lines in her letter of 7 April from Versailles to her brother Charles:

'I go more often than ever to Noisy where the evening walks have now begun: imagine my pleasure as I walk along the avenue, followed by the one hundred and twenty-four young ladies who are there at present.'[3]

One can easily imagine it, for that sentence contains the very essence of the unchanged character of Françoise. During those evening walks she felt herself leading her youthful crocodile into that promised land she herself had only attained the hard way. And as any lesser husband might have done, Louis began to take an active personal interest in her plans. He liked young girls in a disinterested, paternalistic way, found them amusing and touching. He also liked seeing things for himself. One day he paid a surprise visit to Noisy, as in the distant past he had first visited Mme Scarron and his children in their secret retreat at Vaugirard. He was so pleased with what he saw that on Ascension Day he decided to provide the school with a larger home, and to present the pupils with the necessary dowry so that in due course they might marry well.

For neither Mme de Maintenon nor the King wished to found another convent. Although run on severely religious principles under Mme de Brinon, Noisy and later St Cyr, was primarily an educational institution. The revenues of the Abbey of St Denis, 100,000 *livres*, were assigned to it; later another 80,000 were provided from the Royal treasury. For Louis, St Cyr became a hobby; for Mme de Maintenon, a vocation.

Louvois was instructed to find a suitable site; the little village of St Cyr, close enough to Versailles to enable the foundress to drive there daily and sometimes more often, was decided on. Mansard, the architect of Versailles, was commissioned to draw up the plans. The site was badly chosen from the point of view of hygiene, for it was damp and swampy and later led to a great deal of illness amongst the boarders. Nevertheless, building began on 1 May 1685, and proceeded rapidly, so that the great move of the establishment from Noisy took place on 28 July in the following year. This was no small removal; the staff and boarders amounted to around three hundred, and the whole operation was carried out with military precision.

When writing of Mme de Maintenon Saint-Simon dipped his pen fifty per cent in ink and fifty per cent in venom, no more viciously than in his description of her creation of this institution:

> She had a mania for organising that deprived her of the little freedom she had at her disposal, wasting an incredible amount of time on St Cyr and a thousand other convents. She saw herself as the universal abbess, down to the last details concerning various dioceses. These were her favourite occupations, for she imagined herself to be a Mother of the Church, with, in consequence, an ocean of frivolous, illusory, tiresome occupations, infinite correspondence, the direction of elect souls and puerilities of all kinds, generally leading nowhere but occasionally, in important matters, to deplorable mistakes and decisions . . .[4]

Merciless and sweeping as his generalisations were, they did contain more than a grain of truth. In theory and intention the foundation of St Cyr was wholly admirable, but it was as much an outlet for Mme de Maintenon's secret and subconscious lust for power as for her genuinely idealistic motives. She was completely incapable of discriminating between the wood and the trees; intensely jealous of her authority, reluctant to delegate the smallest shred of it to Mme de Brinon or her assistants. For years her letters to Mme de Brinon, to her confessor, her brother and other relatives and friends were filled with such details and trivialities.

The ladies, or instructresses, who were not nuns, wore only a semi-monastic costume in black and white, but around their necks was a chain from which hung a golden cross surrounded by fleurs de lys, under which were engraved, below the crucifix, two lines:

> *Elle est notre guide fidèle*
> *Notre félicité vient d'elle*

lines that ostensibly referred to the Holy Virgin, but by inference could hardly fail to be applied to the foundress.

Saint-Simon also claimed that the whole concept of such an institution had been based on the foundation by Mme de Montespan of a similar educational establishment in Paris, for the Daughters of St Joseph, to which she retired when she was finally obliged to leave Court. His meanest criticism of Mme de Maintenon's motives was that by founding St Cyr she

> hoped to smooth her path to having her marriage made public, by providing herself with an Institution that would entertain and amuse the King as well as herself, and similarly to serve as a retreat for herself should she have the misfortune of losing him, as indeed happened.[5]

In this respect again her implacable detractor did not lie but merely twisted the facts to suit his convenience. It was the usual thing for influential ladies of the Great Century to engage in such good works to benefit their less fortunate sisters, and there was no doubt at all that Louis was at first amused and entertained by St Cyr. During the months preceding his operation he spent many hours with his wife, working out such details as the actual dresses and ornaments to be worn by the boarders. As at Noisy, they were divided into four groups charmingly and almost coquettishly dressed in brown skirts and cloaks, their bodices stiffened by whalebone, their white caps, collars and cuffs trimmed with lace, and ribbons of various colours—blue for the eldest, then yellow, green and lastly red for the littlest ones. At Easter Mme de Maintenon would take them presents of eggs dyed in these various colours. The classrooms and dormitories, with their rows of neat spotlessly sheeted beds, were similarly decorated. So that far from conveying an atmosphere of monastic austerity St Cyr was bright and cheerful. There were other refinements, mainly due to the King's interest in the pupils, who were to enter the great world in due course as model wives to the nobility and, therefore, he commanded, should already be provided with suitable drinking cups and cutlery of silver. The ladies, the teachers, were not to address one another as 'Mother' or 'Sister' but as 'Madame', followed by their respective titles, and d'Hozier, the Court genealogist, was ordered to inspect each candidate's family tree. The King personally undertook to endow the twenty young debutantes who annually left the school with dowries of three thousand *livres* to provide their trousseaux.

The education programme was also less simple than the Foundress had envisaged, for the girls in the highest class, the Blues, having previously learned the usual subjects, were also trained in dancing, deportment, and elocution. Music played a remarkable part throughout the curriculum and in due course amateur theatricals led to an historical event, the writing and performance before His Majesty and the Court of a biblical play, the study of which was ever since imposed on girls' schools throughout France, *Esther*, by Racine.

In the meantime, however, the foundress was faced with a situation worthy of the comic genius of Molière himself—the insubordination of no less a person than the directress she had hitherto so fully trusted, Mme de Brinon.

Mme de Brinon was a *précieuse réligieuse*, who even at Noisy had differed from her benefactress in the emphasis to be laid on education on the one hand and religious ceremonial on the other. At St Cyr, these differences very quickly came into the open. Since the school was obviously giving His Majesty so much pleasure, it rapidly became the fashion amongst the ladies of the Court, princesses, duchesses and all who could gain admittance, to descend on it in chattering flocks. Almost before all the pupils had been transferred there, the Duchesse de Montpensier, the King's first cousin, La Grande Mademoiselle, could not be refused entry. To mark her displeasure at this intrusion Mme de Maintenon decided to remain at Versailles rather than to receive her, an honour she erroneously conferred on Mme de Brinon. The directress was only too delighted to deputise for her on this and other occasions.

Mme de Maintenon spent every possible minute at St Cyr, but not to waste her time on social intercourse, from which even at Versailles she withdrew as frequently as possible. With her personal chamberlain, Manceau, and Nanon Balbien, the servant who had become her trusted deputy and adjutant, she would visit every corner of the building, inspecting, listing and

cataloguing the contents from the linen cupboards to the larders.
But inevitably she was unable to indulge in this minute over-
seeing as often or as constantly as she would have liked, and in
1687 and 1688 matters came to a climax.

Mme de Brinon had been neglecting the girls' secular education more and more. Her passion was the chapel, where the
Holy Sacrament was exposed, its adornment and enrichment,
the embroidering by the young ladies of magnificent vestments
for the clergy, clouds of incense, and above all, endless singing
and religious processions. The time had come to call her to
order: 'You cannot believe, my dear,' wrote Françoise, 'how
sad it makes me to oppose your wishes, but there is no other
house where the children are so constantly at church as they are
here.'[6]

Mme de Brinon, however, did not have the sense to realise
that in an establishment founded by Mme de Maintenon there
could not be two headmistresses. She summoned a priest of her
own choosing to her aid, who rashly endeavoured to plead her
case with Mme de Maintenon herself. It was quite clear that she
had no intention either of ceding or of leaving. She would have
to be dismissed. Mme de Maintenon was subsequently severely
criticised for her method of doing so. She had no difficulty in
persuading Louis that if Mme de Brinon were to remain at St
Cyr all their plans for its future would be wrecked. Having been
so stupidly obstinate in opposing the will of her benefactress,
Mme de Brinon was nevertheless with some justification shocked
and horrified when on 10 December 1688 there arrived at St
Cyr their old friend Mme de Montchevreuil; not, however, in
order to reason with her or reconcile them, but to hand her
that most dreaded of all documents, a *lettre de cachet* signed by
His Majesty in person, commanding her to depart forthwith and
retire to a convent. Unable to bear the disgrace and ignominy of
a public exit the unfortunate woman left secretly, by a little
postern gate. For good measure, Mme de Maintenon had
instructed her confidential chamberlain, Manceau, to accompany her to Paris.

Having achieved her purpose Mme de Maintenon was not

vindictive towards her former very dear friend. She received a pension of 2,000 francs and, wrote the Ladies of St Cyr, as usual putting the gloss on their foundress's actions, 'as she still liked that lady . . . she remained throughout their lives in correspondence with her'.

Five days after Mme de Brinon's summary dismissal Mme de Maintenon was installed at St Cyr, with the reins again firmly in her own hands. From there she wrote a completely heartless note to the confessor in whom she had ceased to have confidence:

> You may not believe, perhaps, that an exclamation is particularly funny, yet I thought I would die of laughing at yours, and your astonishment at what has happened; and after that I do not think you will ever cease to be afraid. If you would like to come back and see at close quarters what has occurred, you will realise that things look larger at a distance and that here, thank God, everything is as one might wish. If you are ill do not force yourself to come, but do so if you feel well enough.[7]

It was the Abbé's consternation and his expression of it, apparently, that had caused her such intense amusement, but in that laughter to which she refers one cannot help hearing a note of triumphant cynicism. She was clearly anxious that he should realise that Mme de Brinon's departure was a relatively trivial incident and that otherwise nothing important at St Cyr had changed. The Abbé Gobelin, her old confessor, was also about to be retired. Mme de Maintenon had already begun to look for another personal confessor as well as a successor as spiritual director of the school. And this quest brought her into closer touch with one of the most remarkable prelates of the period, Bishop Fénelon of Cambrai, with whom she was to commit the grave spiritual error that for two years threatened to break up her marriage.

18 Françoise on the Brink of a Precipice

Mme de Brinon had written some innocuous little plays for performance by her young ladies, since amateur theatricals were part of their education. They were, however, unusually vapid, and her verses doggerel. Mme de Maintenon, who all her life remained a *précieuse*, despised these efforts; nor was anything too good for St Cyr and if her girls were to learn and perform plays they should be the very best.

Jean Racine, France's greatest lyrical dramatist, was born in 1639 and educated at Port-Royal. This famous convent, directed by a group of exceptionally intellectual nuns, provided board and lodgings for some of the greatest philosophers and thinkers of the time, including Pascal. In due course it became the French centre of a form of religious deviationism known as Jansenism, after its creator the Dutch Jansen. The Jansenists were essentially puritanical and against such frivolities as dramatic authorship. But Racine's genius won out over his religious proclivities. He broke with Port-Royal and at the age of 28 began to produce a series of masterpieces, from *Andromaque* in 1667 to *Phèdre*, ten years later. He then had another change of conviction; renounced the theatre, made his peace with the

Jansenists, and married a wealthy woman. In recognition of his genius the Sun King appointed him royal historiographer, with lodgings at Versailles.

Mme de Maintenon requested Racine to provide a suitable play for performance at St Cyr, preferably with a biblical setting and definitely with no love interest. He was reluctant to return to dramatic authorship, but since His Majesty's interest in the theatre was still keen and his benevolent protection of St Cyr evident, the poet could not refuse this invitation. Moreover, in spite of his attempts to renounce worldly vanities, Racine— like his friend and contemporary the critic Boileau—was an astute courtier. Together they chose the subject of the play—the Book of Esther from Holy Writ. And when *Esther* was performed by the young ladies, it was clear to the distinguished audience present by special invitation, that the King, Ahasuerus, and the lowly but virtuous Jewish maiden raised up to be his wife, could hardly fail to be identified with Louis and Françoise.

No expense was spared on scenery and costumes. Esther's cloak was embroidered with the diamonds formerly worn by His Majesty when as a young man he had danced in the Court ballets. A stage was built in one of the larger dormitories, with seating for the audience below. Racine and Boileau rehearsed the performers, none of whom was older than fifteen, and on the first night there was almost a panic of stage-fright amongst them. It took place on 26 January 1689, before the King, the Dauphin, and several high ecclesiastics. After the second performance to such an austere audience, Louis, delighted with the whole production, decided that there should be a third one, for the Royal Family, the exiled King James II of England and his Queen Mary of Modena, who were living at St Germain, and every Court lady who by intrigue or influence could gain admission. The King himself drew from his pocket the guest-list Mme de Maintenon had given him and smilingly checked the names on it as their lucky possessors entered. Mme de Sévigné was one of them, and even received a royal remark: 'I am told, Madam, that you are pleased.' Louis's informant was Mme de Maintenon, who with her usual discretion sat a little behind His Majesty, whispering to him the flattering comments from all over the hall.[1]

Quite naturally this dramatic and social success went to the young ladies' heads. Later, the older girls were allowed to act in the piece, and Mme de Caylus, who had been educated at St Cyr and was by then a veteran married woman aged 17, played *Esther*.

But it was not long before Mme de Maintenon, prompted by the Bishop of Chartres, realised that such frivolity had gone too far. The performances were dropped; the actresses went back to their lessons and discipline. When Racine's second and last tragedy for St Cyr, *Athalie*, was given there in 1691, it was in Mme de Maintenon's private apartments, with neither scenery nor costumes. And other, harsher reforms were pending.

Racine died in 1699. By then he had fallen out of favour with the King. This was chiefly because Louis suspected him of having reverted to the creed of Jansenism, the second heresy of which he so strongly disapproved.

When Mme de Maintenon was seeking a personal confessor to succeed the Abbé Gobelin, she was strongly attracted by one of the most commanding and fascinating ecclesiastics at Court, Bishop Fénelon of Cambrai. The great religious orator Bossuet had been the tutor of the Dauphin; Fénelon held a similar post as spiritual guide to Louis's grandson, the Duke of Burgundy. In the religious drama of Versailles Bossuet's role was analogous to Corneille's in the theatre, Fénelon's to Racine's. The former was nicknamed the Eagle of Meaux, for his swooping flights of oratory, whilst his colleague was known as the Swan of Cambrai for his calm and gentle personality. Fénelon was tall, handsome, eloquent, erudite and emotionally romantic, preaching that God was love and the road to Heaven lay through pure and perfect love. He had no more fervent disciple than Mme de la Maisonfort, whom Mme de Maintenon had chosen as successor to Mme de Brinon.

Mme de la Maisonfort had a cousin, Mme Guyon, and it was to Fénelon's admiration for this lady and her entry into St Cyr

Marie-Anne, Princesse des Ursins
Portrait by Serrur

Elisabeth-Charlotte, Duchesse d'Orléans called 'La Palatine'
Portrait H. Rigaud

Saint-Cyr

Contemporary engraving

that Mme de Maintenon owed the very serious disfavour into which she fell with Louis.

Saint-Simon claimed that Mme de Maintenon was unstable in her friendships with all but a few old cronies; that she took sudden fancies to people and dropped them just as suddenly. And her personal relationship with Mme Guyon certainly indicated that after her second marriage, when more power was thrust upon her than she could always use wisely or with discretion, these criticisms were justified.

Jeanne-Marie Bouvier de la Mothe, whose much older husband was M. Guyon, by whose name she became notorious, was one of the most remarkable women of the Great Century. She came of good family and when her husband died was left a well-to-do widow with three young children. Her spiritual director was a slightly mad Barnabite monk, Father Lacombe, who claimed to have discovered in her profound mystical gifts. From 1681 onwards the two of them travelled around southern France, spreading the doctrine, known as Quietism, that was to be inextricably linked with Mme Guyon's name, but which she had not herself invented. In 1686 the authorities arrested Lacombe and in 1687 sent him to the Bastille. Mme Guyon was sent to the convent of the Visitation, also under detention. But she was well-connected, and through Colbert's three daughters, known for their piety, and close to Mme de Maintenon, she obtained her freedom and the great privilege of meeting the most powerful woman in France.

Mme Guyon immediately made a deep impression both on Mme de Maintenon and on Fénelon, who was the personal director of Mme de la Maisonfort. In a very short time Mme Guyon was installed at St Cyr. She was a prolific writer; her published works totalled forty volumes, but the most popular of them was a little book entitled *Le moyen court et facile de faire oraison, An Easy Way to Prayer*, which set out very briefly the basic principles of Quietism.

This was the simplest imaginable form of transcendental meditation. The inventor of this mystical method of communicating with God was a Spanish monk, Miguel de Molinos.

G

His basic theory was that for the practice of mysticism, the aspirants should place themselves in a state of absolute passivity, of emotional love-surrender to the divine, in which the voice or will of God would then become known. Mme Guyon's simplified version of this mysticism, and her little book explaining how to attain this end, made an instant irresistible appeal to Mme de Maintenon. For some time she carried the booklet about in her apron pocket. Even more extraordinary was the intellectual conversion to quietist theories of Archbishop Fénelon, a theologian regarded at Court as only second to the great Bossuet himself.

Mme Guyon's personal charm and seductive theory of meditation very quickly had a disastrous effect on the ladies and girls of St Cyr. Most of the teachers, like their pupils, were emotionally adolescent. Now, with their foundress's direct approval, they were caught up in a spate of 'meditation'— lessons and religious duties neglected whilst they lay prone in the chapel, or in their rooms, practising this direct relationship through pure love with the Deity.

After the short worldly interlude during their performances of *Esther*, Mme de Maintenon had seen the need to re-impose a stronger religious discipline on St Cyr. As her personal confessor, in succession to the old Abbé Gobelin, she chose the stern and austere Godet des Marais, later through her influence appointed Bishop of Chartres.

It was des Marais who, horrified when visiting St Cyr during the *Esther* period, insisted on the school being thoroughly reformed and placed on a totally unworldly basis. Fénelon remained the personal director of Mme de la Maisonfort, but the young ladies were placed under the authority of the Order of St Vincent de Paul, the Fathers of St Lazare.

In a very short time des Marais and these confessors became aware of the grave danger to their penitents of Mme Guyon's residence amongst them. Quietism was, as Rome in due course ruled, a heresy that threatened to undermine all religious discipline. Mme Guyon's books were strictly forbidden to teachers and pupils alike. After a sharp lecture by her confessor,

Mme de Maintenon, horrified, promptly took out of her pocket the *Easy Way to Prayer*, and threw it down from her as if it were something unclean.

But the controversy had gone far beyond the limits of a young ladies' boarding-school. Fénelon, tutor to the Duke of Burgundy, became Mme Guyon's firmest champion; the formidable Bossuet, his implacable opponent. Still confident in Mme Guyon's rectitude, Fénelon sent her to Meaux, where Bossuet personally examined her and her writings thoroughly, and condemned both. By this time the affair had dragged on into March 1695. The most sensational act, however, was still to come.

Fénelon, convinced still that Quietism was no heresy, said that he would answer for Mme Guyon's honesty and good intentions; finally he went to the length of writing a short work, *Les Maximes des Saints en état d'oraison*, in which he claimed that Mme Guyon was in the line of the most revered orthodox mystics. The controversy was then carried to Rome, for a ruling.

Strangely enough it was only two years later, that Louis became acutely aware of the emergence of Quietism as a successor to the Jansenist heresy which he so much abhorred. In recent years he had been deeply involved in military activities and other governmental affairs. Moreover, ever since St Cyr had ceased to be a hobby with him, since amateur theatricals by charming little girls had been suppressed in favour of a sternly religious curriculum, he had lost interest in it. His religious fervour, that had been so stimulated during the early years of his marriage to Françoise, had also cooled off.

Now, however, the King discovered that two of his most trusted bishops were involved in controversy reaching to the Papal See itself; moreover both were royal tutors, and the Duke of Burgundy, his grandson, adored Fénelon, like all who came under his spell. Who was responsible for his appointment to the Archbishopric of Cambrai? No one but the royal consort Mme de Maintenon, who, as Saint-Simon sarcastically pointed out, had set herself up as a kind of secular mother of the Church.

Until then Louis had blindly trusted Françoise's good sense. When the Court painter Mignard had asked permission to depict her in semi-royal robes for her portrait at St Cyr, the King had smilingly given it. It seemed impossible to him that she of all people should have behaved so indiscreetly; it seriously undermined all his previous confidence in her.

In a regal fury His Majesty demanded an explanation from his wife; in floods of tears she gave it to him, freely admitting her mistakes, and withholding no self-condemnation. But for the King this was not enough. Fénelon was banished from Court after the Holy See had condemned his book; Louis also personally signed the order directing Mme de Maisonfort to retire from St Cyr to a nunnery; as for Mme Guyon, she was sent to the Bastille. As for Mme de Maintenon, for two whole years, in sharpest contrast to their previous marital intimacy, Louis showed her the greatest coldness and indifference. Françoise nearly died of grief and shame. Her women heard her sobbing night after night; years later she admitted that she had never come nearer to disgrace. It was her confessor, Godet des Marais, who seeing how genuine was her repentance, wrote to His Majesty, asking him to forgive her: 'Restore your trust,' he begged him, 'to this excellent companion, imbued with the Holy Spirit, and with affection and faithfulness towards yourself. I know her heart and soul and can guarantee that no one could love you more tenderly or respectfully. She would never deceive you unless she herself had been deceived.'

Quite possibly, had Louis not relented, Françoise might have gone into a physical decline as the result of this shock and sorrow. But at last her husband came to her bedside and smilingly asked her—'Are you going to die of this business, then, Madame?' Françoise smiled back at him through her tears and their marriage was saved.

19 *Social and Military Manoeuvres*

On 6 May 1682 His Majesty announced that from that date his official residence and seat of government would be at Versailles. This fabulous residence, the most famous in all Europe, was the centre of a small city, at any given time housing up to five thousand people. There the Sun King lived from morning till night in the full glare of publicity, from which he only escaped during the hours he spent with Françoise in her relatively modest apartment in the very heart of it. The protocol he himself had established there became so rigid that he began to long for some smaller and less formal residence where he could escape from the close ritual which governed his life.

The rebuilding and decoration of Versailles continued for years. To Louis, with his passion for fresh air and horticultural vistas the gardens were almost as important as the palace. He had never forgotten the marvellous fountains, basins and ponds designed for Fouquet, his fraudulent minister, at Vaux, by Le Nôtre. Their lavishness and beauty must be exceeded by those of the Sun King. In order to provide the necessary water supply the Seine was tapped. At a little village called Marly an enormous hydraulic machine was built to conduct the supply to

Versailles, where in due course torrents gushed from fountains and basins, the mouths of dolphins and horns of tritons; there were canals on which gondolas took gay river-parties for picnics. This extravagant use of the Seine naturally caused acute water shortages elsewhere, in Paris and the surrounding countryside. But the glory of Versailles came before the convenience of the royal subjects.

In visiting the site of the famous Marly machine, regarded almost as the eighth wonder of the world, His Majesty found the village, in a valley enclosed by steep hills on all sides, an ideal retreat in which to build the 'hermitage' where he intended to escape from the formalities of life at Versailles. Louis's ideas of simple country life, however, were no less grandiose than his other plans.

There were to be a central residence, known as The Sun, surrounded by twelve lesser pavilions called after the signs of the Zodiac. And, of course, acres of gardens hardly less elaborate than those of Versailles, which had also to be provided with the necessary irrigation.

The Sun King, Saint-Simon wrote with his usual venomous gusto, enjoyed tyrannizing over nature, to force it to his will by means of men and money. It was Louvois, as Superintendent of Works, who proposed a scheme very much after Louis's taste— to divert the entire course of the river Eure, over a distance of twenty-seven miles, from Pontgouin to Versailles. An enormous aqueduct had to be built, of three-storied arches, on the top of which the water was to run, and which cut right through Mme de Maintenon's property. This did not, however, cause her any displeasure, for since her marriage she had almost ceased to visit it.

The labour for this colossal enterprise, begun in 1684, was provided by an army of thirty thousand soldiers, temporarily unemployed, as the country was briefly at peace. Owing to the marshy ground, thousands of them either died or went sick of malaria.

'Who,' wrote Saint-Simon with almost lyrical bitterness, 'can count the gold and the lives that this intensive enterprise cost over many years . . . it was forbidden under the severest penalties . . . to mention the sick or the dead . . . In 1688, the works were interrupted by war and never resumed.' The expense was in the region of nine million francs. But Marly, like Versailles, was provided with its fountains, lakes, and canals.

At Marly Louis led a less formal life. There Mme de Maintenon, too, emerged from the seclusion of her routine at Versailles. The King relaxed all stringent etiquette; out-of-doors the courtiers privileged to accompany him there—and the royal command to do so was avidly sought by them—were permitted to wear their hats. Indoors the entire company was allowed to sit down in the royal presence. There were no public *levers* nor *couchers*, and at meals Mme de Maintenon took her place at table almost as if she were in fact Queen, surrounded by members of the Royal Family.

The Grand Dauphin, or Monseigneur, always showed his stepmother punctilious respect. Louis's three legitimate grandsons were the Duc of Bourgogne, born in 1682; the Duc d' Anjou, later to become Philip V of Spain, born two years later; and the Duc de Berry from whose birth in 1686 his mother never recovered. Four years later on 20 April 1690, she died. Monseigneur's second marriage, like his father's, was a secret morganatic one, but the bride was as unsuitable as could be imagined: a Mlle Chouin, who had been one of the pretty and naughty Princess de Conti's attendants. Nancy Mitford inimitably described her as 'Ugly, like all his women, she was a fat, squashy girl with a snub nose, an enormous mouth, and huge breasts, on which he would beat a tattoo with his fingers.'[1]

She behaved very well, however, retiring from Court and living quietly with her husband at Meudon. Apparently neither Louis nor Françoise disapproved of this *mésalliance*. When serving in the Army Monseigneur wrote several respectful and even affectionate letters to his stepmother, and in one, on 19 July 1694, he said that he was agreeably astonished that she should write to him of his wife; he was also delighted that the King was pleased with him.

Monseigneur, although a most dutiful and devoted son, was

not in the least gifted, but as dull as his mother, the defunct
Infanta. Neither Louis nor Françoise ever lost their affection
and preference for his eldest illegitimate son, the Duc du Maine,
to whom Mme de Maintenon remained a mother-surrogate.
As he grew into manhood the Duc du Maine did not lose either
his charm or his wit, but he turned out an indifferent and even
cowardly soldier. The criticisms directed at him by his contemporaries and subsequent historians were considerably unfair.
He was, after all, a cripple, had suffered tortures in childhood
from the various unsuccessful cures that he had had to endure,
which were not likely to arouse his enthusiasm for suffering more
excruciating pain from war-wounds.

To the fury of Saint-Simon and most of the aristocrats at
Versailles Louis married off his legitimised bastards to princes
and dukes of the pure Blood Royal. In 1685, the elder of his two
daughters, Mlle de Nantes, married the Duc de Bourbon-
Condé; the younger, Mlle de Blois, made an even more dazzling
match, for Louis had decided that her husband would be the
young Duc de Chartres, his legitimate nephew, son and heir of
the Duc and Duchesse d'Orléans. According to Saint-Simon,
the Duchess regarded this match with one of Louis's daughters,
born on the wrong side of the blanket, as so outrageous, that on
hearing of it she publicly boxed her son's ears. In 1692 the
Duc du Maine married Louise Bénédicte, sister of the Duc de
Condé. Most appropriately, since her husband was so short,
she was a tiny little thing, almost a midget.

The only one of Mme de Montespan's children to make a
love-match was the Comte de Toulouse, du Maine's younger
brother, who was both brave and able and an excellent
naval commander. His wife was Marie de Noailles and it was
also with this distinguished ducal family that Mme de Maintenon made a match for her own niece, Mlle d'Aubigné, the
daughter of her incorrigible brother Charles, and his tiresome
bourgeois wife.

Monseigneur's son, the young Dauphin, more generally
known as the Duc de Bourgogne, was growing up and a bride
was sought for him.

As usual, in choosing a future Queen of France, political con-
siderations were of the first importance. Louis was anxious to
win the alliance of the Duc de Savoie, who had previously
belonged to the League of Augsburg, which had been established
in 1686 by the enemies of France, headed by William of Orange
and including all the leading European nations—the Austrian
Empire, Spain, Sweden and the German princedoms. In 1688
Louis had invaded the Palatinate, on the French side of the
Rhine, north of Alsace, on the claim that it was the property of
his sister-in-law, Madame. In the following year William became King of England, which then also joined the Leaguers.
This consequent war dragged on for nearly ten years. The
alliance with the Duc de Savoie was therefore of considerable
value to France.

The Duchess was already a relative of the House of Bourbon,
since she was the daughter of Henrietta of England, the charming first wife of Monsieur. The little girl who was then affianced
to the fourteen-year-old young Duc de Bourgogne was only ten
at the time. But almost immediately she became the adored
favourite of Louis and Mme de Maintenon.

In 1696 the Sun King had passed his zenith; he was fifty-
eight and Françoise sixty-one. They had by then settled down as
an elderly married couple. Mme de Maintenon was as much
as ever preoccupied with St Cyr and increasingly though
unofficially with religious politics and affairs of State, since
all Louis's conferences with his ministers were held in her
room.

Both she and Louis looked forward with the whetted excitement of two elderly and rather dull-living grandparents to the
arrival of little Marie-Adélaïde de Savoie, the future Dauphine.
And their hope that she would bring a new ray of sunshine to
Versailles was not disappointed. The King attached so much
importance to this event that he set out himself to meet the little
Princess. And immediately afterwards he wrote a long account
of his reception of her to Mme de Maintenon, the only one of his
letters, apart from a few brief notes, that she did not subsequently destroy.

It was dated 'At Montargis, on Sunday at half past six, 4 November 1696.'

I arrived here before five o'clock; the princess did not come until after six. I went to her coach to receive her. She let me speak first, and then answered me very nicely, but with a little shyness that would have pleased you. I took her through the crowd to her room, allowing them to see her from time to time, by having the torches held close to her face. During this walk and under those lights she behaved gracefully and modestly. We finally arrived in her room, where the heat and the crowd were suffocating. From time to time I showed her to those who came closer, and I observed her carefully in order to give you my impressions. She has the greatest charm and the prettiest little figure I have ever seen, dressed like a picture; lively and very beautiful eyes, with admirable black lashes, as pink and white a complexion as one might wish for, with masses of the most beautiful black hair. She is as thin as is appropriate at her age; very red thick lips, with long, white, but very irregular teeth; her hands are well-shaped but the colour of her age [not white, but perhaps slightly chapped and red as little girls' hands tend to be]. She speaks little, at least as far as I could see, but is not embarrassed by being looked at, like someone used to society. She curtsies badly, rather in the Italian manner. There is something slightly Italian about her appearance, but generally pleasing, as I noticed. She is very like her first portrait, but not in the least like the other. To speak to you as frankly as I always do, I find her just as I would wish, and would not like her to be more beautiful. I repeat, everything about her is pleasing, except her curtseying. I will tell you more after supper, when I shall have observed several things more. I forgot to say that she is small rather than tall for her age. Until now I have done wonders, and I hope I shall be able to keep up a certain informality until we reach Fontainebleau, where I am longing to be.

At ten o'clock.

The more I see of the princess, the more satisfied I am. I watched her undress; she has a lovely, one may say perfect figure, and her modesty will please you. Everything went off well regarding my brother; he is very annoyed and says that he is ill.

The reason for Monsieur's behaviour was his extreme anger—and even more his wife's. Until then Madame had ranked as first lady in the land, but His Majesty had decided that in future the little Dauphine would take precedence over her.

'I am pleased to be able to speak well of her to you,' Louis continued, 'for I think I can honestly do so. Not wishing to say all I am thinking I send you a thousand good . . .'[2]

At this point in the letter, the remainder of the sentence was heavily scratched out. But the reader can easily fill it in. No doubt it contained the words kisses or embraces, or loving thoughts. Even although Françoise so scrupulously destroyed every trace of evidence of their marriage, the entire letter is one from a devoted husband to a wife from whom he had no secrets.

And the little Dauphine became the granddaughter of their dreams. Mme de Maintenon took to her as instantly as Louis had done; in no time Marie-Adélaïde became her step-grand-mother's *mignonne*. Mme de Maintenon was *ma tante*.

Saint-Simon described how

> serious and most respectful towards the King in public and demurely well-behaved with Mme de Maintenon . . . in private chattering incessantly, she jumped and pirouetted around them, either perched on the arm of one of their chairs or on their laps, kissing, caressing and rumpling them, messing up their papers with impunity, sometimes reading their letters, bursting in on them even when they were in conference with the Ministers . . .[3]

taking such liberties with His Majesty as his own legitimate children and grandchildren would never have dared, to his huge secret enjoyment. Even in the royal coach or at meals Marie-Adélaïde could not keep still. Her high spirits were only impeded by the bouts of appalling toothache from which she suffered. Mme de Maintenon supervised her diet as carefully as, in the past, the Duc du Maine's.

Three days weekly the Dauphine went for lessons, to St Cyr, where she was known as Mlle de Lastic, and wore the school uniform. She was then twelve; the marriage was not consummated until she was fourteen, two years later.[4]

At Versailles it amused the Sun King to install a menagerie for the Dauphine; at Marly there were a succession of elaborate and extravagant entertainments in her honour—water-parties, ballets, masques, and fancy-dress balls, for like every young girl Marie-Adélaïde adored dressing up. Louis, with his inexhaustible vitality, found these youthful pastimes for the younger generation stimulating. But to Françoise they were merely exhausting frivolities. The older she grew the bitterer became her complaints against Court life and the deeper her longing for retirement to St Cyr. This was not, however, to be for many years yet.

By 1690 during the war against the League of Augsburg Louis had mastered the entire left bank of the Rhine. In the following years he decided that he would himself direct military operations at the siege of Mons. During his absence he allowed Mme de Maintenon temporarily to stay at St Cyr.

'A few days before he left,' wrote Lavallée, 'the King went there to say goodbye to her and told the Ladies of St Cyr, "I am leaving with you the one person who is most dear to me." He left on 17 March.'[5]

During the siege he wrote her numerous letters. Of these only two short notes remained:

> Monday, 9 April, 1691, at half past one in the morning.
>
> The capitulation is signed; so a great matter is ended. Today at noon I shall have one gate, and the garrison will leave tomorrow. Tuesday, at noon. Thank God on my behalf for His grace towards me; I think it will give you pleasure to do so.[6]

And a few hours later, at ten-thirty on the same day, he informed her that he would be leaving on the Thursday morning, arriving on Saturday evening at Compiègne, where he would have the pleasure of seeing her, he hoped, in good health.

On 16 July 1691 Louvois, the War Minister, suddenly died of heart failure after leaving a Cabinet meeting. Louis thereupon decided to take over personally the direction of his army's siege of Namur. But as usual when engaged on protracted military operations he arranged for his own entertainment by taking with him a large retinue of ladies as well as courtiers. When he left on 10 May, he had in his own coach Monseigneur, Monsieur, the Duchesse de Chartres and the two Conti princesses. There were thirteen more ladies in two following coaches. But their presence did not exempt Mme de Maintenon from being of the party, although she was privileged to travel in her own coach. For a woman of fifty-six this trip was no slight ordeal. From Dinant she wrote on 28 May a letter to St Cyr giving a remarkable description of her tribulations:

> After travelling for six hours on a fairly good road, we saw a castle on a rock . . . we went quite close to it without finding any other dwellings, when at last, at its foot, we saw down a precipice, as one might in a deep well, the roofs of what seemed to us like dolls' houses, surrounded on all sides by terrific rocks . . . We had to go down to these horrible dwellings by a worse road than I can describe; all the coaches were madly jumping up and down, enough to break their springs, and the women were holding on to whatever they could reach. After a quarter of an hour of this torture we reached a town containing a so-called Main Street in which two coaches could not pass; there are even narrower ones with no room even for two sedan-chairs. It is inky black and the houses are ghastly,

and the food and water were equally appalling. 'The town is filthy and the cobblestones pierce one's feet.'

The siege of Namur was, however, going well; to her great relief—for she hated war—'with very little bloodshed . . . The King has gout in both his feet, and I assure you that I don't regret it'—for it prevented him from otherwise over-exerting himself. His health was always her greatest preoccupation. 'After this fine description,' she concluded, 'do not worry about me, as I am very well, comfortably lodged and well-served, and wanting to be where God has placed me . . .' And finally, 'there are four hundred steps up to the castle of which I have spoken'.[7]

Both in this letter and one she wrote at the same time to her brother, Mme de Maintenon's complaints were half-rueful and half-humorous. She was undoubtedly enjoying the experience in spite of the discomforts and not a little proud to have weathered it.

After Louis had forgiven Françoise for her blunder over Mme Guyon and Quietism, his devotion to her steadily increased and reached a public climax at the famous review of Compiègne, on 13 September 1698.

The long drawn-out war against the League or Grand Alliance of the European Powers opposed to him ended with the Peace of Ryswick in the previous year. In spite of certain successes Louis was obliged to give up his claim to the Palatinate —allegedly his sister-in-law's possession—for which she was compensated by a large sum. A tricky situation was developing regarding the succession to the King of Spain; the Powers opposed to the Sun King were still very much on the alert for a chance finally to settle their scores with him.

For these reasons Louis thought the moment appropriate to put on a display of military strength; an army of 60,000 men engaged in the three-week long manoeuvres at Compiègne, the pretext for which was the indoctrination of his grandson, the sixteen-year-old Duc de Bourgogne, in the arts of war. Saint-Simon, who was present, slanted his incomparable description of the scene, so as to make it appear to have had an entirely different motive—the apotheosis of the King's morganatic wife.[8]

An old rampart next to the castle was on a level with the King's apartments, and therefore overlooking the whole countryside. The assault was timed for Saturday, 13 September; the King, followed by all the ladies, and in the most glorious weather, stood on this rampart, surrounded by the Court and the most distinguished foreign visitors . . . I was in the half-circle close to the King, at most three steps away, with no one in front of me. It was the most beautiful sight imaginable, the whole army on foot and on horse, and a vast crowd behind the troops in order not to impede them . . . But quite another spectacle, which struck me so that I shall remember it in forty years' time as vividly as today, was given by the King to his entire army and the crowds, as well as those on the rampart itself.

Mme de Maintenon was there, facing the plain and the troops in her sedan-chair, behind its three windows. The

Duchesse de Bourgogne was seated on the left arm of it; on the same side, behind it and in a half-circle stood Madame, the Princesse de Conti, and all the other ladies, with the men behind them. By the right-hand window of the chair stood the King, and in a semi-circle behind him the most distinguished of the men. The King was almost constantly bareheaded and was incessantly leaning down to the window to speak to Mme de Maintenon, to explain to her what she was watching and the reasons for it. Each time she was kind enough to let her window down four or five finger-lengths, but never half-way, for I was observing this spectacle closely, more attentively, I admit, than the troop movements.

Occasionally she let it down to ask the King a question, but it was nearly always he who, without waiting for her to speak, leant down to explain things to her, and when she took no notice he rapped on the window to have her open it. He spoke to nobody but her, except to give a few brief orders, and a few replies to the Duchesse de Bourgogne, who was trying to have someone speak to her, and to whom Mme de Maintenon signed from time to time, but without opening the front window, through which the young princess shouted a few words to her. I looked carefully at all the surrounding faces, all of which were expressing timid, furtive, and embarrassed surprise; everybody behind her chair and in the semi-circle showing more interest in her than in the army ... The King often placed his hat on top of the chair before leaning down to speak to her, which must have been pretty tiring to his back.

Towards the moment of capitulation Mme de Maintenon apparently asked permission to withdraw, the King shouted out, 'The chairmen of Madame'. They came and carried her away; the King left a quarter of an hour later, followed by the Duchesse de Bourgogne, and almost everyone else. Many of them expressed their feelings by looks or nudging, or in whispers, unable to believe their eyes. The same was true of those down below in the plain. Even the soldiers were asking who was in that chair to which the King was constantly bending down; and it was necessary quietly to stop the officers and troops from asking this question. One may imagine what the foreigners thought of such a spectacle, which created a sensation throughout Europe and was as much talked about as the camp of Compiègne itself, with all its pomp and prodigious splendour.[9]

Was Louis, who seldom acted unpremeditatedly, at that moment making it clear to the whole world that the occupant of the chair was his wife, or was he carried away, like any ordinary husband might be, in wishing to explain everything to her and have her share his enthusiasm? Whatever the reason, the one wholly unperturbed person on this occasion was clearly Mme de Maintenon.

It became more and more difficult for all but the Royal Family, the ministers and her own little coterie to gain admittance to her apartments at Versailles; outside her doors there and at St Cyr also, when she arrived or left, there was always a horde of visitors, petitioners, courtiers like Saint-Simon, who found it increasingly hard to be admitted, seeking her patronage, requesting her to pass on petitions to the King, or demanding other favours. Even so her days were crammed with what she regarded as time-wasting, exhausting activities; at the same time she carried on a staggeringly large correspondence. She rose at six or even earlier; went to bed at nine after a light meal, but Louis would often visit her at ten or later. She was permanently weary and increasingly rheumatic and her fibrositis was not diminished when, even on the coldest days or nights, the King insisted on all the windows being flung wide open.

That in spite of all its advantages she found her life burdensome yet considered it a mission with which she had been entrusted, is revealed by a remarkable document found in the archives of St Cyr, a prayer she appears to have composed around 1691.

My Lord God, it is you who have placed me where I am, and all my life I will try to adore your providence and submit to it without reserve. Give me, oh God, the grace to endure my sorrows in a Christian spirit, to sanctify my pleasures, only to seek your glory, and to proclaim it to all the princes in the midst of whom you have placed me; to serve the King's salvation. Do not permit me to give way to the agitations of my restless nature, which wearies and relaxes in the course of my duties and envies the apparent happiness of others. Your will be done, oh God, and not mine! . . . You who hold in your hand the hearts of kings, open that of the King so that I may fill it with the virtue you desire; grant that I may make him happy, console, encourage, and even make him unhappy when it is necessary for your glory; that I hide nothing from him that he should learn from me and that no one else would have the courage to tell him. Grant that I save my own soul and his, that I love him in you and for you, and that he so loves me . . .[10]

'Grant . . . that I hide nothing from him that he should learn from me, and that no one else would have the courage to tell him'—this is the most significant sentence in this remarkable document. Françoise had succeeded at the outset of their marriage in what she considered God had willed her to do, to save Louis from the sins of adultery and fornication he had been committing, and for a short time the Sun King had become almost as pious as herself. But although he scrupulously adhered to the Church, attended communion regularly and listened with rapt attention to the admonitory sermons of his favourite preachers, Louis considered that by doing so he had paid all the necessary respects to his Ally on high. After losing one of his battles, 'how can He do this to me?' he plaintively enquired.

With the sometimes almost brutal candour that was so characteristic of her, after their marriage Françoise did not flinch from telling her august husband the home-truths she thought necessary. Only she, his wife, knew him as a man, with all his human weaknesses; his frequent bouts of depression, his physical sufferings, which he bore with enormous courage; only in her company could he truly relax and be himself. And she was aware, as this prayer proves, of the tremendous responsibility this placed on her. What she was then seeking was a human safety-valve to whom she, otherwise the most reserved of women, could entrust her personal as well as spiritual problems. And in 1694 she found the person who was in her opinion ideally qualified to become her closest confidant, Louis–Antoine de Noailles, Bishop of Chalons. Her many letters to him are the most revealing of her entire correspondence.

Mme de Maintenon's confessor was a saintly, totally unworldly man, of almost monkish habits and outlook, and with little personal experience of the Court and the worldly problems which increasingly preoccupied his penitent.

Among Mme de Maintenon's oldest friends were the distinguished Noailles family. Its head was the Duke and Marshal of France who in 1694 won an outstanding victory over the Spaniards. On 4 June Mme de Maintenon wrote to the Duchess that she had rejoiced in his success 'as a good Frenchwoman' and the occasion gave her the opportunity to remember how very devoted she was both to the Duchess and to her saintly brother-in-law.[1]

He was Louis-Antoine de Noailles, Bishop of Chalons. It was to this highly-born prelate that Françoise then turned as a kind of adjunct to her confessor and in particular as a safety-valve in all her confidential problems. He was then forty-three; she was fifty-nine. Her first important letter to him was written on 22 June. She begged him to read all Mme Guyon's writings and to report to her on them in the greatest secrecy. He did so, and his frankly expressed opinions were as condemnatory of that mystical lady's claims as those of all his colleagues except Fénelon. It was then that Mme de Maintenon removed Mme Guyon from St Cyr. Even before this occurred Françoise was using all her influence with Louis on behalf of the Noailles family, as his mistresses had used theirs for their friends, and what was still odder was the fact that she regularly reported progress in her letters to the bishop. The Marshal petitioned the King to be allowed to retire from his command on the grounds of ill-health. Françoise informed his brother that she had convinced His Majesty that this was advisable. When the Bishop's colleagues had criticised his ordinances to the King, Mme de Maintenon hastened to assure him that she had answered all their objections and, she added, 'this information is for yourself only'.[2]

On 6 August 1695 Harlay de Champvallon, Archbishop of Paris, who had given the blessing at Louis's and Françoise's secret marriage, suddenly died of a stroke.

'Mme de Maintenon,' wrote Lavallée, 'saw the hand of Providence in his death, and without a word to anyone, even to Père La Chaise [His Majesty's confessor] she pressingly begged the King to nominate the Bishop of Chalons to this see. At the same time [on 18 August] she urged him to accept it. This was all done in the greatest secrecy.'[3]

Mme de Maintenon wrote:

> To some extent I understand the weight and importance of the burden to be laid on you, but, Monsieur, one must work. You are young and healthy, and it is not for me to exhort you to sacrifice yourself to the glory of God, the good of the Church, and the King's salvation. I enclose a letter from one of your friends who knows what is going on; you will please keep all this secret. It is sometimes necessary to deceive the King in order to serve him, and I hope that with God's grace we will again deceive him to the same end and in concert with you.[4]

Nevertheless Noailles twice refused the appointment and only accepted it finally at the King's command. A small but curious facet of this odd business was that Louis's two former reigning mistresses, Louise de la Vallière and Mme de Montespan, from the retirement of her Paris convent, wrote to congratulate the saintly new archbishop on his appointment.

However lofty Françoise's motives were, they hardly explained nor excused her, previously the soul of discretion, who continued for years to inform the Archbishop of the most highly confidential events at Court. By the end of 1695 she had become what, in a less worthy cause, might be regarded as his spy; reporting to him, on Père La Chaise, the royal confessor, writing from Marly on 8 November:

> Make a habit, Monseigneur, of enclosing in a separate letter what you wish me to show to the King; you must not mention anything in it revealing our important communications, but only whatever commissions you would like me to carry out on your behalf, since this is what I wish to do.[5]

Her conduct was not only due to her zeal for Louis's salvation. Intrinsically Françoise was extremely lonely. She increasingly dominated everyone around her, including the King. She had never loved any man in the normal manner; the consummation of sexual satisfaction was inaccessible to her. Her love for Louis was largely maternal, the only kind she knew; she was and all her life remained the archtypal governess of France. Yet if she would certainly not have enjoyed being mastered physically by any man there was in her a repressed desire to be emotionally dominated. In all her letters to her confessors this stood out, sublimated as a need for spiritual direction. In Louis de Noailles, fifteen years younger than herself, she found some quality that responded to and gratified this need. He was a man and yet not a man, since he was a priest, and therefore a perfect safety-valve; the only male individual in her life to whom she could fearlessly and confidently look for the comfort for which she yearned; to whom she could confide the secrets that even she, with all her introvertism, self-control and will-power found too heavy to bear. Too often Françoise's apologists and hagiographers overlooked the fact that even Mme de Maintenon, uncrowned queen of France, was a woman who occasionally felt conscious of her own feminine weakness, needing a secure male prop on whom to lean.

In 1698 her bond with the Noailles family became an even closer one. Ever since her marriage to Louis, her brother Charles had become more and more impossible. Whilst in her letters Françoise continued to proclaim her affection for him, she kept him as much as possible from Court and on the rare occasions when he managed to invade it his behaviour was intolerable. To the courtiers he would jokingly refer to His Majesty the Sun King as 'my brother-in-law'. Having insisted on living in Paris he would say the same to anyone who would listen to him in the Tuileries gardens; he also continued his life of profligacy, gambling and visiting whore-houses. Finally Mme de Maintenon arranged for d'Aubigné to live in a kind of home for elderly gentlemen of the lesser aristocracy and in desperation employed a priest to follow him around in the attempt to curb his worst excesses.[6] Much against her liking his wife was relegated to a home for elderly ladies. Françoise always disapproved of her stupid, unattractive sister-in-law, who by descent and upbringing was totally unsuitable to be received in her own circle. But from the moment of the birth of their daughter, Françoise, it was understood that she would adopt her. Judging from their joint portrait, the little girl was remarkably like her aunt in appearance. Unlike her cousin, the Huguenot Mlle de Villette, later Mme de Caylus, whom Mme de Maintenon regarded as a disappointment and married off very shabbily, little Françoise remained a favourite. When the young Duchesse de Bourgogne arrived at Court, she was her constant playmate, companion, and schoolfellow at St Cyr.

In 1698 Mlle d'Aubigné was married in great pomp and magnificence to the young Comte d'Ayen, the eldest son and heir of the Maréchal de Noailles, and the nephew of the Archbishop, who performed the ceremony. No doubt in the distant past the Noailles might have thought twice about such a match with the niece of Mme Scarron. But an alliance with His Majesty's morganatic wife's young relative was a very different matter. Moreover, the bride was also a favourite of the King who appointed her a *dame du palais,* gave her a million francs and the valuable jewels Françoise would not herself accept.

After the wedding banquet, Mme de Maintenon gave a supper party. On that occasion the distinguished guests did include the bride's mother, who presumably only opened her mouth to put food into it; the notable, but unregretted exception, was the Comtesse d'Ayen's father who was not even invited to the wedding.

The future Duc de Noailles became as much Mme de Maintenon's favourite as his wife; he also had a distinguished military career.

Throughout the next two years Mme de Maintenon's correspondence with the Archbishop continued with the same unabated frankness. There was a difficult moment for him when early in 1699 he was accused of Jansenism. On that occasion the Archbishop had the book containing the accusation burnt by the public hangman. He claimed it was inspired by a plot against him on the part of the Jesuits. In this antagonism towards the Jesuits, M. de Paris (bishops and archbishops were always called after their sees) had Mme de Maintenon's full support. Her letters to him during these years show her increasing involvement in ecclesiastical business and intrigue coupled with recurrent complaints against her royal husband. On 22 March 1699 Louis had written her a very nice little note, informing her that the papal bull condemning Fénelon's Quietism had been received from Rome. 'So that business is now over; I hope that it will have no further unpleasant consequences for anybody; I cannot tell you more now, but will keep it for this evening.'[7]

This was his way of conveying to her that she was by then completely forgiven for her own lapse over Mme Guyon. Yet his kindness did not lessen her complaints about him to her confidant.

In spite of Saint-Simon's contentions that Mme de Maintenon was by then more or less running the country, Louis did not easily tolerate anyone's interference in this authority, except by his own direct request. In the summer of 1698 Françoise appears to have been suffering from a mood of unusual depression.

'I can do nothing with regard to practical matters of which I am told hardly anything,' she wrote to the Archbishop. 'I would be more than recompensed for my state of slavery, were I able to do some good.'[8]

Whilst Françoise seldom went so far as to describe her situation as one of slavery, at that particular moment she more than ever needed to unburden herself to Louis de Noailles.

At that time the King was becoming more and more preoccupied with the political problem that was to bedevil all the other leading European rulers as well—the imminent question of the succession to the throne of Spain.

Neither was Mme de Maintenon wholly preoccupied with religious affairs. This situation began only two years after her bitter letter to the Archbishop stating that she had no power at all and was never consulted. But the time was arriving when, incontrovertibly, behind the scenes, she played an extremely important part in this grave political and military crisis.

Essentially the War of the Spanish Succession was a family struggle between the Habsburgs, rulers of the Holy Roman Empire, and the Bourbons of France, for the inheritance of a throne and a kingdom.

Philip IV of Spain left three children: one son, who was sickly from birth, succeeded his father as King Carlos II of Spain at the age of five, and died at the age of forty; and two daughters, Maria Theresa, who married Louis XIV of France, and Margaret, who became the wife of the Austrian Emperor, Leopold I.

At the time of Maria Theresa's marriage to Louis, Mazarin had arranged that in exchange for her colossal dowry she would renounce her rights to the Spanish throne. But as the dowry was never paid in full Louis regarded his late wife's claim as remaining valid.

Her sister Margaret, however, on marrying the Austrian Emperor, did not renounce her rights. After her death the Emperor, Leopold I, married again and had two sons, the elder of whom became Joseph I, in succession to his father, and a younger, who as Charles VI succeeded his brother. But before he did so, there was terrific diplomatic battle in Madrid between the Bourbons and the Habsburgs for the succession to the Spanish throne.

On 1 November 1700 Don Carlos II died childless, but leaving a will in which he appointed Louis XIV's grandson, Philippe d'Anjou, as his successor. When informed of this happy event, a week later, Louis immediately called a council in Mme de Maintenon's room to discuss the matter.

The fact that Spain would pass under French domination was not likely easily to be accepted either by Austria or by the protestant William of Orange, one of Louis's bitterest enemies, who in 1690 had succeeded the deposed King James II as King of England.

During the haggling for the partitioning of Spain that preceded Carlos II's death, Louis had signed treaties with the reigning Austrian Emperor Joseph I and William, which, if he now allowed his grandson to accept the Spanish throne, would be broken, when war between them would inevitably follow.

To an absolute ruler of Louis's temperament—a Bourbon first and foremost, the Sun King of France, and for so long the scourge of his enemies, it was hardly likely that this risk would prove a deterrent. Spain was too great a prize to let slide for the sake of a treaty or two. Nevertheless, Louis, as was his custom, held prolonged consultations with his Ministers on this tremendous issue, as usual, in the privacy of Mme de Maintenon's apartment, at Fontainebleau.

There she sat, in her little niche, embroidering or spinning or even pretending to read, whilst the future of Spain was debated in her presence. In spite of her claims that she had no part whatever in political decisions, on this historic occasion it was to her that her husband finally turned for the casting vote—should or should not Anjou accept the Spanish succession? Those present at this dramatic council were, in addition to His Majesty, the Dauphin, father of the future King of Spain, the Duc de Beauvilliers, Governor of the Princes and one of Louis's most trusted confidants, and two Ministers, de Torcy, Minister for Foreign Affairs, and the Chancellor, Pontchartrain. The Duke and the Foreign Minister did not conceal from His Majesty their view that the acceptance of this offer would almost inevitably lead to war with the European Powers. Unusually, however, the Dauphin, who as a rule showed little interest in foreign affairs, and seldom opened his mouth on such occasions, made a surprising intervention. He was dazzled by the prospect of becoming the father of the King of Spain. As Maria Theresa's son he himself was half-Spanish and should have had the succession which she had formally but not literally renounced. As the future King of France this was not his intention, but it seemed obvious to him that his second son was fully entitled to this brilliant inheritance and he would not have him deprived of it.

Whereupon Louis, turning to the wife whose good judgement he so deeply trusted, asked her point-blank, '*Qu'en pense votre Solidité?*'

Madame Solidity, this was the nickname he alternately used when smilingly consulting her, to 'Madame La Raison'.

Although in many respects her judgements were reasonable and based on solid premises, Mme de Maintenon was not and never had been, as objective as Louis liked to believe. Moreover, in this respect Saint-Simon was incontrovertible: she was basically incapable of taking decisions on such weighty matters, very far removed from such organisational problems—at which she undoubtedly shone—as the administration of St Cyr or the day-to-day affairs of the Church. The Dauphin, although not one of her greatest favourites, had always stood well with her and no doubt she was secretly grateful to him that unlike the Duc and Duchesse d'Orléans and lesser members of the Blood Royal he had always shown her the greatest deference and respect. Nor was she less conscious of the glory of the Bourbon tradition because she was only a morganatic participant in it. Finally, she was acutely aware of Louis's own feelings in the matter. Had she sided with the Ministers it might have made little difference and only irritated him without influencing his own decision. One cannot, therefore, agree with those who accused her of the sole responsibility for the disastrous consequences for France that were to ensue from the council.

Once the decision was taken to accept the Spanish throne whatever doubts of its wisdom she might previously have stifled, appeared to vanish. On 25 November she reported to her confidant, now the Cardinal de Noailles:

'I regard our union with Spain as a new source of pleasure ... I wish the King of Spain had already left, and if I had a voice in the matter he would by now be on the road to take possession of his kingdom.'[1]

To all intents and purposes Spain was to become another French dominion. The young King was to be accompanied to his capital by the French Ambassador, another trusted courtier, the Marquis d'Harcourt, who was given a dukedom for the purpose, and the young Comte d'Ayen.

In a long letter from St Cyr Mme de Maintenon wrote to the Duc d'Harcourt that although the young King showed good sense and judgement, 'his tone of voice and slowness of speech were very disagreeable; perhaps they would be less shocked by this in Madrid than at Versailles'.

The Duc d'Anjou officially received the Spanish Ambassador at Versailles, and there, in the greatest pomp and splendour the Sun King beamed his pleasure and approval as the Ambassador fell to his knees and kissing the hand of his future monarch exclaimed with typical Spanish fervour, 'Ah, Sire, the Pyrenees have ceased to exist!'

To Louis kingship was hedged with divinity; he had shown for years the same respect to one of his few equals, the deposed James II of England, for whom he had provided a home at St Germain and an income out of his own pocket. So the King of Spain, to whom throughout his life hitherto his grandfather had rarely vouchsafed a pat on the head or a kind word, must now walk at his side ahead of the entire Court, sit next to him at all meals and banquets, and kneel beside him in chapel. At Mass one morning, seeing that no cushion had been placed beside his own for the King of Spain to kneel on, Louis offered it to him. The boy was unable so soon to adapt himself to this singular honour and accept it, whereupon His Majesty pushed it away and knelt beside him on the bare carpet.

On 4 December, Philip V left Versailles for Madrid. Louis accompanied his grandson as far as the splendid palace at Sceaux, belonging to Philip's half-brother, the Duc du Maine. They were joined by most of the royal family, including of course Monseigneur, the new king's brothers, the Ducs de Bourgogne and de Berry, and the Duchesse de Bourgogne.

There was, however, more than a matter of etiquette and protocol in this scene of departure. Louis had always shown the greatest affection and loyalty to his descendants. It was, therefore, not surprising that when, according to Dangeau, it came to the final farewells, all these magnificently arrayed personages, under their ermine and velvets and satins, their periwigs and plumed hats, broke down and wept as copiously as any lesser human beings on such occasions. Even the Sun King, normally in perfect command of himself on all public occasions, was obliged to hold his hand in front of his eyes to hide his tears.

The parting over, the King of Spain, whom his brothers were to accompany as far as the frontier, managed to mount his gilded coach with apparent alacrity, perhaps secretly relieved at ending this emotional scene. Before he did so, his grandfather had also mastered his feelings, and after having embraced him warmly stepped back, ceremoniously bowing to the fellow-monarch from whom he was finally parting.

As he did so and watched the cavalcade disappear, Louis may have felt great pride in having brought off this coup—the virtual annexation of Spain as another French colony through the Bourbon connection. Yet he had no illusions that this would proceed without difficulties. The Emperor in Vienna would hardly let this prize be wrested from his own brother without a struggle; already he and his English, German and Dutch allies were organising their armies for the war of the Spanish Succession, which was to last for the next thirteen years. Louis too had taken the precaution of ordering sixty battalions to Milan. And another fifty squadrons of marines were sent to Toulon.

This bitter and fierce war began in the following year. The Great Century was over, and with it had gone most of Louis's most brilliant generals, to whom he chiefly owed his European

reputation of invincibility in battle, and the equally able statesmen, such as Colbert and Louvois, with whom the later members
of the Cabinet—who were unable to prevent Louis from committing this last *folie de grandeur*—were not to be compared.
When the greatest European commander of the day, John
Churchill, later Duke of Marlborough, took the field against
France, Europe was to be avenged for the losses and sufferings
millions of people had endured as the price of the Sun King's
glory.

At the beginning of 1701 Mme de Maintenon was as busily cor-
responding as ever. During the first three months she was mostly
writing to her nephew-in-law, the Comte d'Ayen, who was
giving her regular reports on all the doings of the Spanish Court,
and to the Duc d'Harcourt. Some of her earlier letters to
d'Ayen were, for her, positively frivolous. She was trying to
divert him during the long and tiresome journey to Spain by a
little harmless gossiping. But the following letter reveals a rare
glimpse of her own intimate circle or, as it was called, *cabale*, the
few highly privileged women who surrounded her morning,
noon, and night, as a queen's ladies-in-waiting might have
done:

> . . . Mme de Dangeau distracts herself with backgammon,
> Mme de Roucy is pregnant, Mme de Nogaret is getting fat,
> Mme d'O remains in bed since her husband went away, to
> look at his place beside her where he no longer lies . . . Mme
> du Chatelet is pregnant. Mme de Montgon is red in the face,
> Mme de Lévis is skinny, the Comtesse d'Estrées bursts out
> laughing, the Comtesse d'Ayen [her niece] is talking in
> *falsetto*, the lady-in-waiting has gout, and the *dame d'atour*
> does not neglect her spinning. That, my dear Count, is the
> state of our little Court that gathers every evening in my
> apartment around the young Princess [the Duchesse de
> Bourgogne, who spent most of her time there] who is growing
> taller in front of our eyes, and a little less quickly in good
> behaviour.[2]

This lighthearted passage may well have been inspired by the
frivolous and impetuous young Duchess herself; for Mme de

Maintenon spoilt her almost as much as Louis. It also shows, however, the side of Mme de Maintenon's character which had made her so attractive in her youth and which, although generally so carefully concealed by her in her ultra-discreet behaviour and normally serious correspondence, nevertheless was enduring into her seventies, largely explaining how for so long she had kept her husband entertained and amused.

But in the following letter she revealed the irritation and boredom she was increasingly feeling. She was writing to him, she said, in the short interval allowed her before the invasion of her apartment by visitors. Whilst she dined with her two cronies, Mme de Dangeau and Mme d'Heudicourt, Monsieur would call and discuss every mouthful they were eating; the princesses who had not gone hunting would arrive with their friends to await the King's return to dinner; they would be followed by a crowd of hunters who would all simultaneously discuss the chase at the top of their voices. And as she concluded by asking him to convey her humblest New Year greetings to the Prince she added bluntly, 'for one must follow the customs although I admit that I do not feel the tender affections by which everyone else is transported on New Year's Day.'[8]

On 16 January the first misfortune in the King's closest circle occurred. Bontemps, his first valet, who had so faithfully served him all those years and was present at his secret marriage, died of an apoplectic stroke at the age of seventy-five.

Four days later Mme de Maintenon was writing to the Duc d'Harcourt, begging him to send her a 'horoscope' or forecast as to whether or not war was likely to ensue. In spite of all her expressions of joy at the Duc d'Anjou's becoming Philip V of Spain, from the beginning of that year there was a note of apprehension in her correspondence on the subject, an intuitive foreboding of the outcome of Louis's colonialist policy towards Spain. She never hid her dread and horror of warfare, not even from the King, although over the years she had been compelled to accept it as the executive instrument of his personal statecraft. Louis, still obsessed by his visions of military glory, personally took over the direction of his generals and armies. And although she wrote to the Duke that His Majesty was anxious that their enemies should not have the impression 'that the King is governing Spain as well as France' this was nevertheless his obvious intention, a policy that could not for long be concealed from the Spaniards nor from his powerful European enemies.

James II died at St Germain on 16 September 1701. Louis, who was most attached to him and the ex-Queen, Maria of Modena, visited him on his deathbed and there unhesitatingly announced that he was recognising the 'Prince of Wales', later known as the Old Pretender, as the rightful King of England. If anything had been needed further to infuriate the English this gesture would have sufficed. But a month earlier, in spite of the illness of William III, Parliament had decided on war with France. The Hague Treaty with the Emperor and the United Provinces was signed on 7 September.

In spite of Louis's contention that he did not intend to rule Spain as well as France, he gave that country a Queen as well as a King. The bride he chose for Philip V was the much younger sister of the Duchesse de Bourgogne, another daughter of the house of Savoy. His motive in hurrying on this match was to provide Spain with a Bourbon heir to Philip V as quickly as possible.

Less than a week after the signing of the treaty by Louis's enemies, the future Queen of Spain was on her way, leaving Turin under the care of her appointed lady-in-waiting, the Princesse des Ursins.

This woman, who was to play so large and disastrous a part in the matter of the Spanish succession, was Marie-Anne de la Tremoille, daughter of the Duc de Noirmontier, who as a young, beautiful and aristocratic bride had known little Mme Scarron years before, when Françoise had been a protegée of the d'Albrets. After the death of her first husband, the Prince de Chalais, she married the Italian Prince Orsini, but used her title in the French style as Princesse des Ursins. The Princess was a natural schemer and intriguer, devoted to the Bourbon cause, and Louis, realising how useful she could be to him in

Italy, paid her a pension. She had already earned this before the death of Carlos II by convincing influential Spaniards in Rome and Naples that the successor to the Spanish King should be a Bourbon prince.

It was therefore natural that having also taken part in the intrigues leading to the engagement of Philip V of Spain and the little Duchesse de Savoie, Mme des Ursins should be appointed first lady-in-waiting to Spain's future Queen.

Whilst, according to protocol, Louis himself might only deal with the Spanish court through the ambassadors of the two nations, he still saw how useful a role the princess could continue to play for him. In spite of the fact that Mme des Ursins's love life was somewhat notorious, Mme de Maintenon also approved of her intelligence and devotion to the Bourbon cause. It was chiefly on Louis's instructions to his wife that there then began the famous correspondence between the two women, by means of which unofficial information came weekly from Spain and equally unofficial instructions were sent to the Queen's lady-in-waiting by Mme de Maintenon.

This correspondence caused some historians to view in a sinister light Mme de Maintenon's role in the most disastrous events of Louis XIV's later reign. Yet, it is difficult to see how, as a devoted and dutiful wife, she could have refused to comply with her husband's request.

Françoise de Maintenon as an old woman

Louis XV, King of France, as a small child
Portrait by Rigaud

It was now Louis's turn to endure and suffer. In addition to the disasters of the Spanish War, there occurred during the following years a series of appalling personal losses for a man so devoted to his family. These included the deaths of his brother, son, and grandson, and even the little Duchesse de Bourgogne.

The first of these tragedies was the death at St Cloud on 9 June 1701, of Louis's brother, the Duc d'Orléans, following a stroke.

In spite of Monsieur's notorious homosexuality, Louis had always been very fond of him. But for some time previously he had his Secret Police intercept several of his wife's letters to her German relatives. Some referred to Mme de Maintenon as 'the old spider' or 'the old rag bag'. After her husband's death Lise-Lotte was terrified that as a result of these appalling indiscretions she would be sent packing, back to Germany. The King's punishment, however, was more subtle; he handed the correspondence to Mme de Maintenon, with the request to have a few words on the subject with its writer. Mme de Maintenon, who had never feared nor had reason to fear Madame's enmity, was

H

by that time so securely in power that the situation even appealed to her sense of humour.

Mme de Maintenon went to visit Madame in her apartment at Versailles after dinner. She had asked Mme de Ventadour to be there also. Madame rashly opened the conversation by complaining that the King had recently shown marked coldness towards her. Mme de Maintenon replied that his coolness would cease if he were more satisfied with her behaviour.

Lise-Lotte then vehemently affirmed her undying loyalty and devotion to her august brother-in-law. Then, with perhaps a slightly feline gesture, Mme de Maintenon calmly drew from her pocket Madame's letter to her aunt, the Duchess of Hanover, in which she had written that no one precisely knew the relationship between the King and Mme de Maintenon; whether it was indeed marriage or concubinage, together with a few other ill-chosen comments. As Mme de Maintenon quietly read out this incriminating letter to her, Madame 'nearly passed out on the spot' with shame and terror.

Mme de Ventadour then pointed out to her that her wisest course was to make a full confession and to ask Mme de Maintenon's forgiveness, which, with sobs and tears she proceeded to do. Françoise also reminded Madame that it was she who had turned the late Dauphine against her when she had been her *dame d'atour*. There were more tears and lamentations, but seeing Madame reduced to this humiliating condition Mme de Maintenon showed no vindictiveness at all. With a generous gesture she promised to report Madame's repentance to His Majesty. Louis never mentioned it to his sister-in-law; with his usual kindness he settled large pensions on both the widow and her son, the Duc de Chartres, who had succeeded his father as Duc d'Orléans; Madame, realising that she owed this happy ending, instead of the disgrace she had had every reason to fear, to Mme de Maintenon, then wrote her several letters expressing her undying gratitude and devotion.

King William, for so long the Sun King's bitterest opponent, died on 19 March 1702. Under Queen Anne British foreign

policy underwent no change. Only two months later, on 15
May, England, Holland, and the Austrian Empire declared
war on France.

The effects of this war did not immediately make themselves
felt. Court life continued much the same, with its daily ritual,
the King's public *levers* and *couchers*, his hunting and outings to
one or the other of his castles, notably to Marly, his daily and
nightly sessions with his ministers in Mme de Maintenon's
apartment, which continued, to her great distaste, to be invaded
by the daily calls of the princes, princesses and their followers.

She was an old, rheumatic woman; Louis, only a few years
younger, showed no signs of physical strain or fatigue. Yet not
only was she obliged to conceal the fact that she was feeling
increasingly weary. During the next few years her wifely duties,
which she had always found so distasteful, were to weigh more
and more heavily on her.

'Is she not fortunate?' She ironically wrote of herself in the
third person singular. 'She is with the King from morning till
night. But those who say so do not remember that princes and
kings are men like any others, that they too have their sadness
and sorrows, which one has to share with them.'[1]

At first there were some apparent compensations and even
moments still of joy. On 25 June 1704 the Duchesse de Bourgogne, after several miscarriages, gave birth to a male baby,
the infant Duc de Bretagne, Louis's first great-grandson. This,
however, was only a brief interlude of happiness.

For on 21 August arrived at Versailles the news of the utter
defeat and rout of the French army in the battle of Blenheim.
Two thirds of the troops were lost in this bloody defeat. The
victor was John Churchill, who was rewarded by a grateful
nation with the dukedom of Marlborough and a palace built by
Vanbrugh, bearing this glorious name in British military
history.

The Emperor had a statue built on the battlefield bearing the
inscription 'Let Louis know that no man before his death should
be called either happy or great'.[2]

No one but Mme de Maintenon dared break the news of this

catastrophe to His Majesty. Yet seasoned campaigner that he was, even in his decline, the Sun King was not prepared to accept one defeat as definitive, nor certainly to allow the world to assume that he did so. The interrupted celebrations of the birth of his great grandson culminated in the usual fireworks, dancing and feasting throughout the country. A note of almost incredible irrelevance was the King's reprimand to certain Court ladies for not appearing at the theatre in full Court dress.

More to the point and quite comprehensibly, three years later, Mme de Maintenon was to write to the Princesse des Ursins with reference to a very small success, 'I am delighted to hear that eighty Spaniards defeated four hundred English. Naturally I like the Spaniards especially in present circumstances and I hate the English. I would never have believed myself capable of such narrow-mindedness; nevertheless I cannot stand them.'

The infant Duc de Bretagne did not survive to fulfil Louis's hopes; he died in 1712.

Louis suffered a further disappointment. His policy in arranging the matches between his two grandsons, the Duc de Bourgogne and the King of Spain, to the Savoy Princesses, was intended to keep their father the Duke, whose territory was an important buffer between himself and the Emperor, on the side of France. But six months later, in the same year, the Duc de Savoie defected to the enemy camp.

According to Dangeau, the capture of Gibraltar by the English did not then appear to the French as more than a source of displeasure. But it was a more serious matter, when, a year later, the Archduke Charles of Austria took Barcelona, had himself proclaimed as Carlos III of Spain and was preparing to march on Madrid.

In the following year Vendôme, who had had some successes in Italy, was given a hero's welcome at Versailles. Louis took every such minor success as an opportunity to re-affirm his belief in ultimate victory. Fête succeeded fête at Versailles. When on his return to Italy in the following year Vendôme won another small victory, even Mme de Maintenon appeared to have discarded her gloom and wrote quite gaily that 'the battle won in Italy decided me to dress up; I will wear green if we regain Barcelona, and pink if we capture the Archduke.' Even she was for a brief moment seeing life through rose-coloured spectacles. But not for long.

There were soon further reverses in Italy, but these were trifling compared to the next terrible disaster of Ramillies in Holland on 23 May, when Marlborough utterly smashed and routed the French under Villeroy. Mme de Maintenon was not slow in applying her own peculiar standards to this crisis.

Discussing the Ramillies defeat in a letter to the Duc de Noailles on 12 June she appeared almost glad of it for the sake of the King's greater good—his spiritual salvation.

> The King is bearing this reverse with touching Christian courage which gives great pleasure to those even more interested in his salvation than in his success in this world. As for myself, my dear Duke, I was until now prostrated and stupefied by the news but I have managed to regain my courage and feel to some extent the grand-daughter of Agrippa.[3]

One hardly knows what to make of that extraordinary statement. In Françoise's voluminous past correspondence there was barely a reference to her intransigent Huguenot grandfather, Agrippa d'Aubigné. Now, in the adversities crowding on her husband in his old age, Mme de Maintenon, who had not hesitated to support the Revocation of the Edict of Nantes, who had kidnapped her own nephews and nieces and more or less forcibly converted them to Catholicism, was drawing courage from Agrippa's memory. Possibly her admiration of Louis's regal fortitude caused her to search for some matching quality in her own ancestry to make her worthy of sharing it.

Her main theme did not change—'God's will be done' was the leading strain in all her letters. Even so, as the war continued and the reverses as well, she became more and more conscious of its horrors and suffering. There was almost a note of rebellion in one of her letters at this time to the Princess:

'How cruel is war and the mutual persecution of one another

by these princes one has to witness, with the destruction of so many lives! I am extremely unhappy and can only see the horror of it.'4

The Princesse des Ursins, however, was not given to religious philosophising or moral scruples. She was a straightforward intriguing and mischievous politician, whose ambition knew no limits and who feared neither God nor the devil. Young King Philip, with Louis's approval, was despatched to the command of the Spanish troops in Italy in order to gain military experience. His youthful Queen was appointed regent during his absence, which in fact meant that Mme des Ursins, who completely ruled her, was the actual Governess of Spain. Not unnaturally this seizure of unofficial power by a woman and a foreigner bitterly antagonised those Spanish grandees who had originally invited the King of France's grandson to become their ruler. But almost incredibly, Mme des Ursins did not for a moment hesitate to interfere with Louis's own appointed representative at the Spanish Court. She prevented the French Ambassador from obtaining an interview with the Queen. When he indignantly protested to his Royal master at this insolence, Mme des Ursins had his accreditation cancelled. The post was then conferred on the Ambassador's nephew, the Abbé d'Estrées, who in a very short time was complaining as strongly as his uncle of the Princess's hostility. But then she overplayed her hand, by having the diplomatic bag from France seized and brought to her, breaking the seals and reading the highly confidential instructions it contained. This was the last straw. Louis ordered her immediate dismissal and return to France.

But Mme des Ursins was not yet defeated. She claimed that throughout she had acted with no personal motive but solely in the interests of Bourbon supremacy. She knew she could rely on the Queen of Spain, to whom she had made herself indispensable. Less frivolous than her sister, the Duchesse de Bourgogne, the young Queen had certain determination of her own and insisted on the Princess's reinstatement. Although she was obliged to obey the Royal command and return to Paris, Mme des

Ursins, with her audacity unshaken, pulled every possible string to be restored to Louis's good graces; she appealed to Philip V, who wrote to his father, the Grand Dauphin, to intercede on her behalf, to everyone else who might influence His Majesty and especially to Mme de Maintenon who even then had not lost faith in her correspondent's good intentions. Within a few days of the Princess's return she appeared no longer as a disgraced interfering sixty-year-old female busy-body, but, granted an audience by the King, made such good use of it that she fully won him over. In spite of her age, Mme des Ursins was still a handsome woman; in spite of his, Louis was still susceptible to feminine wiles and flattery. Very soon the Princess re-appeared at Court, almost as magnificently received as might have been a Royal favourite in the old days. By whatever arguments she pressed and won her case she put it over so brilliantly that within a matter of weeks she was given the Royal command to return to her post. She even affected a certain reluctance to obey it which the King overcame by doubling her revenue and as a crowning mark of favour present-ing her with thirty thousand *livres*.

Mme des Ursins's reluctance to return to Madrid may not have been altogether assumed. Although Louis's marked atten-tions to her at Versailles and Marly had not seriously disturbed his wife, Françoise had nevertheless written to the Duc de Noailles on 12 June 1705 that 'there is something about Mme des Ursins that I don't understand: one cannot get her to leave.'[5] Perhaps she did not wish to understand too much at that point. For a year later, when the Princess had resumed her post in Madrid and the two women were again writing to one another as intimately as previously, Mme de Maintenon in-formed her of a highly amusing rumour that had been reported to her, 'which', she wrote ironically in brackets, 'you will find very sensible and reasonable: namely that in my innocence I do not realize that your intention is to bring the King and Queen of Spain back to France, where you will then usurp my place with the King, either by disgracing me at Court or poison-ing me or after my death, which cannot be very far off'—since she was then seventy-two. And she added, 'would you like to explain yourself in this matter to me?'

To which the Princess replied that she had never had such a good laugh in her life as when she read those lines.

Françoise clearly knew when writing them that where there's smoke there's fire. And it was typical of Mme de Maintenon to use this facetious method of informing her dear friend that she was not unaware that she just might have had some ideas of the sort.

There were, however, more serious and less personal differences between the two women. Profoundly religious as she was, Françoise saw God's will in France's suffering and reverses even more than in Louis's successes. The longer the war dragged on the more she longed for it to end. Two years later in 1708 she was to write: 'You foresee a glorious peace which will set us all joyously at rest, but I fear one even sadder than the war.'[6] And although she claimed not to understand politics, she was right.

In spite of an occasional minor success here and there France lost Italy as well as Belgium, when at the battle of Turin the French were defeated owing to the incompetence of their generals, Marcin and La Feuillade. The titular head of the army was the Duc d'Orléans, the former Duc de Chartres.

He was not responsible for the defeat in Italy, where he was wounded on the battlefield but when he was subsequently sent to Spain the Duke was accompanied by his mistress, a former actress, Mlle de Sery. Wishing to remain on good terms with him, Mme des Ursins foolishly asked Mme de Maintenon to obtain the King's approval to this lady of easy virtue's appointment as *dame d'atour* to the Queen of Spain.

Mme de Maintenon had lived too long at Court not to have become used to the laxity of morals that continued to prevail there, even after the King himself had been saved from further debauchery by their marriage. She could not have been unaware that the Princess herself had had several lovers and that her secretary, d'Aubigné, a young man years younger, was Mme des Ursins' acknowledged *cavalier servant*. But however much she wished to keep the young Queen of Spain under French influence this suggestion went too far.

'Do not think,' Françoise answered the Princess, 'that I am a pious old woman afraid of this girl's sins, but you know as well as I do that even among sinners there are certain more decent ways of behaving than others.'[7]

A temporary setback to the Princess's domination of Spain occurred in 1706 when the self-styled Carlos III, the Habsburg Pretender, succeeded for three months in occupying Madrid, but in due course the young Bourbon sovereigns returned there where two years later the Queen was to give birth to a son, the Prince of the Asturias. This infant was just a year younger than his cousin, the new little Duc de Bretagne, another great-grandson for Louis.

The death of Mme de Montespan, on 27 May 1707, touched Louis hardly at all. It was not in his nature to look back to the past with nostalgia. The present was sufficiently disturbing.

In 1708, another setback occurred when Louis's hopes of establishing a Catholic monarchy in England were disappointed. At his own enormous expense he had fitted out a fleet and provided six thousand troops to invade Britain on behalf of the Pretender. But this expedition came to grief, when arriving at the Firth of Forth it turned tail and fled back to Dunkirk rather than face the inimical reception that was awaiting it. The Pretender's later attempts to regain the throne were equally frustrated.

In 1709, the Almighty, far from granting Mme de Maintenon's prayers and hopes for some miracle to transform the situation, inflicted on France one of those catastrophic winters that go down as landmarks of disaster in climatological history.

The sea froze on the beaches, rivers were sheets of ice. Even as far south as Provence, whole orchards, olive groves and vineyards became blackened stumps. Under their blanket of snow, winter cereals rotted in the ground. After a slight thaw, with flooding and inundation, the black frost returned in the spring.

'How can you say, Madame,' Mme de Maintenon wrote des-
pairingly, 'that God is not against us when He sends us a winter
such as there has never been for the past hundred and five or
six years . . . The poor are dying and we are helpless to save
them because our soil no longer produces food for them.'[8]

And indeed the people lay dying in thousands, in hovels and
garrets and cellars all over the country. But not without protest.
Rebellion was growling in the alleys of Paris, and although
revolution was not imminent, there was an ominous forecast of
the events that did occur eighty years later, when a mob of
desperate women demanding bread marched from Paris to
Versailles, although the soldiery turned them back at Sèvres.

Even the army was suffering; sentries froze to death in their
boxes, and disease was rife in the barracks.

The upper classes had better means of protecting themselves
against the disasters of that terrible winter. They owned forests
which they could cut down in order to send a blaze up their vast
fireplaces. They had certain reserves of corn and vegetables,
and bought what additional foodstuffs they could obtain on the
Black Market. They were accused by their enemies of making
large scale speculations in cereals. As the people's suffering and
fury mounted, even Mme de Maintenon herself did not escape
this calumny. *Lèse-Majesté* was perpetrated when a sacrilegious
mock Lord's Prayer appeared.

> Our Father that art at Versailles
> Thy name is no longer hallowed
> Thy Kingdom is no longer so great
> Thy will is no longer done either on earth or on sea.
> Give us our daily bread which we can no longer obtain
> Forgive our enemies who have beaten us,
>   and not our generals who have defeated us.
> Do not fall into the temptations of the Maintenon
>   but deliver us from Chamillard. Amen.

It was however no laughing matter. Four years earlier Louis
had already realised that victory was unlikely and had then
begun peace negotiations which he now resumed in earnest.
But the terms imposed by the enemy were so harsh that his

pride would not stomach them, and when the matter was debated he could not refrain from publicly weeping in Council. The Exchequer was nearly empty. Bernard, the wealthy banker, whom His Majesty had not disdained to entertain magnificently at Marly, in order to borrow several millions from him, was bankrupt. Money had to be raised. Well aware of the appalling suffering that the continuing struggle would impose on his subjects, Louis took an unprecedented and dramatic step. Once again one seems to detect Mme de Maintenon's influence in this humiliating yet noble gesture. For the King, the hitherto unquestionable despot, decided to issue a Proclamation placing the facts fully and candidly before the people of France.

As our sources of revenue are almost exhausted I place myself before you to ask for your advice and collaboration. Let us by our united efforts prove to our enemies that our fortunes are not as low as they hope, and with your help we will compel them to make a just and lasting peace to our own benefit and that of the whole of Europe.[9]

The King thereupon set his subjects an example they could hardly refrain from following. He sent his own gold services to be melted down, dining on porcelain or silver plate, and even pledged the Crown Jewels; at Versailles, Marly and the other Royal residences stringent economies were introduced.

In June Mme de Maintenon wrote to the Princesse des Ursins:

We have endured a series of misfortunes from which France can only recover in long years of peace, and famine, the last and greatest of all, has us at bay. I admit that all my fears never went as far as to foresee that we should be reduced to wishing the King and Queen of Spain to be dethroned; no words, Madame, can express the sorrow I feel at the very thought of it.[10]

Exceptionally for him, Louis was actually showing physical signs of the appalling strain he was enduring and to his anxious doctor, Maréchal, he frankly admitted that he was indeed feeling miserable.

Still the Princess remained unmoved, and under her domination Philip V repudiated his grandfather's request that he should abdicate.

The crunch came with the famous battle of Malplaquet, described by Marlborough as a 'very murdering battle'. France was now fighting not in defence of Spain but of her own soil. For the little village of Malplaquet lay close to Mons, within the frontiers of the realm, just across the Belgian border. The Allied attackers, under Marlborough, Prince Eugène and the Prince of Orange, had under command German, Austrian, Dutch, Irish and English troops, well equipped, well trained and well seasoned. For most of them however this was merely another battle in the war of attrition. For the French it was a very different matter. Their commander was Villars, who had already distinguished himself by certain successes in Spain. Marshal Boufflers, then seventy, although his senior in rank, had ceded the command to him.

The decisive struggle took place on 11 September. The French fought with desperate patriotism and the situation looked favourable for Villars when he was seriously wounded in the leg. Even then he insisted on continuing to direct the troops from a chair until he lost consciousness and was carried from the battlefield. The Allies promptly took advantage of the situation by launching renewed attacks. Although Boufflers threw in fresh cavalry to stem them, he made the fatal error of withdrawing too early. Defeat for France and victory to the Allies. The carnage was frightful; twenty thousand Allied troops and twelve thousand of the finest French officers and men were lost. The sole gain to France was a breathing space, for the Allies temporarily refrained from pressing home their advantage.

'M. de Boufflers,' Mme de Maintenon wrote on 14 September, 'described this battle as glorious and unfortunate, for we lost it in spite of the valour of our troops, not one of our soldiers having deserted either in action or retreat.' And she explained that the French had been defeated by the greater number of their enemies, as she had always feared would be the case. Nevertheless, in spite of her tribute to their military prowess, she foresaw very clearly the ghastly consequences to a France that was dying not in battle but of famine. 'God's will,' she repeated, 'is so obviously clear, that we would be resisting it were we not to make peace, and you know even better than I do, Madame, that to safeguard the people's welfare is the King's first duty.'

Yet in spite of the fact that Louis was by then entirely in agreement with his wife's hopes and forebodings, another three long years were to drag on before Françoise's prayers for peace were granted.

23 *Majestic Stoicism*

Three of the principal witnesses to the secret marriage of Louis and Françoise twenty-seven years previously, Harlay de Champvallon, Archbishop of Paris, Louvois, and the King's confidential valet Bontemps, who had served the nuptial mass, were dead. During the appalling winter of 1709 on 20 January, Louis also lost his confessor Père La Chaise, who had performed the ceremony. He was an ardent Jesuit and in later years, as her letters to the Cardinal de Noailles revealed, Mme de Maintenon disliked him increasingly and feared his influence over the King.

His successor as the royal confessor was another Jesuit, Père Tellier. Whether or not he was chiefly responsible, it was during that year of internal and external agitation that in spite of all his other preoccupations, Louis finally settled his score of nearly fifty years against that abhorred centre of Jansenism, the famous convent of Port-Royal.

This was the third of the heresies so abominated by the King. By the Revocation of the Edict of Nantes he had robbed himself and the realm of the services of some of his most brilliant and industrious Protestant subjects. In his stamping out of Quietism he had dismissed Fénelon, the Duc de Bourgogne's tutor and one of his most saintly bishops and subjects, and had nearly broken Françoise's heart as well. She was however no friend of the Jansenists, as her agitation, when the Cardinal de Noailles showed leanings towards them, proved.

After the various stringent steps taken against the nuns of Port-Royal and their illustrious boarders between 1660 and 1669, a ten-year lull occurred. In 1679 the intransigent nuns were commanded to dismiss their boarders and forbidden to take novices. When in 1705, Louis received from the Pope the authority to compel them to sign a document condemning Jansenism, these religious female rebels chose martyrdom rather than to do so. Whereupon, four years later, they were forcibly removed from their sanctuary by the police, and Port-Royal, which had housed such glorious leaders of French thought, philosophy and literature, as Blaise Pascal and Jean Racine, was razed to the ground. According to Saint-Simon, the villain responsible for this act of spiritual and physical vandalism was Père Tellier, whom Fagon, the royal doctor, melodramatically described as a 'bird of prey', whom he would not care to meet on a dark night.[1] But the principal beneficiary of the destruction of this famous religious centre of learning was Mme de Maintenon, for the grounds were donated to St Cyr.

In the family circle however the year 1710 opened auspiciously. Although the war was dragging on and the economic plight of the French people continued to worsen, grave anxieties were discarded for rejoicing, when, in the second week of February, the future Louis XV was born. Five years after the birth of the second Duc de Bretagne, Marie-Adélaïde gave birth to another male baby, the Duc d'Anjou.

Since the former duke who held that title had become Philip V of Spain, it had reverted to the second son of the Dauphin and Dauphine. This birth was the last and most difficult of her confinements.

On 16 February Mme de Maintenon was writing to her crony in Madrid, you will already have heard by courier, Madame, of the happy delivery of the Duchesse de Bourgogne, during whose labour however we went through some very bad moments . . . Her pains lasted so long and were so dreadful, that several of the men left the room, unable to endure the scene,[2]

for such royal births were public occasions, the reason being that in order to secure the legitimacy of the succession, it was necessary for several witnesses to be present. This can hardly have mitigated the suffering of the unfortunate young mother, in a room crowded not only with doctors, surgeons and nurses, but also several leading members of the Royal family, and statesmen.

Some time beforehand, Marie-Adélaïde had been showing signs of calming down and growing up, a development in her character which gave Mme de Maintenon the greatest satisfaction.

Louis was already regarding her as a successful future queen of France.

The next important family event in that year was the marriage of his youngest legitimate grandson, the Duc de Berry, to Marie-Louise Elizabeth d'Orléans, whose mother had been Mlle de Blois, Louis's daughter by Mme de Montespan. The Duchesse de Bourgogne had shown less sense than Louis had credited her with, by making a protegée of this young cousin. For although at the time she was barely fifteen, scandalmongers claimed that she had an incestuous passion for her father. She was physically unattractive and even in that age of gluttony her greed and tendency to drink as well as eat too much later became positively scandalous.

Although Louis and Mme de Maintenon were supposed to be unaware of the young Duchess's vices, she was certainly the supreme example of those women of a younger generation whose manners and morals Françoise, like ageing ladies in all periods, roundly condemned.

'I must admit to you, Madame,' she had previously written to Mme des Ursins, 'that I find the young women of today intolerable; the outrageous and immodest way in which they dress, their tobacco habits, their drinking, their greed, their vulgarity and laziness. I find all this so utterly distasteful, and as it seems to me unreasonable, that I cannot stand them.'³

As the King grew older, more careworn, and was spending more time in his wife's private apartments, most of this wilder set found Versailles so boring that on every possible occasion they withdrew to Paris where they were safe from royal disapproval, since both the King and Mme de Maintenon detested the capital and strenuously avoided it.

Nor was Monseigneur, Louis's heir, attracted by such dissipations, but was living quietly and happily at Meudon with his devoted morganatic wife, the big-bosomed Mlle Chouin. When his second son was proclaimed King of Spain, at the Dauphin's insistence, he had danced like a boy with pride and joy; and at their parting, when the young king set out for Madrid, he had wept as copiously as if he had a presentiment that they would never meet again.

It had been predicted of him that 'Son of a king, father of a king, he would never himself become a king'.

When Philip's throne was threatened Monseigneur had begged his father to be allowed to join the army and fight on his son's behalf, but Louis thought his heir's life too precious to be risked. So Monseigneur dutifully returned to Meudon and resumed his idle but innocuous existence. On an outing there on Wednesday 8 April 1711 accompanied by his daughter-in-law, the Duchesse de Bourgogne, he chanced to pass a priest carrying the Sacrament. After having dismounted in order to bend the knee to Christ, the Dauphin enquired to whom the Father was going, and was told 'that it was to a man dying of smallpox'. This made a considerable impression on him, so much so that on returning that evening he informed his doctor, Boudin, that he would not be surprised if he himself had caught the infection, of which during that winter an epidemic was raging throughout Europe, and which had already carried off many victims in

France. The very next day, as he was dressing to go wolf-hunting, he suddenly fell back in a faint, whereupon his doctor immediately had him put to bed. Louis was informed by his own doctor Fagon of his son's condition, but seemingly not considering it serious, went off to Marly after dinner where he was sent the latest bulletins from Meudon by the Duc and Duchesse de Bourgogne, who, in spite of the risk of infection, devotedly remained by their father's bedside. Three days later it was clear that Monseigneur's premonition that he was going to die of smallpox was indeed true. Although he had appeared to rally for a short time, he was dead within the week. He was fifty-three years old.

Louis could not bring himself to believe in this tragic possibility, but on hearing that his son was rapidly sinking, he hastened to Meudon, where Mme de Maintenon followed him.

'What a sight, Madame, met my eyes when I entered Monseigneur's cabinet! The King was sitting on a day-bed, dry-eyed but shaking from head to foot,' surrounded by the weeping members of his family and their attendants. Before her arrival, Mme de Maintenon continued, the King had entered his dying son's bedroom three or four times, terrified that he might expire before Père Tellier was able to give him Extreme Unction.

In spite of his grief and anxiety Louis had gone to supper, but immediately after the meal Fagon rushed in to tell him that all was lost. The King then at once returned to the Dauphin's apartment insisting on visiting his son's death-chamber. At the Princesse de Conti's urgent plea that His Majesty must now think only of his own safety, he finally gave way and threw himself on to a couch in the ante-chamber, where he was soon joined by Mme de Maintenon. Louis insisted that Père Tellier be sent for to administer the Last Sacrament, for none of the doctors and attendants dared to inform His Majesty that it was by then too late. And when Tellier returned from visiting the unconscious man, in order to console the King, he assured him that Monseigneur had received the last rites.

Whether or not he believed it, Louis found an outlet for his heartbreak at his son's tragic death, by sharply rebuking his medical attendants. Mme de Maintenon then led him out to the courtyard where one of Monseigneur's carriages was waiting to take him to Marly. However another coach was sent for, since it would have only added to Louis's grief for him to have ridden in the late Dauphin's. Yet, characteristically even then he had sufficient command of himself and of the situation to summon his minister Pontchartrain and to order him to arrange council to take place two days later. It was already clear what he had in mind, for he also sent word to the Duchesse de Bourgogne at Versailles that she was to meet him in the court-yard between the two stables there, as he was passing through.

Late as it was, when they arrived at Versailles, the young Duchess was awaiting them in her own coach, and immediately stepped out of it and up to his Majesty's. But the ever watchful Mme de Maintenon letting down the window next to her, shouted to her, wrote Saint-Simon, 'for goodness sake, Madame, whatever are you doing? Do not come near us, we may be infectious!'[4] And so the Duchess immediately retired.

Word had apparently not been sent to Marly to prepare the King's apartments, so that on their arrival it was some time before either light or warmth could be provided. Meanwhile it was no longer necessary to keep up appearances. The man who sat on a couch in Mme de Maintenon's cold, unlit private apartment, in front of an empty grate, miserably weeping, was an old, bereaved father, mourning the loss of his son and heir. By next morning although his grief had not lessened, in a voice broken by sobs, he requested his Council's agreement to his proposal that his eldest legitimate grandson, the Duc de Bourgogne, should be officially recognised as Dauphin, since this title was traditionally reserved for the King's eldest son. The ministers of course agreed to His Majesty's proposal, and his heir was promoted to the title, the young duchess becoming the Dauphine.

From the point of view of the European conflict, an even more important victim of that year's smallpox was the Emperor

Joseph. By a curious coincidence he and the Dauphin both fell ill on the same day, but Joseph's death did not occur until a few days after Monseigneur's. Having no male heir, his successor was his brother Charles, who in Barcelona had already proclaimed himself King of Spain. The prospect of the union of these two great Catholic empires immediately aroused alarm among the Protestant members of the Alliance.

In spite of the victory of Malplaquet, owing to the enormous losses in men and money suffered by the Allies as well as the French, Marlborough had been unable to force the war against France to a successful conclusion. The situation was further complicated by the political struggle for power between the Whigs and the Tories. The mood of the country was summarised in the blunt statement by the Earl of Peterborough that 'We are all great fools to get ourselves killed for two such boobies'[5] as the Bourbons and the Habsburgs. In consequence, under Tory rule, in April 1711, England seceded from the coalition.

Despite this temporary lull in the Spanish war, at the beginning of 1712, Louis needed every ounce of his faith and courage to face the greatest tragedy he and Françoise had to suffer during their whole married life. Less than a year after the death of his heir, for whom the court was still in full mourning, the young Dauphine fell ill. At the beginning of that year she was still presiding with her usual vivacity over the glittering festivities at Versailles. Yet, it was true, Mme de Maintenon wrote to the Princess on 11 January, that Marie-Adélaïde was feeling some strain and was aware that her high spirited youthful gaiety was becoming cloudy. Her adoring Aunt however was so unaware of any impending calamity, that she was confident the Princess's natural *joie-de-vivre* was inexhaustible and that she might look forward to a life of happiness for many years to come.[6]

But within less than a week after this letter was written, Saint-Simon reported that the Dauphine was again having one of her recurring attacks of acute inflammation of the jaw. On joining Louis and Françoise at Marly, she had gone to bed, but when the King sent for her to preside over his evening party, she rose and came down to do so, her face swathed in scarves. After a brief visit to Mme de Maintenon's apartment she returned to bed. During the following week the inflammation appeared to subside, but re-erupted with increased violence on 6 February. Within thirty-six hours she was suffering the most excruciating pain just below the temple, which was so agonising that when Louis came to visit her, she begged him not to enter her room. These symptoms appeared to indicate intense neuralgia quite possibly due to a chronic infection of the middle ear which by then had become acute.

A horrifying aspect of the poor young Princess's condition was the so-called treatment she was given by the royal physicians. Years previously Molière, Louis's favourite dramatist, had ridiculed the medical profession of his day. Nothing could have been more absurd and less unfunny than their ministrations to the dying Dauphine. She was given tobacco to smoke and chew, weakened by emetics and bleedings. The only remedy that might conceivably have relieved, although not cured her, was opium, and when her pain was temporarily eased, she said that it was even more awful than her recent labour.

Mme de Maintenon never left her bedside, except when Louis was spending his usual afternoon sessions in her private apartment. When it became tragically clear that their favourite was dying, it was decided that the time had come for her to receive Extreme Unction. In spite of her suffering she herself had not realised that her life was in danger. Those who loved her so dearly broke it to her as gently as possible that it was time for her to make her last confession, and after she had done so, the prayers for the dying were said, Mme de Maintenon holding Marie-Adélaïde's hand and giving the responses.[7]

After these last sad rites had taken place, Françoise was compelled to tear herself away from the death-bed in order once again to take her husband, to whom she owed her first duty, to Marly, since it was against royal protocol for His Majesty to remain in the same building as a corpse.

As they sorrowfully drove away, Françoise needed to draw on

all her faith and devotion to enable Louis to support this almost intolerable loss. She was seventy-seven and the King seventy-four. Since that happy occasion when Louis had gone to meet his grandson's child bride, Marie-Adélaïde had been their darling, the living spark that for so many years had ignited all the fun and games at Court. Her whims and fantasies, however crazy, had never failed to amuse and entertain Louis and although Françoise with her usual clear-sightedness had occasionally criticized the spoilt young woman's most extravagant vagaries, she too had adored her as much as her natural reserve would allow her to love any human being. With Marie-Adélaïde's death the sunshine went out of the Sun King's life.

Françoise was so shattered by this tragedy that she was unable personally to write of it to the Princesse des Ursins. Instead, the news was given her by Mlle d'Aumale, her private secretary'[8]

As if this dreadful loss had not been enough to crush even Louis's remarkable self-control and constitution, as if like some hero of a Greek tragedy he was being pursued by avenging furies, his grandson and heir, the Dauphin, was to die only a week later.

He had adored his wife, who when she died was again pregnant, and it was only with the greatest difficulty that, until the very end, he was occasionally led from her room for a breath of fresh air. Finally he joined the King at Marly. On arrival there, wrote Saint-Simon, everyone including Louis, was appalled at his appearance. It was clear that the Dauphin was also suffering from some acute infection. This was at first thought to be measles, at that period a deadly disease. As his condition continued to worsen, his will to live appeared to be weakening as rapidly as his physical resistance, and it seemed as if he was positively welcoming death in which he would be reunited with his beloved wife. He died on 18 February. On leap year day, the 29th, Mme de Maintenon wrote 'the King is overwhelmed by sorrow and the whole of France is stunned'.[9]

But the furies had not yet finished with Louis XIV. A mere three weeks later his two little great grandsons, the five-year-old

Duc de Bretagne and his baby brother, the Duc d'Anjou, also fell ill; this time it almost certainly was of measles. Neither had yet been christened and this ceremony was now hastily performed, both of them being given the name of Louis, since the elder would clearly not survive. Almost miraculously in spite of his frailty, the infant did so and in due course became Louis XV.

The deaths of the Dauphine and the Dauphin had been so dramatically sudden as well as tragic that there were inevitably rumours of poisoning. And there had been an odd incident on one occasion when Marie-Adélaïde appeared to be rallying a little. She had asked one of her ladies-in-waiting to fetch her an exceptionally pretty little snuff-box containing some rare Spanish snuff which the Duc de Noailles had presented to her a short time previously. It had however disappeared and was never found again.

Whether or not it was due to this incident, sinister rumours soon arose in Paris that the Dauphin had been poisoned. His suspected murderer was his cousin, Philippe, Duc d'Orléans, whose daughter was married to the Duc de Berry. Philippe's motive allegedly was to secure the succession for the Duchesse de Berry's children, in the event of the death of the baby Duc d'Anjou, or if this infant did survive, to have himself appointed Regent during his minority.

Philippe's relationship with his daughter was sufficient cause for scandal; he also happened to be a dabbler in alchemy and the distillation of scents and perfumes, into which poison might so easily be inserted. There was not however a shred of evidence against him, and with justified indignation Philippe demanded that His Majesty should hold an enquiry into these allegations and, if his guilt were proved, shut him up in the Bastille. Louis himself, whilst disapproving of his nephew's profligacy, never for a moment thought him guilty of the murder of his cousins. In order however to clear up the matter, autopsies on both the royal victims were held, by a committee of sixteen of the royal physicians. As might have been expected, no traces of poison were found, and Philippe's name was cleared of suspicion.

His indignant mother, Lise-Lotte, did not hesitate to accuse Mme de Maintenon and the Duc du Maine of having started the calumnies against her son. By that time Françoise could well afford to ignore the Duchess's spitefulness. Her allegations were both false and absurd. Yet it was undoubtedly true that there did exist considerable enmity between Philippe d'Orléans and Louis du Maine, both of whom already had an eye to the future and the opportunities of power it might offer them after the death of Louis the Great.

Mme de Maintenon did not exaggerate when writing that Louis was overwhelmed by sorrow. But although privately and in her loving arms he might allow himself the luxury of his unmitigated grief, Saint-Simon correctly expressed the admiration of all his subjects in saying that he had never more fully earned his right to be known as Louis the Great. He continued with exemplary stoicism unremittingly to fulfil every one of his duties and obligations. The public *levers* and *couchers*, the council meetings, the reviews, continued punctiliously. His strength was rooted in the tradition of monarchy. He had succeeded to the throne of France at the age of five, had occupied it for nearly seventy years during which the grandeur and glory of his station and his obligations had been uppermost in his thoughts. That grandeur and glory were now waning, but the tradition remained and never before did he appear more admirable to his contemporaries and to posterity.

The chief witness, naturally, of Louis's grief and superb self-control was Mme de Maintenon. In the past her main preoccupation had been his spiritual salvation, but now like any anxious wife, her first thoughts were for his health. She wrote on 27 March,

> The King is doing all he can to keep up his strength, but his sorrow returns again and again, and sharing it with him, as you can imagine, increases my own. Nevertheless his health has not broken down and he has not failed in any of his duties . . .[10]

Even the incorrigible Lise-Lotte was compelled to admit the solicitude and devotion with which Françoise was caring for her husband:

> Although the old lady is our worst enemy, I nevertheless wish her a long life on account of the King, for everything would be ten times worse, were the King to die now. For he has loved that woman so dearly that he would certainly not survive her.

24 'After I Am Gone I Can Do Nothing For You'

In the early summer life at last began to take on a more cheerful aspect. Writing to the Princess Mme de Maintenon was making constant references to the peace negotiations which seemed at last to be leading somewhere, although far too slowly for her taste.

Owing to the tragic loss of Monseigneur and the Dauphin, Louis was placed in an acute dilemma. For in the event of his baby great-grandson dying before he could succeed him, Philip V of Spain would ascend the throne of the Lilies. Louis had no intention of allowing the King of the Spaniards also to become the ruler of France. Possibly under the influence of the Princesse des Ursins or owing to his own Bourbon obstinacy, Philippe was reluctant to renounce his rights.

Writing to his ambassador in Madrid, M. de Bonnac, on 18 April 1712, Louis roundly declared: 'The peace will be absolutely destroyed if the King of Spain does not renounce his rights to my throne, and if the Duc de Berry does not renounce, at the same time, his to the crown of Spain. It only remains to decide whether I want peace at this price or a continuation of the war.'[1] Only when Louis threatened to join Austria against Spain, did he, on 8 July, bring his grandson Philip V to heel.

It was not until the end of July 1712 that really good news from the battlefield arrived at Fontainebleau. Villars, the hero of Malplaquet, had won a smashing victory at Denain and later at Douai over the famous Prince Eugène, the principal commander on the enemy side. In consequence, for the first time since the King of France had attempted to come to terms with his enemies, he was in a relatively favourable position for the conclusion of peace negotiations. Indeed it seemed as if at last Divine Providence had relented towards him; nor did he fail to order thanksgiving services to be held throughout the land.

When peace did finally come, early in 1713, Mme de Maintenon was surprised to find, as she wrote to the Princess, that the pleasure and relief she was feeling were not nearly as great as she had hoped they would be.

For the terms of the various treaties concluded at Utrecht in Holland put an end to the domination of Europe by Louis XIV. After this exhausting ten-year war, which had drained France of men and money, he did succeed in preserving her frontiers but in little more. The Netherlands where he had previously won some of his most glorious victories, passed under Austrian domination. Both Nice and Savoy were surrendered. Perhaps the bitterest blow was the emergence of England's future maritime power. For the strategic naval bases of Gibraltar, Newfoundland and Nova Scotia passed into English possession. Worse still from Louis's point of view, he was obliged finally to recognise the Protestant succession and to renounce all efforts to replace his protegé, the Old Pretender, on the former throne of the Stuarts.

At this awful cost, Louis had achieved his original objective since Philip retained the throne of Spain, even though losing most of his Empire. It was unlikely that his loyal but implacable mentor who had governed him for so long, the Princesse des Ursins, would accept the situation without a struggle. Still posing as merely the faithful adherent of the Bourbon monarchs, with her usual audacity she sent her confidential secretary, d'Aubigné, to Versailles, with a view to persuading the King to support Philip in his efforts not to lose his Dutch possessions. Louis and Mme de Maintenon received this envoy with due politeness but no more.

The final blow to Louis's hopes of being succeeded by one of his legitimate grandsons came when, on 4 May 1714, the Duc de Berry was killed in a hunting accident, and shortly afterwards his wife, who was pregnant at the time, gave birth to a female baby who did not survive. Philippe d'Orléans might well then have thought that his chances of becoming Regent or even ascending the throne, should the little Duc d'Anjou die, were bright.

To Louis however this possibility was not alluring. Philippe had shown himself unlikely to be a satisfactory Regent or successor. Once again both the King and Mme de Maintenon regretted that the Duc du Maine, their favourite, was barred from the throne by his birth.

Louis therefore decided in June 1714, despite considerable parliamentary opposition, to confer on the Duke and his younger brother the Comte de Toulouse, the rank of Princes of the Blood Royal. But in the following August he went even further. In order to anticipate any future intrigues by Philippe d'Orléans, he decided to draw up his Will. In this he appointed a Council of Regency, consisting of fourteen members, including the two new princes. M. du Maine was given further powers. He was to supervise the education of Louis XV and receive the oath of allegiance of the Royal Guard on his behalf.

Stamped with the seven royal seals, the Will was handed by His Majesty to the First President of the Paris Parlement, with orders that it be preserved behind locked and barred gates of iron in the wall of one of the towers of the Palais de Justice.

Yet Louis had no illusion that in spite of all his stringent precautions his wishes would be carried out after his death. To Maria of Modena, widow of James II, he remarked with insight: 'I have made my will, but I know just how little it is worth. While we are alive we can do as we please, but in making arrangements for the future we are worse off than an ordinary citizen'[2] and to his favourite son, Louis du Maine: 'However great I may make you during my lifetime, after I am gone I can do nothing for you.'[3]

Having made his will, he was still so much concerned with his successor's future, that he attempted to strengthen his testament by adding two codicils to it. As if foreseeing that after his death events would prove his forebodings to have been justified, and that Louis du Maine might not be in a position to carry out his instructions, in the first of these codicils, dated 13 April 1715, the King directed that immediately after his own death, Maréchal de Villeroi should be put in charge of the new King, taking him to Vincennes, which was as much a fortress as a palace, presenting him to the Parlement of Paris on the way there. The second codicil was written in Louis's own hand on his deathbed, on the following 23 August, appointing the young King's confessor and tutor.

With regard to all these important dynastic events, Françoise preserved her usual sphinx-like silence. She was certainly aware of Louis's decisions and fully concurred in them, whether or not, as her enemies maintained, she was responsible for them.

On St Valentine's Day, 14 February 1714, the young Queen of Spain died. This was a considerable blow to the Princesse des Ursins, since her official position all those years had been that of her first lady-in-waiting. By then she had exhausted her usefulness to Louis. Unquestionably it was he who decided that the time had come to put an end to her importunities and that it was on his instructions that Mme de Maintenon wrote on 16 June 1714 in no uncertain terms:

> I would have you know that we here think peace with Holland is as necessary as you think it is disgraceful. Therefore it would be as well for you to make up your mind, Madame, lest it be said that you are the only person responsible for the continuation of the war[4] . . .

She attempted to soften the blow by continuing: 'I fully appreciate that you are being asked to make a great sacrifice, yet peace, to which the King has pledged himself, is also of the greatest importance.'[5]

Nevertheless, as she had always done when it was suggested to her that she might be meddling in affairs of state, Françoise once again emphasised that this was far from the case. A fortnight later she was explaining to the Princess that she would be quite incapable of doing so owing to her physical condition. And to prove her point she drew a pitiable portrait of herself as she then was:

It is the plain truth, Madame, that I am not my own mistress in matters concerning affairs of state. You were quite right in saying that I do not care for them and that as far as I possibly can I am living in retirement. If you could see me, I am sure you would agree that the only thing for me to do is to hide myself away; I can hardly see any longer, and my hearing is even worse. What I say is barely intelligible because since I lost my teeth I can only mumble. My memory is beginning to go and I can no longer remember people's names, I am constantly getting things mixed up; and our misfortunes, together with my age, make me weep like any other old woman.[6]

This self-portrait, as touching as it is striking, may well have been true, yet Françoise was not failing intellectually to the extent she would have the Princess believe. For several years previously her rheumatism and other minor ailments had provided her with the excuse she needed to withdraw from public life. Yet in their closing years together, Louis was relying on her more heavily than ever.

On one point at least she was in complete agreement with the Princess. This was the re-marriage, very shortly after his first wife's death, of Philip V. As a young widower he must not be allowed to become the prey of some designing mistress.

The Princess's motives in favour of this second marriage were not on the same moral plain as Mme de Maintenon's. According to Saint-Simon, at the age of seventy-two, she had at one moment contemplated marrying the thirty-two-year-old King herself. But ruthless as she was, even she could hardly seriously have considered such a plan. As for his suggestion that Mme de Maintenon, when hearing of it, had said: 'I hope that we shall soon find Mme des Ursins a queen, and this time officially,' this can only be dismissed as the *reductio ad absurdum* of Saint-Simon's malice towards her.[7]

Yet to remain in power the Princess did require the alibi she had used for so long as a lady-in-waiting to a docile young Queen. She thought she had found another perfect instrument in Elizabeth Farnese, Princess of Parma, and so dispatched an envoy to Italy to conclude the matrimonial arrangements on behalf of the King of Spain. It was an unfortunate choice, for the envoy in question, the apparently insignificant Abbé Alberoni, who later became the extremely powerful Cardinal, was secretly in league with the Princess's enemies, including the Grand Inquisitor. The future queen, far from being the desired pliable instrument, was an ambitious girl who was only too pleased to fall in with their plans. On 22 December Mme des Ursins accompanied the King to meet his bride; a day later, at their very first interview, the would-be lady-in-waiting met her match.

Arrayed in full court dress she presented herself before her future mistress. Elizabeth Farnese ordered all her other attendants out of the room. Then, after only a few moments' interview, she herself rushed to the door, crying out, 'Take this madwoman away at once!'

Without even a chance to change her dress, Mme des Ursins was bundled into a coach, surrounded by seventy-two guards, with strict orders not to stop until they had crossed the Pyrenees.[8]

Whether or not Louis and Mme de Maintenon were secretly relieved that this turbulent governess of Spain had at last been removed, Françoise wrote to her with every appearance of sympathy on 12 January 1715: 'Although for some time you have been preparing me for your retirement, I must admit that I would never have dreamed that you would leave Spain like a criminal.' But, she added, 'we must submit when our misfortunes are due to those whom God has made our masters.'[9]

As might have been expected, by the time she had crossed the Pyrenees, Mme des Ursins had fully recovered her usual arrogance. She presented herself at Marly, not with the humility of a refugee, but with the pride of an ambassadress. Louis did receive her on two occasions, but with a marked lack of enthusiasm. Clearly she was no longer welcome in France and decided to resume residence in her ducal palace in Rome. There again she held court to cardinals and princes until her death, at the age of eighty, on 5 December 1722.

25 *End of Two Reigns*

During the spring of 1715 Louis seemed in his usual rigorous
health, but in the early summer he began to show the first signs
of serious decline. His formerly vigorous appetite was falling off
and other symptoms appeared. As Louis was still living in the
full glare of court publicity, it was soon noticed that he was now
looking what he was, an old man of seventy-six. Rumours of his
failing health quickly spread throughout Europe. In the London
clubs, the English, who had no love for the King of France, were
blithely betting that he would not last out the year. But as if to
give the lie to the hopes of his enemies, with his usual indomitable willpower Louis made a pretence of eating the food he
could hardly any longer swallow.

'. . . As he behaved as usual,' wrote Dangeau, 'went out
driving, followed the hunt in his carriage, and reviewed his
troops, he did not seem ill enough for us to fear for his life'.[1]
He propelled himself in his three-wheeled chair in the gardens
and inspected the statues that he continued to install there.
Every evening he attended the concerts given in Mme de
Maintenon's apartment. He was also continuing to work there
as usual with his ministers.

In the evening of 10 August, however, not feeling so well, Louis decided to return to Versailles.

A fortnight later Dangeau described the change in his appearance with dramatic vividness:

> Since Saturday 10 August when he returned from Marly he was so weak and depressed that he was scarcely able to walk from his cabinet to his *prie Dieu*. And on the Monday when according to his usual custom he wished to dine in public at ten o'clock, going to bed at midnight, as he was being undressed he looked to me like a corpse. Never did a vigorous body decay so rapidly. Seeing him naked, his flesh appeared to have melted away.[2]

On 13 August he took to his bed.

Potations of ass's milk and such like remedies, prescribed by Fagon and the other doctors summoned in dozens from Paris, were as ineffective as they were ludicrous. By then he was suffering acute pain in his left leg, which Maréchal attributed to sciatica. In spite of massage and swathing in hot towels soaked in Burgundy, the pain worsened, and on the following morning the royal *lever* was cancelled. Two days later he was a little better. He was carried to Mass in his chair and was even able for the last time to attend the concert in Mme de Maintenon's apartment.

The first ominous symptom appeared on the 19th, when Maréchal noticed a black spot on the King's foot, indicating the fatal gangrene that rapidly spread until his whole leg became black. By then amputation would have been pointless and would only have increased Louis's suffering.

Françoise was with Louis when he spoke what were perhaps his most famous last words. As his leg was being dressed he happened to see in the mirror his valets weeping at the foot of his bed.

'"Do they think," he asked with gentle irony, but no trace of self-pity, "that I am immortal?"'

By the 25th it seemed that his end was imminent.

During the whole of their long life together Madame de

Maintenon had never entered her husband's bedroom except when he had 'taken medicine'—purgatives administered to him monthly, or when he was suffering from gout or some other minor ailment. Now however, Louis gave orders that a bedroom adjacent to his own was to be prepared for her. Mlle d'Aumale, her secretary, was with her at the time. Mme de Maintenon, she said, never left the King throughout the day except to hide her tears from him when she could not bear to witness his suffering, and also spent several nights at his bedside.

Since the King's salvation had always been Françoise's main preoccupation, she now decided that the time had come for him to make his last confession. At first Louis was a little surprised at his wife's suggestion. 'He said,' wrote Mlle d'Aumale, 'that it was surely a little premature, since he was feeling quite well.' Nevertheless, he added, he was quite willing to do so.

Whilst they were awaiting the arrival of the Cardinal de Rohan to hear it and to administer the Last Sacrament Françoise with her usual thoroughness took care that Louis would omit nothing from the record. 'She reminded him,' said Mlle d'Aumale, 'of several sinful incidents in his life that she had witnessed, in order that he should not forget to ask God's forgiveness for them.' And she added 'Louis thanked her for doing so'.

Having made his peace with God, His Majesty next took farewell of his family, friends and courtiers. The first to be admitted to his presence were the Princes and Princesses of the Blood Royal. The courtiers then arrived and knelt at the foot of the royal bed. As the curtains were withdrawn to give them their last glimpse of the Sun King who had for so long dazzlingly reigned over them, the dying monarch, propped up by pillows, addressed them. Although his voice was weak, shreds of his former magnificence remained as he thanked them for their loyalty and asked their forgiveness for any injustice he might have done them.

The most moving of all these farewells occurred when the

five-year-old heir to the throne was brought to the King's bedside by his governess, Mme de Ventadour.

The touching scene was described by Dangeau.

At noon His Majesty sent for the little Dauphin, and after having embraced him, said to him: 'My pet, you are about to become a great King, but your happiness will depend on your submission to God and the care you will take of your people. For this reason you must as far as possible avoid making wars for it is the ruin of nations. Do not follow my bad example in this respect. I often went to war too irresponsibly and kept it up through vanity. Do not imitate me, but be a prince of peace. Your chief concern should always be the well being of your subjects. . . '[3]

'He then,' Dangeau continued, 'with tears in his eyes, kissed the child twice and gave him his blessing!'

Louis XIV's advice to his successor was further embodied in a letter which, according to Voltaire, was later framed and hung over the bed of Louis XV, and which, he claimed, he had carefully copied.

This brief speech to the future little King might well have been dictated by Mme de Maintenon herself. It certainly shows that by then she had completely converted Louis to her own point of view. It is remarkable for its humility and self criticism. Looking back over the past, Louis did not refer in a single word to his glory but to his mistakes.

He had been the greatest patron of the arts and sciences in Europe, encouraged, protected and given freedom to express themselves to men of letters: Vauban, who built his fortifications, was the greatest military engineer of the day; Versailles remains France's most magnificent showpiece, as it was Louis's most grandiose architectural conception; the grounds there and at Marly laid out by Le Nôtre set a new standard for landscape gardening. Few monarchs so generously gave full reign to the men of genius of their period as did Louis XIV. At the height of his military glory, his generals won victory after victory. He had also shown an unusual flair in choosing his ministers. He might well have prided himself on all these achievements.

.   .   .   .   .

Both Louis and Françoise were still acutely worried that Philippe d'Orléans would be in almost total charge of the next King in spite of the precautions Louis had already taken in his will and first codicil to avert this. On 23 August he added in his own shaky hand a second short codicil to his will, appointing Père Tellier as the little Dauphin's confessor and Fleury, Bishop of Fréjus, as his tutor.

This codicil gave Saint-Simon the occasion for a further calumny on the woman to whom he referred as 'the wicked old fairy', Mme de Maintenon, of course. According to his story, uncritically quoted by Miss Nancy Mitford, when

> Louis XIV was too tired to stand up to them she and Du Maine forced him to add a codicil to his will, putting Du Maine in charge of the new King's education. . . . Two people, President de Mesmes and Lauzun, told Saint-Simon that the King was heard to say 'I have bought some rest. They gave me no peace until I signed . . . at least they won't torment me any more.'[4]

Fortunately however we have an eye-witness account to give the lie to this calumny. Dangeau, who was present until the last moment, gave the names and functions of all those who on that day were admitted to audience, even listing the exact times they spent with His Majesty, from a quarter to half an hour respectively. The King had a little desk placed on his bed, and whilst he was writing there was at first no one in his room, but his Chancellor, Daniel-François Voisin. The door leading to the ante-room where the princes and the courtiers were waiting was only half ajar, and none of them saw Mme de Maintenon entering the bedroom. She remained there while the King, having finished writing, handed the codicil to the Chancellor, who took it to the further room, read it out to the Duc d'Orléans, and then replaced it in his pocket.[5]

Dangeau did not exaggerate when he wrote that on his deathbed Louis behaved 'with such firmness, presence of mind and magnificent self-possession as had never been known.'[6]

One last thing remained to be done—the burning of all his secret and confidential papers. Mme de Maintenon and he systematically destroyed together all their love letters, with the exception of one or two fairly non-committal notes he had sent her during his various campaigns.

It was possibly also then that they burned the secret reports sent to the King in 1678 by La Reynie, dealing with the Affair of the Poisons, in which Mme de Montespan was so deeply incriminated. This was done not to protect the reputation of that departed mistress, but for the sake of their children, the Duc du Maine, the Comte de Toulouse and their sisters.

Going through their intimate papers together they also found such trivialities as old guests' lists from Marly, which, said Mlle d'Aumale, made the King smile, and remark '"We can burn all this rubbish"'. They also found one of his rosaries, which Louis handed to Françoise, saying tenderly; '"I am giving it to you not as a relic but as a souvenir."'[8]

Mlle d'Aumale wrote:

I myself heard almost everything he said to her, talking with all the affection and confidence he had always shown her. Mme de Maintenon treasured every one of his words and wrote them down. They were later found recorded in her own handwriting with her will:

'He said goodbye to me three times,' wrote Mme de Maintenon, 'the first time saying that he regretted nothing except having to leave me, but that we should meet again very soon. I begged him to think only of God. The second time he asked my forgiveness for not always having treated me kindly; he had not made me happy, but he had always respected and loved me dearly.'

From the third conversation noted down by Mme de Maintenon it was clear that Louis was still considerably worried regarding his aged wife's future, short as it might be.

'"... he said, what would become of me, since I had nothing? I answered him that I was nothing, that he should not concern himself with me but with God."'

She was about to leave the room, but on second thoughts turned back. For secretly, in spite of her denials to him, she did share Louis's anxiety. And in the circumstances nothing was more natural. Within a matter of days, or even hours, Philippe

d'Orléans would be in power; and Françoise was only too well
aware that ever since her marriage to Louis, he and his mother
had been her bitterest enemies.

Therefore, she wrote, she had only taken a few steps when she
decided to request the King to intercede on her behalf with the
Duc d'Orléans. Louis was only too willing to do so.

'My nephew,' the King said, 'I commend Mme de Maintenon to your care. You know how highly I esteem and respect
her; she has never given me anything but good advice, which
I would have done well to follow. She has served me in all
things, and especially for my salvation. Do all you can for her,
her family, friends and connections. She will not take unfair
advantage of it and I wish her to address herself personally to
you for all she may require.'[9]

Françoise instructed Mlle d'Aumale carefully to attach the
record of these last conversations to her own testament. They do
not reveal however her love for the King, but almost exclusively
his devotion to her. In the last account particularly, a defensive
note had crept in, partly due to the fears for her own future she
was admittedly feeling, but partly also as if she were defending
herself to posterity for not having loved him as he loved her.

During his final days Louis was no longer in great pain and
said to her, '"I am beginning to believe that it is not as difficult
to die as I had imagined."'[10] According to Mme de Maintenon's French biographer Cordelier, Françoise's reply was, to
say the least of it, uncompromising: '"It is not easy," she answered him, "for everyone when one has to begin with the
catechism for a dying man who has led an impious life who is
still clinging to old attachments, with hatred in his heart, and
needs to make amends."'[11]

The fact that Françoise had persuaded Louis to make his
final confession and receive the sacraments a week before his
death, proves that her main concern was, as ever, his salvation. It is
possible that at that stage she may have used uncompromising
terms. It is hardly credible and contrary to all the evidence of
their characters and their relationship during more than thirty
years that the scene took place as described by Cordelier. 'We

imagine,' he wrote in the editorial plural, but speaking for himself only, 'this eighty-year-old woman, her arms akimbo, leaning over the dying man, and screaming her reply at him.'[12]

Others might find such a scene unimaginable. The same author quotes a letter written by Mme de Maintenon to the Princesse des Ursins in which she first described the type of woman she most detested, and continued: 'I like women who are modest, reserved, cheerful, serious or light-hearted in turn, polite, occasionally teasing but with implied praise when doing so; kind hearted and lively conversationalists.'[13]

If these words were not an indirect self-portrait, they indicated very clearly Françoise's feminine ideal, and perhaps even more so her attraction for Louis during the years of their companionship. It seems therefore all the more improbable that during their closing days together she would have fallen so far short of her own standard.

Equally cruel and unfair to Françoise was Saint-Simon's spiteful contention that 'the wicked old fairy' abandoned her dying husband four days before his death.

Once again we need only refer to the eye-witness account of Mlle d'Aumale.

'When Mme de Maintenon saw that the King was unconscious,' she wrote,

> when he was no longer asking for her and his death was momentarily expected, she decided to leave for St Cyr with me. Before doing so she insisted that her own confessor, M. Briderey, should see the King and confirm that she could do nothing more for him. . . . She instructed me to take him to the King's bedside; and after having seen him he returned to Mme de Maintenon saying 'Yes, you may leave now, for there is nothing more you can do for him.'

And, added Mlle d'Aumale, 'she left Versailles before the King's death because she feared that in those last sad moments, in spite of her submission to God's will, she might break down.'[14]

Louis died at eight o'clock in the morning on 1 September 1715, four days before his seventy-seventh birthday.

He had lived and ruled too long. When his sun finally set the glories of his reign were dimmed. From 1700 onwards, and especially during and after the ghastly winter of 1709 and the war of the Spanish Succession, the burdens the French people suffered aroused resentment and hatred against him, and Mme de Maintenon was included in this popular antagonism.

Françoise was by then nearly eighty, a very tired old lady indeed. Not surprisingly at that first moment of her widowhood, she was seized by panic.

'She was,' continued Mlle d'Aumale,

apprehensive for another reason. This was that she might be insulted during her journey, for with her great experience and having a very low opinion of herself, she thought that she might be treated as had happened to others who had been in favour and who had lost everything. That was why she instructed me, when it was time for her to travel to St Cyr to order another coach rather than her own. She left in M. de Villeroy's, and he also provided her with an escort. In addition he placed guards along the route. These precautions proved quite unnecessary and were only taken to set her mind at rest.

When we were in the coach she said to me; 'although my sorrow is very great, I feel calm and peaceful. I shall often weep for him but they will be tears of affection, for in my heart I feel great joy that he did die like a true Christian. . . . Since he became ill I never prayed for his life but for his salvation.'[15]

And writing to Mme des Ursins from St Cyr she informed her with pride that the King had died 'like a saint and a hero'.[16]

With Louis XIV's death two reigns ended. For, during more than seventy years he had reigned over France; during thirty-five of those years Françoise had reigned over him. Her comment to Mlle d'Aumale that during his illness she had never prayed for his recovery but for his salvation was not the callous remark of a tired old widow, glad to be relieved of a burdensome husband. It was simply the summing up of what Françoise de Maintenon truly believed was the mission to which God had called her. To the end she had fulfilled this duty, and duty was the one word in the human vocabulary that throughout her life meant most to her.

26 End of a Life—Birth of a Legend

The Maréchal de Villeroi kept his promise constantly to inform Mme de Maintenon of the King's condition. It was Mlle d'Aumale who early in the morning of 1 September gently broke the news to her that Louis had died. She did so indirectly by telling her that the whole of St Cyr was at prayer in the chapel, and Mme de Maintenon understood immediately what this meant. In due course she herself attended an official service for his late Majesty.

After his lying in state, Louis's body was carried from Versailles to St Denis, the traditional burial place of the kings of France. Dangeau noted that owing to the height of the catafalque one of the gates of the Bois de Boulogne had to be demolished in order to let it through.

He also expressed some surprise that Louis, who had taken such tremendous pains over his last will and testament, had given no specific orders for his funeral rites. The King had however donated his heart to the Jesuit community in Paris, final proof if any were needed that they retained their hold on him to the very end. Since the Duc d'Orléans, the new Regent, had no other specific instructions, it was decided to inter Louis

XIV at St Denis according to the ceremonial used on the death of his grandfather Henry IV and his father Louis XIII.

Mme de Maintenon did not attend the funeral. Indeed after her final retirement, she never again left St Cyr. Yet she was not completely out of touch with the world.

Louis's and Françoise's suspicions of the intentions of Philippe d'Orléans were fully justified.

The King had died on the Sunday morning. On the following Monday, wrote Dangeau, the Duc d'Orléans visited the Parlement of Paris: 'Before the late King's testament was even opened, he requested that he be appointed Regent . . . although in Louis's will he had only been nominated as Head of the Council of Regency.'

This request was immediately granted by the Parlement, in return for certain concessions and privileges.

Four days later, on 6 September, at 8 o'clock in the morning, the new Regent paid an official call on his Uncle's widow at St Cyr.

They began by exchanging the usual polite compliments. He then came to the point, with regard to which Mme de Maintenon was most anxious.

> He told me that he had taken the necessary steps for me to be paid exactly the same income as I had been receiving from the King's privy purse [48,000 *livres*] to which I replied . . . that it was too large a sum in the present state of the country's finances and that I did not wish for so much. He answered that although it was true that finances were in a bad state, this was a mere trifle.

Philippe was aware that Mme de Maintenon had never fully trusted him and her reply to his apparent generosity was a slightly veiled allusion to her estimate of his character.

He parried her thrust in reposting that, indeed, he was already feeling the burden of his new responsibilities, and Mme de Maintenon replied: 'I told him they would become even heavier in the future'. Whereupon he assured her that his one and only ambition during his regency would be to hand the country over to the new King in a better financial state than it had been left by the late one. Moreover, no one was more deeply concerned than he was with the well being of the young king, and when the moment came to assign full power to him he would be only too happy to do so. Mme de Maintenon then said with her usual inflexible candour that 'if he had not that insatiable desire to reign of which he had always been accused, his future would be a hundred times more glorious'.[3] And as if feeling the necessity to defend himself against this open statement of his allegedly secret ambitions, Phillippe answered that 'if the young king were to die, he would be unable to reign in peace, and war with Spain would be inevitable'.

Mme de Maintenon then proceeded from attack to defence. 'I begged him not to listen to anything that might be said regarding my own motives towards him; that I was only too well acquainted with human malice. I had nothing more to say; I was thinking only of my retirement'.

As Mme de Maintenon assured the Regent, she intended to give most of her income to charity. According to Saint-Simon she could well afford to do so. Her revenues included the benefits of the estate of Maintenon, and of various pensions due to her as former governess of the royal bastards, and later, as lady-in-waiting to the Dauphine. In addition, she claimed, the charter of St Cyr stipulated that, should Mme de Maintenon in due course retire there, the institution should provide board and lodging for the foundress and her entire household, free of charge and also free heating and lighting, including logs and candles.

Even so, Mme de Maintenon had no intention, and, she said, no need, of any longer keeping up an elaborate establishment.[4] She therefore decided to sell her coach and horses.

'"At a time when so many of the poor nobility are dying of hunger, I do not consider myself justified in feeding six horses".'[5] She did not however dispose of her coach until early in 1716. Her niece, Mme de Caylus, had retired to a little house in Paris, but remained in close touch with her.

Mme de Maintenon wished her to sell the coach there, where she would get a better price for it. She was clearly dissatisfied with an offer that Mme de Caylus had sent her, for on 16 February 1716 she wrote indignantly,

> What you tell me was said about it [obviously that it was old and shabby] is very unfair. It is well constructed, well upholstered, with the finest window-panes in the world, very comfortable; the damask lining will last another four or five years, and it can also be re-upholstered in velvet. It seems to me that you are not a very good bargainer.[6]

Although Françoise had given up worldly vanities, she would not have been a true Frenchwoman if she had not still kept a keen eye to a business proposition. Economy had always meant a great deal to her, and years of affluence had not wiped out memories of her earlier poverty. Now she was reducing her personal expenditure to the minimum.

"'My maids tell me,'" she wrote to Mme de Caylus, "that I am short of chemises. But I do not feel like buying any at present." And she asked her to have some made for her more cheaply.'[7]

She gave away all but the plainest and most essential of her clothes; some to Mme de Caylus. The rest, including some of the finest flowered muslin that she had worn at Versailles, she handed over to Mme de Fontaine, the Headmistress of St Cyr, to be given to those girls whose education was finished and who were about to return to society.

Françoise also gave up cosmetics and perfume, saying that she had lost him for whose pleasure she previously used them.

One of her earliest economies was the dismissal of her staff, thanking them for their services, retaining only two of her women servants and one valet to act as her outside messenger. The only luxury she allowed herself was to keep her silver plate.

In making these economies she may well have had misgivings that Philippe would not honour his promises to her, and these forebodings proved justified within three years of her retirement.

Françoise remained amazingly vigorous almost to the end. She still held herself as upright as in her youth, and walked, her companions noticed, with a spritely step of a far younger woman.

'I have given up the spectacles I have been wearing for the last thirty-five years,' she wrote to Mme des Ursins, 'and I work at my tapestry night and day for I sleep very little.'[8] When her maids came to dress her at seven o'clock, they would often find that she had been stitching away since five in the morning.

At the age of eighty-one she was still keeping up part of her large correspondence in her own hand.

In the past Françoise had found relaxation in playing backgammon or piquet with Mme de Dangeau and other ladies of her intimate circle. Even now she still longed for some slight entertainment. So after dinner, in her private apartment, she would play with Mlle d'Aumale and Mme de Glapion, at that time directress of the school.

Françoise's chief interest at St Cyr however continued to be the education of the pupils. Almost to the very end, even when she was tired or far from well, she delighted in joining them during their period of recreation. It was then that, surrounded by the fascinated circle of her young acolytes, she would occasionally tell them something of life at Court and in the highest society.

Nor did she mind apparently the noise made at their games by the younger children or even their untidiness, when she occasionally invited some of them into her private apartment.

This was all the more remarkable because, although Mme de Maintenon had reduced her personal expenditure to the last degree, her suite retained a magnificence not far short of her former residence at Versailles. Ever since the founding of St Cyr, when she had given up all intention of ending her days at Maintenon, she had been preparing for her final retirement there. There were two principal spacious rooms, her salon and her bedroom. The former, where she received such privileged guests as Maria of Modena, was dominated by a portrait of the King as well as one of herself. A handsome bookcase contained behind its ornamented grill her collection of religious and secular books. Two large mirrors also hung on the walls. Six armchairs were provided for distinguished visitors, and six tabourets for such ladies or girls privileged to be invited there occasionally as well as a day-bed upholstered in crimson damask and a pile of six cushions on which the children sat while playing their games.

Both Mme de Maintenon's rooms were kept well warmed by logs in large fireplaces and on the overmantles stood her collection of 182 pieces of precious Chinese porcelain.

The bedroom was even more elaborately furnished, containing eight armchairs, six folding stools and four tabourets, a table and mirror as well as Madame's bed. This was covered with a bedspread of blue damask lined with pure English wool. At its foot stood a crucifix beneath which was another small portrait of the King.[9]

Françoise still needed, as she had done throughout her life, a little girl to pet, fuss over and educate.

'Some time after her retirement here,' wrote the Ladies of St Cyr, in their records, 'a little girl called La Tour came to us, as if she had been specially sent by Providence to give her pleasure, for she was pretty, charming and well behaved.' Although Mme de Maintenon was old enough to be her great-grandmother, she 'treated her as if she were her own daughter and even allowed her to call her *Maman*.'[10] Little Marie was only seven, the youngest entrant to St Cyr. She was a rather delicate child and fearing that she might catch cold in the chilly classrooms, Françoise took her to live with her, bringing her up herself. 'Mme de Maintenon was so fond of her,' wrote Mlle d'Aumale, 'that she kept her beside her until she died, and in her will wrote "I commend the care of the little La Tour girl to the Head of the House and the whole community."'[11] Mlle de la Tour took the veil in 1732 and remained in St Cyr until her death in 1760.

Mme de Maintenon's attitude to the Ladies was a very different one. Françoise never suffered fools gladly. Regarding St Cyr, she was always a perfectionist, intent on making it a model institution, watching like a lynx the slightest incompetence or slackness on the part of the teachers. No doubt many tears were shed when Madame, as she was always known there, found it necessary to administer a reprimand. But the greatest sufferer from her implacable will and stern code was Madeleine de Glapion, whom she had been training and grooming for nearly twenty years for the highest post there.

This beautiful, charming, and intelligent girl had entered St Cyr in the days of its early and more relaxed rule. In the production of *Esther*, Racine having discovered her lovely voice, cast her for the part of Mardochée. When, with His Majesty at their head, the whole court had crowded in to this fascinating performance, a young page had fallen madly in love with her and sent her some passionate love letters. The innocent girl took them as in duty bound to her superior. A terrific scandal ensued. The unfortunate boy was horse-whipped for his presumption. At the age of nineteen Mlle de Glapion entered the Novitiate. Allegedly Mme de Maintenon was not forcing her to do so, and Madeleine was free to leave St Cyr, had she wished. In fact such a decision on her part was almost ruled out. Poor and friendless as she was, she could hardly have returned to the world. She had already by then surrendered herself completely if not yet to God, certainly to Mme de Maintenon, from whom she found it impossible to tear herself away. Nevertheless, she continued for years to suffer agonies of doubt and perplexity. For a short time Madeleine found some emotional outlet in a passionate friendship with another of the Ladies, Mme de Saint Aubin, who died of smallpox in her arms. Mme de Maintenon's reprimand was swift and sharp. 'I am displeased with you. Do you wish it to be thought that your relations with Mme de Saint Aubin were too intimate? What will your life be if you require years to recover from each death in which you are interested?'[12]

Madeleine found no comfort in religious orthodoxy. Christian faith seemed no compensation to her for the sufferings of humanity. Her reading of both sacred and secular history only increased the doubts in what was obviously an unusually intelligent and enquiring mind.

Mercilessly Madame once again reproved her. 'Intellectualism is not for you. It is only vanity which makes you desire it.

What will the reading of history do except disgust you with pious work and fill your mind with dangerous ideas?'[13]

As if this were not enough, when Madeleine confessed her loss of faith to her spiritual director, he instantly forbade her all further reading. Her voice was still as beautiful as Racine had found it to be. And for consolation, in her loneliness and misery, she turned to music. St Cyr was famous for its choral singing and Nivers, the school organist, had composed a motet on the Song of Solomon. Mme de Maintenon, finding this work far too erotic, had forbidden it to be performed. To her indignation, when passing the music room one day, she heard it being sung nevertheless; the culprit none other than Madeleine de Glapion. Forthwith, like a female Jove, she thundered at her. 'Christians should love nothing with passion, still less nuns who have made the vow of chastity.'[14]

By this merciless training, amounting almost to spiritual and emotional torture, Françoise reduced Mlle de Glapion to a passive and, curiously, willing instrument of her own will. Having done so, she then raised her to the highest post, appointing her headmistress of St Cyr.

In so ruthlessly preparing Madeleine for this vocation, Françoise was undoubtedly convinced of the purity of her own motives. One of her most endearing traits was her complete lack of hypocrisy. But if she was mistress of herself and all her subjects from the King to Mme de Glapion, she was no more aware than they of her own subconscious motives. She may or may not have forgotten that at sixteen she herself had chosen marriage to that disgusting little cripple Scarron, rather than enter the convent. Her determination that Madeleine de Glapion, temperamentally as unsuited to this vocation as she had been, should take the veil, might well have been due to her repressed guilt feelings at not having done so herself.

Her rationalisation was her firm conviction that in this sinful life Christians had no right to happiness, but only the duty of obedience to God's will.

Having moulded her to her liking with the greatest severity, occasionally even with cruelty, in her last years Mme de

Maintenon made Mme de Glapion her most trusted and intimate friend, speaking to her far more freely about her own life than to any other human being. Madeleine piously wrote down every word of these conversations, or *entretiens*, with her benefactress.

'It is true certainly,' she recorded Mme de Maintenon as saying, 'that I have my crosses, but by that I do not mean lacking the necessities of life, physical pain or being humiliated . . . On the contrary, I am surrounded by affluence, magnificence, favour and popularity; I do not have to suffer anything hurtful to my pride!'[15]

Françoise's fear, even in her old age, was still that she might find disfavour in God's eyes by committing what she dramatically described as 'the sin of Lucifer', this terrible pride which connects everything with oneself and makes one wish to pose as a divinity.

She knew, she said, that at St Cyr she was worshipped, and this also gave her cause for concern.

After the King's death and her retirement, she gave Mme de Glapion a most doleful account of her life with Louis.

'What martyrdom I endured. Whilst everyone thought me the happiest woman on earth, the very contrary was true.'[16]

Her happiness at the beginning of her marriage was interpreted by Cordelier as due to her having experienced sexual satisfaction in it. On the contrary, from her complaints to her confessor, she clearly found her marital duties more and more burdensome.

During that week at Fontainebleau, after the Queen's death, she was obviously extremely uncertain of her future. But within a week Louis made it clear to her, to her amazed pride and joy, that he loved her so much that he intended to marry her, whereupon her serenity immediately returned. But this was more a passive emotional state than passionate physical happiness. It must also be born in mind that Françoise was by then forty-eight years old, an age at which a woman no longer experiences the physical emotions of a young girl. Even whilst accepting the tremendous honour of becoming His Majesty's morganatic wife, Françoise may still have been dreading, rather than looking forward to physical intercourse with him.

Even granting the doubtful premise that after Scarron's death she had a brief affair—and leaving out the absurd list of her alleged lovers given by Saint-Simon—men never attracted Françoise. It is probable that she knew about sex when she was quite young, but certainly had no direct experience of it when at the age of sixteen she married Scarron. If that poor middle-aged cripple's body was her first intimate contact with the male, it would only too naturally have disgusted her, and this might well have set up a trauma regarding sex that lasted throughout her life.

She also had a minor but nevertheless, to her, very important, grievance against Louis.

'I do not think that he [Louis] found it difficult,' she told Mme de Glapion,

> to love someone who only thought of pleasing him, who was always ready to obey his least wishes, of whose honesty he was convinced, who asked nothing from him in return, who sacrificed her entire freedom to him, and yet left him completely free.
>
> It is true that he loved me more than anyone, but only as far as he was capable of loving. For men, when they are not feeling physical passion, have very little capacity for tenderness.[17]

The resentment so clearly expressed in these words, is explained by the fact that nature had not fitted Françoise to be a wife, but a governess. She was incapable of feeling deep emotional attachments to adults. Throughout her life all the love and affection she was capable of giving were only aroused by children.

After the strict seclusion of the first few months of her widowhood, Mme de Maintenon began again to receive her most favoured relations and friends; her nephew by marriage the Duc de Noailles, Maréchal de Villeroi, and the ladies, who for so long had been her intimates at court.

'Clearly one can have no social intercourse,' she wrote to the Princesse des Ursins, 'with people who never had any personal experience such as mine, brought up as they had been all their lives in this house, and knowing only its rules.'[18]

For years Maria of Modena, former Queen of England, had been one of her greatest friends. When she visited her at St Cyr, the two old ladies sat in identical armchairs, as became persons of equal rank. These visits, which lasted until the Queen's death in May 1718, may well have kept Mme de Maintenon informed of current affairs.

'"It is impossible for me," she admitted to Mlle d'Aumale, "to remain indifferent to what is going on."'[19]

She did however remain peculiarly indifferent to a great event which occurred in the spring of 1717, the arrival in Paris of Peter the Great, Emperor of all Russia. In his way Peter was an even more remarkable absolute monarch than Louis XIV. It was the great Russian writer, Pushkin, who coined the splendid image that when the Czar founded St Petersburg in 1703 he 'threw open a window on Europe'.

At the age of twenty-five, he had already made several trips to the shipyards of Holland and England with the intention of providing himself with a first class fleet. An immensely popular German opera, *Czar and Carpenter*, by Lortziny, perpetuated the story of how he mingled with the common shipwrights as one of themselves. For Peter was centuries ahead of his time. His thirst for practical information was as keen as that of any twentieth-century reporter. He was very conscious of his immense power and authority, yet he preferred to live rough, sleeping in camp beds, wearing the simplest clothes, and drinking beer rather than wine. When he was in a hurry, he threw protocol to the winds, and would jump into the first available cart or carriage, and be off, when his courtiers frequently lost his trail.

These highly original and unconventional facets of the Czar's personality provided no little shock for the etiquette-bound French, when in 1717, at the age of forty-five, Peter arrived in Paris. In his account of this visit, Saint-Simon expressed the general amazement, but he also paid tribute to the Czar's enormous intelligence and passionate interest in detail. '. . . His inexhaustible curiosity . . . his infallible judgement of what was and was not important . . . aroused general admiration.'[20]

Peter the Great's primary motive for this visit to France was to discuss with the Regent a defensive alliance between their two countries. But whilst there he went sightseeing with charactertic thoroughness. In Paris he visited the Opera, and the Invalides, where he tasted the food and chatted through his interpreter with the inmates.

He paid several visits to the little King Louis XV. The colossal luxury and magnificence, to the verge of decadence, did not however impress him. He showed great concern both for the King and France, wrote Saint-Simon, and said sorrowfully that 'such extravagance could not fail very soon to lead to ruin'.

Peter the Great also visited St Cloud, Marly, Meudon and in particular Versailles. When he first arrived there on 25 May, Louis XIV's masterpiece did make a great impression on him. A less favourable impression however was created by certain of his retinue: 'Apparently,' wrote Dangeau, 'members of his suite brought women along with them and actually went to bed with them in the apartments formerly occupied by Mme de Maintenon. Blouin, the Captain of the Versailles guard, and all the King's gentlemen who saw this, were highly scandalised.'[21]

The Czar returned there a second time on 3 June, remaining for a week. It was then that he decided to visit St Cyr and the old woman living there in retirement, who had for so many years dominated the Sun King and his court.

The Czar, Dangeau wrote on 4 June, was very anxious to visit Mme de Maintenon. Although she had not the least desire to receive him, it would have been impolite not to have done so. Yet, if this gossip regarding the desecration of her former private apartment had reached her ears, her displeasure would not have been unjustified. She did her best to put Peter off but a week later Dangeau recorded that 'The Czar refused to leave until he had seen her!' For the Emperor of all Russia was not used to having his wishes thwarted.[22] And see her he did. Yet that was about all. For the woman who had ruled Louis XIV for more than thirty years was not intimidated by this enormous barbaric monarch from the Steppes, about whom she knew nothing and cared less. Her description of this event, in a letter to Mme de Caylus, is a combination of irritability and sardonic amusement: '. . . M. de Bellegarde informs me that he wishes to come here after dinner, if that suits me . . . I did not dare to say no but I shall receive him in bed!'[23] For she had decided to parry the Czar's insistence by pretending to be ill. 'I know nothing more, whether he is to be received officially, or wishes to see the House and the young ladies . . . .etc; I am just leaving everything to chance!' And after His Imperial Majesty had departed with his curiosity presumably only very slightly satisfied, Françoise continued her letter.

'The Czar arrived at seven o'clock and sat down beside my bed.'

As Peter spoke no French nor Mme de Maintenon a word of Russian, or his only foreign language, German, their brief conversation was conducted through his minister Kourakin, acting as interpreter. 'He enquired whether I was ill to which I replied "Yes". He then asked what my illness was, to which I answered, "Old age and physical weakness".'[24] Quite clearly Mme de Maintenon was still mistress of the art of conveying a rebuff as well as a compliment, for, she continued, 'he did not know what to say in reply and so he pretended not to hear what I had said. His visit was a very short one; I think he is still somewhere in the house, but I do not know where.'

She then went on to discuss Mme de Caylus's health, ending her letter: 'Goodnight my dear niece, I am now going to drink my milk,' adding the postscript: 'I forgot to tell you that the Czar had the curtains of my bed drawn back, to get a better view of me; let us hope that this satisfied him.' In these few sentences Mme de Maintenon dismissed what was surely one of the oddest interviews in the lives of these two extraordinary characters.

.   .   .   .   .   .

Françoise's favourite visitor remained Louis du Maine, who, as Saint-Simon noted, 'would spend three or four hours at a time with her. As soon as he was announced she was wreathed in smiles, and embraced her pet, as she had always continued to call him, with the greatest affection.'[25]

As Louis himself had only too clearly foreseen the feud between Philippe d'Orléans and Louis du Maine had broken out almost immediately after his death. As soon as Philippe was officially appointed Regent he set about depriving du Maine of his appointments, leaving him only temporarily as guardian of the little King's education. On 1 July 1717 he dealt a further blow to the Duke and his brother the Comte de Toulouse, depriving them of their rank as Princes of the Blood.

Finally on 28 August 1718, the Regent removed the Duke from his last remaining influential post as Superintendent of Louis XV's education.

The Duchesse du Maine was a Bourbon-Condé, with all the arrogance of her race. These insults inflicted on her husband infuriated her. The view was later taken that it was she, 'that devilish little doll', and not the Duke who was primarily involved in the plot against the Regent.[26] Yet even if du Maine's participation in it was merely passive, he could not possibly, as his defenders claimed, have been totally unaware of it.

The essence of this intrigue was the attempt to overthrow Orléans and to bring France back into the Spanish orbit; the very policy to which Louis XIV had been so implacably opposed. The charge against the du Maines was that they had conspired with the Spanish Ambassador, Cellamare, and Cardinal Alberoni to restore the throne of France to Philip V of Spain.

This hair-brain scheme was du Maine's downfall.

The plot was discovered fortuitously. A fraudulent Spanish banker, who had escaped from London, had joined Cellamare's envoys carrying the ambassador's dispatches to Spain. The English requested the French to arrest this man before he reached the frontier. In consequence the entire party was stopped and the ambassador's letters were taken from his messengers. On demanding their return on 9 December 1718 Cellamare was refused them on the grounds that they included certain highly incriminating papers. Shortly afterwards he himself was arrested and taken to the Franco-Spanish frontier under escort.

This was the death blow to Spain's ambition to reconquer France and also to the attempt by the Duke and Duchesse du Maine to remove Orléans from the Regency.

On 29 December Louis du Maine was arrested at Sceaux and imprisoned in the fortress of Doullens. The Duchess was not spared either. She was held in custody at Dijon.

During the earlier part of the year, when her *mignon* was still visiting Mme de Maintenon, he discussed his grievances with her, and even showed her the brief he had drawn up to place his case before the Paris Parlement. The Duchess never visited St Cyr, and apparently Mme de Maintenon was unaware of the Cellamare conspiracy until after the storm had broken. But her worst fears of Philippe d'Orléans were already confirmed. The date of her last meeting with her beloved Duke is unknown. But, said Mlle d'Aumale, she felt his misfortunes and his disgrace acutely.[27] Her unhappiness must have been greatly increased by the knowledge that she was unable to protect him as she had done throughout Louis XIV's life. As the months passed she did hear rumours and tried desperately to find out the true situation, but with no success.

Then, news came at last. Mme de Glapion was with her when a messenger brought a sealed letter from the Maréchal de Villeroi, informing her of du Maine's arrest. This she handed to Mme de Maintenon who took it, read it, and without a word, went straight to the chapel. On following her there an hour later, Mme de Glapion found her deep in prayer.

Possibly Mme de Maintenon gained a grain of comfort from the fact that the Duke was bearing his sufferings with great courage. After several years in prison he was finally released and survived until 1736, but Françoise was never again to see this most beloved of all her adopted children.

Early in 1719, Françoise became conscious that her physical

strength was ebbing, although mentally she was as alert as ever. She therefore decided one day to burn all the remaining letters from Louis she had kept until then, particularly those he had written to her during the siege of Mons, in 1691. Whilst she was doing so she said to Mlle d'Aumale, '"Let us leave as little behind as we can."' And when she had destroyed most of them she remarked with satisfaction, '"Now I can no longer prove that I was on good terms with the King, and that he did me the honour of writing to me."' [28]

Mlle d'Aumale noted however that when the little girls of St Cyr said to her, '"Madame, we have been told that you were married to the King," she never denied it, but simply said, "Who told you that?"' [29]

As her health began to fail, her main preoccupation became the making of her will. She sat writing it out whilst little Marie de La Tour at her side pretended to be doing the same. Both documents were then sealed by them and placed in a little coffre. This of course was only a game, although possibly rather a morbid one for an old lady to play with a little girl, and when the child had left the room, Mme de Maintenon said to Mlle d'Aumale; 'Remove the little La Tour's testament from my coffre, for if it were left there it would make mine look ridiculous.' [30]

She had been working at it for some time and was not finally satisfied with it until a few days before she died.

On 13 April Mlle d'Aumale wrote. 'She read through the whole of it, had me seal it and with her own hand wrote on the document the word Testament, smilingly remarking as she did so, "my hand still appears to be pretty steady." And she added, "It would have been better not to have made a will at all, rather than one like mine, and to have left nothing, rather than so little ... People will laugh at it, for it really is not like a will at all."' She altered the word Testament, describing the documents as a form of disposal of her possessions. [31]

Nor did she omit to provide out of what little she had left for her charities and pensioners.

To Mme de Glapion she said one day, '"It has given me

great pleasure to pay these pensions in advance and to think that even after my death I will still be giving away alms, in order to tide over these poor people until they find other benefactors.'' '32

On hearing of her aunt's failing health, Mme de Caylus had come from Paris to Versailles visiting Mme de Maintenon at St Cyr every day. Françoise was clearly under no illusion at all about her condition, discussing it with the utmost calm and clarity. She told Mme de Caylus that although at the time she was hardly running a temperature, she knew she would not recover. She had made her will and put her affairs in order. She then told her in detail all the arrangements she had made for the disposal of her furniture and the little money she had left, and what she was leaving to her in particular. She also mentioned that in one of her coffres there were letters from certain princes which she had kept. ' "This was perhaps a little vain of me," she admitted, "but I am leaving them for Mme de Glapion who has a weakness for that kind of thing." ' '33

The provisions she made with her usual thoroughness were precise and detailed: 'I wish to be buried with the Ladies of St Cyr and I am leaving them a thousand livres to have Masses said for me.' '34 She left certain small bequests to her servants, to the poor of Maintenon, to the two sisters of the little La Tour girl and to the Benedictines of Moret. Her personal silver and her furniture would be divided between Mme de Caylus and Mlle d'Aumale. 'I leave to Mme de Noailles,' she continued, 'the diamond I have always worn.' The crucifix standing at the foot of her bed, with Louis's portrait above it, she left to the Bishop of Chartres, instructing him that it should be permanently held in veneration and gratitude.

Although Françoise had apparently destroyed most of her private papers by then, she directed that her 'secret little notebooks' '35 should be given to Mme de Perou, a former head of St Cyr, requesting the Bishop of Chartres to allow her to keep them. According to Mlle d'Aumale Mme de Maintenon's fortune at her death was a modest 32,000 livres.

During those last few days Mme de Glapion never left her

bedside. 'Really Madam!' Françoise gently remonstrated with her, 'I am taking too great an advantage of your kindness. If you never leave this room what will become of your other duties?'[36]

Her nephew, the Duc de Noailles, was also constantly visiting her.

She was not in any pain, and her mind was completely lucid. But at seven o'clock on 14 April, a terrific thunderstorm burst over St Cyr which caused an immediate rise in her temperature. As a result she became only partially conscious, except for brief intervals. At midnight her confessor brought her the Last Sacrament. When he asked her whether she wished to make her confession before receiving viaticum, Mme de Maintenon replied that she had done so only two days previously and had nothing more on her conscience.

'She had told me more than a hundred times,' Mlle d'Aumale recorded,

> that she was longing for death; that she could not convince herself that after all His grace towards her, God wished to condemn her to damnation. I sometimes said to her that I feared God's wrath and to be in Hell. 'Oh My God, how can anyone imagine such a thing? she said. Such a thought has never entered my head. I have not led so good a life as you have, but I have done my best, and I am sure that is all God demands of us. No I find it quite impossible to think that I shall be damned.'[37]

Towards the end, during a conscious interval, Françoise saw that Mlle d'Aumale, Mme de Glapion and her confessor were around her bed, whereupon with a whimsical phrase of her old humour, she asked them, 'Am I at my last gasp, that you should be all standing around like this?'[38] She was in fact very close to it, but, as if to reward her lifelong devotion, she was spared all pain. She quietly passed away as if in her sleep, at five o'clock in the evening of 15 April 1719.

Her body was embalmed and lay in state in her bedroom for the following two days. The Duc de Noailles personally took charge of the funeral arrangements, giving instructions that they were to be kept as simple as possible to comply with Mme de

Maintenon's own wishes, and for this reason he advised the Ladies of St Cyr that there should be no funeral oration. Nevertheless the ceremony was sufficiently dramatic.

At nightfall on the 17th, the bier was taken to the chapel by the Ladies of St Cyr, followed by the two hundred and fifty young pupils carrying torches and silver sconces and lighted candles. Singing was always one of their most noted accomplishments. But on this last occasion their voices were so broken by sobs and tears that they were unable to pay this farewell tribute to their beloved foundress. Foreseeing this, M. Bonnet, the spiritual director of St Cyr, had arranged to provide a male voice choir of seventy priests and clerics.

On M. de Noailles's instructions, Mme de Maintenon's marble memorial slab was inscribed with an epitaph composed by the Abbé Vertot, a member of the Académie Française. After referring with slight exaggeration to her 'noble birth', the Abbé did give an accurate description of her personality.

> She was of a wise, modest and gentle nature, which never varied, throughout the changing circumstances of her life. Always following the same rules and principles with the same virtue. Unwavering in her piety, calm amidst the turbulence of the Court. Simple amidst grandeur, poor although surrounded by wealth, and humble when most highly honoured. Revered by Louis the Great. Enveloped by his *gloire*. Taken into his most intimate confidence and the recipient of his favours. Yet she never took advantage of her power except to do good ... A mother to the poor and a refuge to the unfortunate. So illustrious a life has ended in a saintly death before God. Her body remains in this Holy House which she founded leaving to the whole world the example of her virtue. Deceased 15 April 1719, born 28 November 1635.[39]

In founding St Cyr Mme de Maintenon laid the whole basis for the higher education of both the young French women of the impoverished nobility, and later for the daughters of the higher bourgeoisie. To the Ladies and pupils of St Cyr, her friends and admirers, Mme de Maintenon appeared as little less than a secular saint, all sweetness and light. Yet to her enemies she was little less than a she-devil.

It was Saint-Simon who noted the ironical fact that her death caused hardly a ripple of interest in the world from which she had retired only four years previously.

That famous *femme fatale* Mme de Maintenon died at St Cyr on Saturday 15 April. What a sensation the event would have caused in Europe had it occurred a few years earlier! Although Versailles was so near it was ignored there, and barely mentioned in Paris. So much was said about this unfortunately notorious woman at the time of the King's death, that nothing remains to be added. During thirty-five years without a moment's break she played so great and sinister a role at court, that everything about her was remarkable until she finally retired.[40]

Although he occasionally paid unwilling tribute to Françoise's gifts Saint-Simon maintained that her influence on Louis XIV was disastrous. He claimed that before the King received his ministers in Mme de Maintenon's apartments, she had previously instructed them regarding the advice they were to give him. And that whilst she sat in her little *niche* embroidering away she was keeping a sharp eye and ear on them, to see that they were obeying her instructions.

The most sensational accusation he brought against her was that she never forgave Louvois for having prevented Louis XIV from making their marriage public. He gave a positively lurid description of the war minister's disgrace and death. The accusation against Mme de Maintenon appears to be irrelevant regarding the former. For some time Louvois had been exceeding his authority. A remarkable scene took place in Mme de Maintenon's apartment, after the siege of Mons, when Louvois tried to persuade his master to destroy the ancient city of Trèves. Louis was furious and grabbing the poker was about to attack Louvois, when Françoise intervened, thereby possibly saving the minister's life.[41] When Louvois died suddenly of a heart attack in 1691, Saint-Simon claimed that he had been poisoned and that at the King's orders no autopsy was held.

The calumny that Mme de Maintenon had instigated his murder was enthusiastically propagated by her old enemy Lise-Lotte, Duchesse d'Orléans, who wrote with relish:

'The old slut croaked at Saint-Cyr last Saturday, 15 April, between four and five in the afternoon. The old witch had Louvois poisoned for opposing the public announcement of her marriage'. And for good measure she added: 'That wicked old devil Fagon poisoned the Queen in order that the old cow should step into her shoes.'[42]

But this suggestion was as improbable as it was spiteful. Kingship was Louis's vocation and profession. He held his sovereignty by divine right. He was born to it, brought up to it and exercised it with diligence and authority. Louis believed that it was by virtue of the Blood Royal that flowed in his veins that he was set above his subjects. This mystique of the Blood Royal was then fully shared by all Frenchmen and Frenchwomen, not least by Françoise de Maintenon. Although she had attempted, by a faked pedigree, to link her own and her brother's genealogy to that of the slightly more aristocratic family of d'Aubigny, she knew that by birth she was totally disqualified from aspiring to become Queen of France.

As Louis grew older and the war of the Spanish succession bore more and more heavily on him, his self doubts and uncertainties increased. 'He has a very low opinion of himself,' Mme de Maintenon confided to Mme de Glapion in 1707. 'He does not regard himself as indispensable, and is convinced that anyone else could do as well as he, or better in many ways . . . He does not feel as much pride in one year as I do in one day.'[43]

Françoise knew that this innate pride, this passion for standing well in the eyes of the world she had had since her childhood, was her chief fault. Her guilt feelings over it became immeasurably increased when Louis fell in love with her and insisted on marrying her. She sublimated these by convincing herself that it was God who had called her to this station—she was not great, she was merely 'raised up'. She was never in love with the man, nor any man; she was in love with the King, and only half in love with this glorious image since the other half of her love was given to God. To bring the King to God was to unite her emotional and spiritual halves. Yet, one wonders, was

Françoise ever aware of an even greater passion concealed in her character, a passion for power?

In her youth she was timid and shy and blushed easily. After her marriage and elevation as consort to His Majesty, she developed an acute inferiority complex. This took the form of advertising her dislike of Court life and longing for privacy and retirement as ostentatiously as the Montespan had flashed her diamonds. For if she was never in love with luxury nor any man, she was in love with Power, almost as voluptuously as any other woman with her partner in sex.

On his death bed Louis had asked her forgiveness for not having made her happy. The fault was not his, but hers. With all her compassion, generosity, affectionate impulses—loving and being loved did not come easily to her. The final impression remains of a woman surrounded by a multitude of men and women throughout her life, who died as she had lived, intrinsically alone. Her life was one long success story. Only one thing eluded her—the secret of happiness.

Postscript: Unquiet Grave

'So long as there is a king in France,' Mme de Maintenon had told the Ladies of St Cyr on one occasion, 'you will never want'. And indeed, for a hundred years this was the case.

The Regent died in 1723. The government was taken over by the Duc Louis Henri de Bourbon, who amongst several other retrenchments made severe cuts in the income of the Ladies of St Louis, so that great economies had to be exercised at St Cyr. With his dismissal however by Louis XV their prosperity was restored. In fact the King's fiancée, the Spanish Infanta, was educated there for some years. When the engagement was broken off, Marie Leczinska, his future Polish queen, was also a boarder there. And her mother, the Queen of Poland, for a time took over a whole wing of the establishment. She even entertained the ambition of becoming a second Mme de Maintenon to the Ladies, but they considered the foundress irreplaceable, and continued to venerate her as before.

In 1786 the centenary of St Cyr was celebrated with great magnificence and pomp. By then it had become immensely rich, owning vast estates and employing more than two thousand peasants. Three years after the celebrations, under the unfortunate Louis XVI, the Revolution erupted. Yet, in their semi-monastic seclusion, the Ladies of St Cyr were in almost total ignorance of the violent political events about to sweep to their gates.

In July 1789 the peasants revolted. The woods on the estate were felled, and the game killed by poachers. The village of St Cyr itself came under a revolutionary Council which forebode worse to follow. From 1789 to 1792 the National Assembly passed a series of laws dispossessing the clergy of their lands and properties. Since it was obvious that the end was near, in August of that year, the pupils began to leave St Cyr. During the following months, although they were not personally attacked, the Ladies who of course were nuns, began to prepare for their departure. They gradually removed from the house their personal belongings. Books and manuscripts—including those in the Chapel and in Mme de Maintenon's former apartment—relics, all were taken away and carefully preserved. Before their final departure they said a farewell prayer at their foundress's tomb in the Chapel. The last to leave, on 1 May 1793, were the Superior and the Treasurer.

Throughout this exodus the villagers reacted according to their personal feelings. The revolutionaries jeered, whistled and made contemptuous remarks, although they did not personally molest the Ladies. Women and children, to whom they gave clothes, odd bits of furniture and alms, wept to see them go.

The National Assembly had previously passed a law confiscating the wealth and property of the monastic orders. Officials were sent to St Cyr as elsewhere to make an inventory of those possessions of the community that had to be nationalised. Immediately after the Ladies' departure the Mayor of St Cyr took charge of the large collection of silverware and other valuables which had accumulated during the past hundred years, and handed them over to the Convention which by then had succeeded the Assembly.

The outer fabric remained undamaged, but it was decided to transform the buildings into a military hospital. The interior was completely gutted. The classrooms and dormitories of the

K

little Reds, Blues, Greens and Yellows were to be turned into hospital wards bearing such revolutionary names as *Marat, Bonnet-Rouge, William Tell, Sans-Culottes,* etc. These alterations lasted until the middle of 1794 and cost 236,000 francs.

Since the Revolution had abolished Christian worship, the Chapel itself was to be divided into two hospital wards. Altar, reredos, pews, organ and all religious symbols were ruthlessly removed. One day the workmen engaged in these demolitions found beneath the rubble and debris piled on the floor, a black marble slab, the tomb of Mme de Maintenon.

'This', wrote Lavallée,

> they smashed, they opened the tomb and the two coffins of lead and wood within it, and tore out the body of the foundress. It was perfectly preserved, still wrapped in its burial clothes, smelling sweetly of the unguents in which it had been embalmed. With savage oaths and imprecations they bound a rope around the neck, dragged it out into the courtyard, and broken and mutilated as it by then was, roughly threw it into a hastily dug hole in the cemetery.[2]

Lavallée added that the chief perpetrator of this desecration, the head mason Delauney, later defended himself for this brutal act by stating that he only wished to clear the new hospital ward of an unwanted tomb.

After the Revolution, St Cyr was again transformed. At the beginning of the nineteenth century it became the famous military establishment for the education of officers of the French army.

In 1802, after the freedom of religious worship had been restored to France, Mme de Maintenon's remains were rescued from their ignoble pit and reburied in a pretty little grave surrounded by weeping willows in a little garden facing her former apartment. But she was not to lie there in peace for long. Three years later St Cyr was commanded by General Duteil. Whether or not he was a Huguenot, he had no love for its foundress, and ordered that the tomb of 'that fanatic who was responsible for the revocation of the Edict of Nantes' be destroyed.[3]

With almost unbelievable callousness, Mme de Maintenon's bones were once again disinterred and thrown into a wooden packing case which was taken up to one of the attics where it was pushed behind a lot of other superfluous rubbish and where it was to remain for the following thirty-one years.

Not until 1836 did the then Commandant of St Cyr, Colonel Baragauy d'Hilliers, obtain permission from the Ministry of War to have Mme de Maintenon's remains decently interred in the chapel. This however was done very simply, with no religious ceremonial. The crate containing her bones was placed in a black marble tomb, on a white marble base, surmounted by a cross, with the bare inscription:

Here lies
Mme de Maintenon
1635 – 1719

And so, by a singularly ironic twist of fate, Françoise de Maintenon who, it might be claimed, was one of the most sincere precursors of pacifism, who all her life had hated war, at last came to rest in the heart of France's most famous military establishment.

Appendix: Fiction and Fact

Although Mme de Maintenon's death caused so little interest at the time, she was not to remain in oblivion for long. Françoise's posthumous fame was partly due to the talent to which she owed her whole career, her accomplishment as a letter writer. Had she never become the wife of Louis XIV her correspondence would still have rivalled in interest and extent that of her friend and contemporary Mme de Sévigné.

At the time of her death, she left more than sixty thousand letters. Even Saint-Simon noted that 'she wrote singularly well'.[1] But the first literary man to make this discovery, sixty-nine years previously, was Paul Scarron. As he himself wrote to her, he fell in love with 'the little Indian girl' after having been shown her first letter to her friend in Paris, Mlle de Saint-Hermant. 'I have always suspected that the little girl who came to see me six months ago, in a dress that was too short, and who burst into tears, I really don't know why, was as intelligent as she seemed to be . . . To tell you the truth, I never thought that one might learn, either in the American Isles or at the convent at Niort, to write so well.'[1]

It was this talent that won Françoise her first husband and

even more remarkably, her second. Louis's dislike of her as a *précieuse*, an intellectual female, was already partly broken down by her devotion to his children. His growing interest in her was considerably increased by the letters she wrote to him when she took his crippled little son to Barèges for his cure. Mlle d'Aumale also recorded the impression Mme de Maintenon's letters made on those privileged to receive them:

'. . . The people to whom she wrote, even the most distinguished, all kept her letters. Many of them were given to St Cyr, in the firm belief that they would one day be collected together.'[3]

And in fact the Ladies did preserve in their archives every scrap of paper in their foundress's writing, which, incidentally, was of an almost masculine firmness, intellectual, uncompromising, with hardly a trace of femininity.

Yet by a freak of literary history, for many years Mme de Maintenon's notoriety rested less on her own genuine correspondence than on a series of elaborate forgeries.

Louis Racine, the son of the great dramatist, had intended to write a memoir on Mme de Maintenon. For this purpose he obtained from the Ladies of St Cyr a collection of her letters and other relevant documents. But he was more a collector of literary curiosities than a writer, and had not yet begun the memoir when he received a visit from another minor author, aged 25, whose name was La Beaumelle. Born in Languedoc in 1726, La Beaumelle was a Protestant and was then a professor of French Literature in Copenhagen. He was visiting Paris in connection with some vague literary project, when he called on Racine. Flattered by La Beaumelle's interest, Louis Racine showed him his miscellaneous documents, including those concerning Mme de Maintenon.

Although thirty-one years after her death Madame continued to be worshipped as fervently as ever at St Cyr, outside this pious little enclave, her image was a very different one. The legend first started by Saint-Simon and the Duchesse d'Orléans that 'the old witch' had been Louis's evil genius, was by then widely believed. It was she who was held responsible by the

Huguenots for the revocation of the Edict of Nantes; the persecution of the Jansenists and the demolition of Port Royal; the war of the Spanish Succession and all the want and misery of the people which during her lifetime had so distressed her. When Voltaire published his famous *Siècle de Louis XIV* in 1740, he was criticised for having taken too generous a view of 'this odious woman'. But even Voltaire was shortly to change his opinion of her.

La Beaumelle had a natural flair for a good story. Louis Racine's documents inspired him with a very simple but ultimately a highly successful plan of presenting Mme de Maintenon to a later generation, not as she really was but as they would wish her to have been. Louis Racine generously allowed him to take away the genuine documents and letters in his possession. With calm effrontery La Beaumelle then re-edited these to suit his purpose, not hesitating to add certain spicy or scandalous letters of his own invention to her alleged intimates and referring to quite fictitious sexual adventures she was supposed to have had in her youth. In 1752 he published in Frankfurt three volumes: two containing her letters, and one a Memoir. These did contain certain authentic material he had obtained from Louis Racine interspersed with his own fabrications so cleverly that their genuineness was not challenged, even by Voltaire.

La Beaumelle had already attacked the *Siècle de Louis XIV*, arousing Voltaire's lasting and bitter enmity. His suspicion that La Beaumelle had stolen the original documents, although he did not know from whom, was expressed in a letter to a friend: 'It was rumoured some years ago that Mme de Caylus's letters and recollection of her aunt had been stolen. Do you know anything of this?'[4] Yet even Voltaire did not suspect that La Beaumelle's publications were largely a forgery.

Had I seen these letters before, I would have had to cast my portrait of Mme de Maintenon in darker colours. . . . Ignorance, weakness, deceitfulness, ambition, intrigue, masses, sermons, love affairs, clannishness—these are the characteristics of this Esther.

And this was the portrait of Mme de Maintenon which was to endure for sixty years. Yet even La Beaumelle could not entirely destroy the evidence of her integrity, for added Voltaire: 'This Esther writes well, and I was pleased to note that she was bored by being queen. While I prefer Ninon, Mme de Maintenon is well worth while.'[5]

In spite of this initial success, La Beaumelle ran into political difficulties on other grounds. Later in 1752, he was imprisoned for six months in the Bastille, for a libel on the Regent, in another of his works. On his release, encouraged by the success of the first edition of Mme de Maintenon's letters, he persuaded the Ladies of St Cyr and the Duc de Noailles to open their archives to him. Three years later he published in Amsterdam a second and much enlarged edition. The recipe was as before, an artful blend of genuine and forged material. But this time the consequences for La Beaumelle were disastrous.

Louis Racine had suspected that the first edition, of which La Beaumelle had not even sent him a copy, contained several forgeries, and on comparing the published letters with the copies in his possession, found this to be the case. But not wishing to become involved in a literary controversy, he had not raised the issue, nor did he do so when the second edition appeared. The Ladies of St Cyr and the Duc de Noailles were also unfavourably impressed, but as the work had been published in Amsterdam and not in France, could take no steps to have it suppressed. It was Voltaire who now struck at his enemy.

He did not take the letters seriously. But Mme de Maintenon's so-called memoirs aroused his fury. They contained a passage which gave him the opportunity to destroy La Beaumelle. This referred to the poisoning of the Prince of Bavaria in Brussels at the instigation of the Court of Vienna. Voltaire took it upon himself to report this passage to the Austrians, who immediately demanded satisfaction from the French government for this libel. In consequence La Beaumelle was again arrested and sent to the Bastille, this time for a year. On his release he was forbidden to reside in Paris and was sent back to his native Languedoc. There, in spite of his record, he married a rich widow. In due course he was pardoned and returned to Paris, where he died in 1773.

But now comes the most extraordinary part of this tale of literary forgery. Mme de Maintenon might well have gone down in history as La Beaumelle portrayed her. The fact that she did not do so she herself might have attributed to the mercy of the divine intervention in which she had always so fervently believed, a belief that might well be justified by the facts.

For when he was freed from the Bastille, La Beaumelle left behind him a mass of papers. On investigation these were found to include the copies he had made at St Cyr of some of Mme de Maintenon's authentic letters, together with copies of his own forgeries of them.

'They remained in the Bastille until it was stormed on 14 July 1789. Carried away with other loot, they passed from hand to hand, and were sold and resold several times.' And almost it might seem by a miracle, sixty years later came into the hands of a distinguished literary scholar, Théophile Lavallée.

He himself told this story in his preface to *Correspondance Générale de Mme de Maintenon* which he published in 1865. In this admirably edited and annotated work Lavallée produced as well as Mme de Maintenon's authentic letters several of La Beaumelle's forgeries, based on Louis Racine's collection and with Racine's own commentaries on them. Lavallée became the leading nineteenth-century authority on Mme de Maintenon. His works also include a history of the d'Aubigné family and of St Cyr.

Bibliography

AUMALE, MARIE JEANNE D', *Mémoire et lettres inédites de Mademoiselle d'Aumale* (see HAUSSONVILLE, vol. 1).

BEAUMELLE, ANGLIVIEL DE LA, *Mémoires pour servir à l'histoire de Madame de Maintenon*, 6 vols., Paris, 1737.

BOISLISLE, A. DE, *Paul Scarron et Françoise d'Aubigné, d'après des documents nouveaux*, Paris, 1894.

BRUNET, C. (ed.), *Correspondance complète de Mme la duchesse d'Orléans*, 2 vols., Paris, 1886.

BUSSY-RABUTIN, ROGER DE, *Correspondance avec sa famille et ses amis*, Paris, 1859.

CAYLUS, COMTESSE DE, *Souvenirs et correspondance de Mme de Caylus*, Paris, 1881.

CORDELIER, JEAN, *Madame de Maintenon*, Paris, 1955.

CRONIN, VINCENT, *Louis XIV*, London, 1964.

CRUTTWELL, MAUD, *Madame de Maintenon*, London and New York, 1930.

DANGEAU, PHILIPPE DE COURCILLON, MARQUIS DE, *Journal, avec les additions inédites du duc de Saint-Simon, 1684–1720*, 19 vols., Paris, 1859.

GEFFROY, A., *Mme de Maintenon d'après sa correspondance authentique*, 2 vols., Paris, 1887.

GERARD-GAILLY (ed.), *Lettres de Madame de Sévigné*, Paris, 1953.

HASTIER, LOUIS, *Louis XIV et Madame de Maintenon*, Paris, 1957.

HAUSSONVILLE and HANOTAUX (eds.), *Souvenirs sur Madame de Maintenon*, 3 vols. Vol. 1 contains *Mémoire et lettres inédites de Mademoiselle d'Aumale*, Paris, 1896–1902.

LANGLOIS, M., *Louis XIV et la cour*, Paris, 1926.

LANGLOIS, M. (ed.), *Mme de Maintenon: Lettres*. Paris, 1935–9.

LAVALLÉE, THÉOPHILE (ed.), *Correspondance générale de Madame de Maintenon*, 4 vols., Paris, 1865–6.

LAVALLÉE, THÉOPHILE, *Histoire de la maison royale de Saint-Cyr (1685–1795)*, Paris, 1865.

LAVALLÉE, THÉOPHILE, *La Famille d'Aubigné et l'enfance de Mme de Maintenon*, Paris, 1863.

LAVALLÉE, THÉOPHILE (ed.), *Lettres historiques et édifiantes de Madame de Maintenon adressées aux dames de St Louis*, Paris, 1856.

LOUIS XIV, *Oeuvres de Louis XIV*, 6 vols., Paris, 1806.

MITFORD, NANCY, *The Sun King*, London, 1966.

MONGRÉDIEN, GEORGES, *Mme de. Montespan et l'affaire de poisons*, Paris, 1953.

MONMERQUE (ed.), *Lettres de Madame de Sévigné*, Paris, 1862.

ORLÉANS, DUCHESSE D', *Correspondance complète* (see BRUNET).

SAINT-SIMON, DUC DE, *Le Cour de Louis XIV*, Paris, 1911.

SÉVIGNÉ, MME DE, *Lettres de Mme de Sévigné* (see GERARD-GAILLY and MONMERQUE).

TAILLANDIER, MME SAINT-RENÉ, *Madame de Maintenon*, Paris, 1923.

URSINS, PRINCESSE DES, *Lettres inédites de Mme de Maintenon et de Madame la Princesse des Ursins*, 4 vols., Paris, 1826.

VISCONTI, PRIMI, *Mémoire de la cour de Louis XIV*, Paris.

VOLTAIRE, *Siècle de Louis XIV*, Paris, 1852.

WOLFE, JOHN, *Louis XIV*, London, 1968.

Notes

1. *The Little Indian Girl*

1. Crutwell, *Mme de Maintenon*, p. 15.

2. *Rebellious Convert*

1. Quoted by Cruttwell from Lavallée, *Conseils et Instructions aux Demoiselles de Saint-Cyr*, Vol. I, p. 98.
2. Lavallée, *Lettres et entretiens sur l'éducation des filles* (1854), Vol. II, p. 347.
3. Lavallée, *Correspondance générale*, Vol. I, p. 33.

3. *The Chivalrous Cripple*

1. Cruttwell, p. 29, from Scarron, *Oeuvres* (1752), Vol. I, p. 154.
2. Lavallée, *Correspondance générale*, Vol. I, p. 38.
3. Ibid., p. 38.
4. Ibid., p. 39.
5. Ibid., p. 41.
6. Voltaire, *Siècle de Louis XIV*.
7. D'Aumale, *Mémoire et lettres inédites*.

7. *The Mysterious House at Vaugirard*

1. Lavallée, *Correspondance générale*, Vol. I, pp. 131–2.
2. D'Aumale, p. 53.

3. Caylus, *Souvenirs et correspondance*, p. 38.
4. D'Aumale, pp. 53–55.
5. Cordelier, *Madame de Maintenon*, p. 81.
6. Lavallée, *Correspondance générale*, Vol. I, p. 155.
7. Ibid., p. 154.
8. Sévigné, *Lettres*, Vol. II, p. 464.
9. Ibid., p. 196.
10. Ibid., p. 299.
11. Ursins, *Lettres*, Vol. I, p. 114.
12. Cordelier, p. 85.
13. Lavallée, *Correspondance générale*, Vol. I, p. 162.
14. Ibid., p. 165.
15. Ibid., pp. 177–8.
16. Caylus, p. 59.

8. Governess at Court

1. Lavallée, *Correspondance générale*, Vol. I, pp. 182–3.
2. Ibid., p. 183.
3. Ibid., p. 187.
4. Ibid., p. 191.
5. Ibid., p. 192 footnote.
6. Ibid., p. 196.
7. Ibid., p. 201.
8. Geffroy, *Mme de Maintenon d'après sa correspondance authentique*, Vol. I, p. 42.
9. Lavallée, *Correspondance générale*, Vol. I, pp. 221–2.
10. D'Aumale, p. 61.
11. Lavallée, *Correspondance générale*, Vol. I, p. 232.
12. Ibid., p. 234.
13. Ibid., p. 237.
14. Ibid., p. 238.
15. Taillandier, *Madame de Maintenon*, p. 103.
16. Lavallée, *Correspondance générale*, Vol. I, p. 248 footnote.

9. Royal Soul in Peril

1. Sévigné, Vol. III, p. 433.
2. Lavallée, *Correspondance générale*, Vol. I, p. 254 footnote.
3. Louis XIV, *Mémoirs*, p. 226.
4. Taillandier, p. 104.
5. Lavallée, *Correspondance générale*, Vol. I, p. 264.
6. D'Aumale, pp. 66–68.
7. Ibid., p. 56.
8. Lavallée, *Correspondance générale*, Vol. I, p. 268.
9. Lavallée, *Lettres historiques et édifiantes de Mme de Maintenon*, Vol. II, p. 73, and *Correspondance générale*, Vol. I, p. 689.
10. Lavallée, *Correspondance générale*, Vol. I, p. 265.

10. The Indispensable Madame de Maintenon

1. Lavallée, *Correspondance générale*, Vol. I, p. 276.
2. Loc. cit.
3. Ibid., p. 280.
4. Ibid., p. 290.
5. Sévigné, Vol. III, p. 480.
6. Ibid., p. 504.
7. Lavallée, *Correspondance générale*, Vol. I, p. 285.
8. Caylus, p. 46.
9. Sévigné, Vol. III, p. 534.
10. Op. cit., Vol. IV, pp. 222–3.
11. Ibid., p. 223.
12. Ibid., p. 224.
13. Lavallée, *Correspondance générale*, Vol. I, p. 260.
14. Cruttwell, p. 96.
15. Sévigné, Vol. IV, p. 543.
16. Ibid., pp. 527–8.
17. Lavallée, *Correspondance générale*, Vol. I, p. 308.
18. Sévigné, Vol. V, p. 9.
19. Ibid., p. 38.
20. Lavallée, *Correspondance générale*, Vol. I, p. 321.

11. The King on the Brink of a Precipice

1. Lavallée, *Correspondance générale*, Vol. I, p. 335.
2. Sévigné, Vol. V, p. 17.
3. Lavallée, *Correspondance générale*, Vol. I, p. 337.
4. Ibid., p. 340.
5. Ibid., p. 345.
6. Ibid., p. 346.
7. Ibid., pp. 355–6.
8. Ibid., p. 365.
9. Op. cit., Vol. II, pp. 15–23.
10. Ibid., p. 47.
11. Visconti, *Mémoire de la cour de Louis XIV*, p. 205.
12. Ibid., pp. 205–8.
13. Mongrédien, *Mme de Montespan et l'affaire des poisons*, pp. 155–6.
14. Visconti, p. 124.
15. Mongrédien, p. 157.
16. Ibid., p. 158.

12. The Great Poison Trials

1. Mongrédien, pp. 32–33.
2. Ibid., pp. 116–17,
3. Ibid., p. 21.

4. Lavallée, *Correspondance générale*, Vol. II, p. 97.
5. Ibid., p. 106.
6. Ibid., p. 95.
7. Ibid., p. 96.
8. Ibid., pp. 94–95.
9. D'Aumale, p. 77.
10. Sévigné, Vol. VI, p. 475.
11. Lavallée, *Correspondance générale*, Vol. II, p. 93.

13. Ruthless Conversions

1. Lavallée, *Correspondance générale*, Vol. II, pp. 93–103.
2. Ibid., p. 135.
3. Ibid., p. 135.
4. Caylus, ix, x.
5. Lavallée, *Correspondance générale*, Vol. II, pp. 139–40.

14. Morganatic Marriage

1. Caylus, pp. 105–6.
2. Saint-Simon, *Le Cour de Louis XIV*, p. 439.
3. Lavallée, *Correspondance générale*, Vol. II, p. 166.
4. Ibid., p. 301.
5. Ibid., pp. 301–2.
6. Ibid., pp. 302–3.
7. Caylus, p. 135.
8. Lavallée, *Correspondance générale*, Vol. II, p. 304.
9. Ibid., p. 308.
10. Ibid., p. 313.
11. Ibid., p. 323.
12. Cronin, *Louis XIV*, p. 241.

15. Living with Louis

1. Lavallée, *Correspondance générale*, Vol. II, p. 366.
2. Ibid., p. 389.
3. Saint-Simon, p. 430.
4. Lavallée, *Correspondance générale*, Vol. II, p. 344.
5. Saint-Simon, p. 443.
6. Lavallée, *Correspondance générale*, Vol. II, p. 410.
7. Lavallée, *Lettres historiques*, Vol. II, p. 163.

16. Revocation of the Edict of Nantes

1. Saint-Simon, p. 416.
2. Lavallée, *Correspondance générale*, Vol. II, pp. 245–6.

17. *St Cyr—Ambition Achieved*

1. Lavallée, *Correspondance générale*, Vol. III, p. 9.
2. Cronin, p. 292.
3. Lavallée, *Correspondance générale*, Vol. II, p. 399.
4. Saint-Simon, p. 411.
5. Ibid., p. 419.
6. Lavallée, *Correspondance générale*, Vol. III, pp. 77–78.
7. Ibid., p. 161.

18. *Françoise on the Brink of a Precipice*

1. Taillandier, pp. 184–5.

19. *Social and Military Manoeuvres*

1. Mitford, *The Sun King*, p. 130.
2. Lavallée, *Correspondance générale*, Vol. IV.
3. Saint-Simon, pp. 210–11.
4. Mitford, p. 197.
5. Lavallée, *Correspondance générale*, Vol. III, pp. 276–7.
6. Ibid., p. 293.
7. Ibid., pp. 333–5.
8. Op. cit., Vol. IV, pp. 248–9.
9. Ibid., pp. 249–50.
10. Op. cit., Vol. III, pp. 319–20.

20. *Spiritual Safety Valve*

1. Lavallée, *Correspondance générale*, Vol. III, p. 394.
2. Op. cit., Vol. IV, p. 10.
3. Ibid., pp. 11–12.
4. Ibid., p. 12.
5. Ibid., pp. 33–34.
6. Lavallée, *Correspondance générale*, Vol. IV, p. 232.
7. Ibid., pp. 278–9.
8. Ibid., p. 256.

21. *Louis Gives Spain a King*

1. Lavallée, *Correspondance générale*, Vol. IV, p. 347.
2. Ibid., pp. 361–2.
3. Ibid., pp. 367–8.

22. *Years of Disaster*

1. Cordelier, p. 443.
2. Cronin, p. 318.
3. Cordelier, p. 452.
4. Loc. cit.
5. Ibid., p. 466 footnote.
6. Ibid., p. 471.
7. Ibid., p. 469.
8. Taillandier, p. 235.
9. Cronin, p. 323.
10. Ursins, Vol. I, p. 430.

23. *Majestic Stoicism*

1. Mitford, p. 221.
2. Ursins, Vol. II, pp. 35–36.
3. Cordelier, p. 469.
4. Saint-Simon, p. 166.
5. Mitford, p. 234.
6. Ursins, Vol. II, p. 253.
7. Taillandier, p. 244.
8. Ursins, Vol. II, p. 266.
9. Ibid., p. 269.
10. Ibid., p. 227.
11. Cordelier, p. 504.

24. *After I Am Gone I Can Do Nothing For You*

1. Wolfe, *Louis XIV*, p. 660.
2. Cronin, p. 334.
3. Cronin, p. 343.
4. Cordelier, p. 489.
5. Ursins, Vol. III, pp. 75–76.
6. Ibid., Vol. III, p. 83.
7. Cordelier, p. 490 footnote.
8. Ibid., pp. 490–1.
9. Ursins, Vol. II, p. 163.

25. *End of Two Reigns*

1. Cruttwell, p. 349.
2. Dangeau, *Journal*, Vol. XVI, p. 118.
3. Ibid., p. 125.
4. Mitford, p. 240.
5. Dangeau, Vol. XVI, pp. 121-3.
6. Ibid., p. 119.

7. D'Aumale, pp. 219–20.
8. Loc. cit.
9. Ibid., p. 202.
10. Cordelier, p. 517.
11. Ibid., p. 518.
12. Loc. cit.
13. Ibid., p. 469.
14. D'Aumale, p. 203.
15. Ibid., p. 204.
16. Ursins, Vol. III, p. 179.

26. *End of a Life—Birth of a Legend*

1. Dangeau, Vol. XVI, p. 163.
2. D'Aumale, p. 208.
3. Ibid., p. 309.
4. Saint-Simon, p. 510.
5. D'Aumale, p. 212.
6. Loc. cit.
7. Ibid., p. 216.
8. Geffroy, Vol. II, p. 379.
9. Taillandier, p. 280.
10. D'Aumale, p. 109.
11. Ibid., p. 221.
12. Cruttwell, p. 264.
13. Loc. cit.
14. Ibid., p. 265.
15. Ibid., p. 285.
16. Lavallée, *Lettres historiques*, Vol. I, p. 456.
17. Ibid., pp. 456–7.
18. Geffroy, Vol. II, p. 379.
19. D'Aumale, p. 222.
20. Dangeau, Vol. XVII, p. 80 footnote.
21. Ibid., p. 95.
22. Ibid., pp. 101, 104.
23. Geffroy, Vol. II, p. 389.
24. Loc. cit.
25. Saint-Simon, p. 505.
26. Taillandier, p. 276.
27. D'Aumale, p. 223.
28. Ibid., p. 112.
29. Ibid., p. 87.
30. Ibid., p. 234.
31. Ibid., p. 233.
32. Ibid., p. 232.
33. Ibid., p. 231.
34. Ibid., p. 241.

35. Ibid., p. 242.
36. Ibid., p. 234.
37. Ibid., p. 229.
38. Ibid., p. 235.
39. Ibid., pp. 239–40.
40. Saint-Simon, p. 505.
41. Ibid., p. 333.
42. Taillandier, p. 279.
43. Lavallée, *Lettres historiques*, Vol. II, p. 198.

Postscript

1. Lavallée, *Correspondance générale*, Vol. I, p. 257.
2. Lavallée, *Histoire de St Cyr*, p. 297.
3. Ibid., p. 298.

Appendix

1. Saint-Simon, p. 507.
2. Lavallée, *Correspondance générale*, Vol. I, p. 39.
3. D'Aumale, p. 149.
5. Loc. cit.
6. Lavallée, *Correspondance générale*, Vol. I, p. xxxiii.

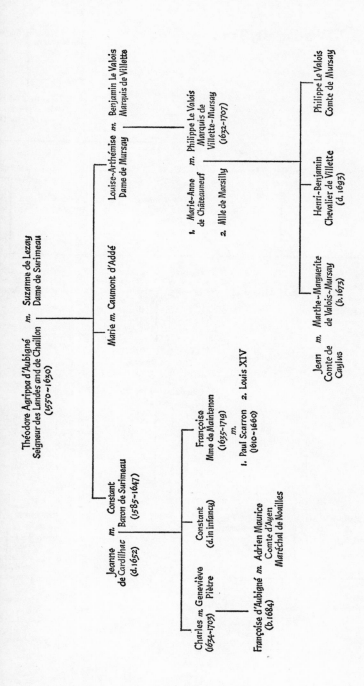

Mme de Maintenon's Family Tree

LOUIS XIV's Family Tree

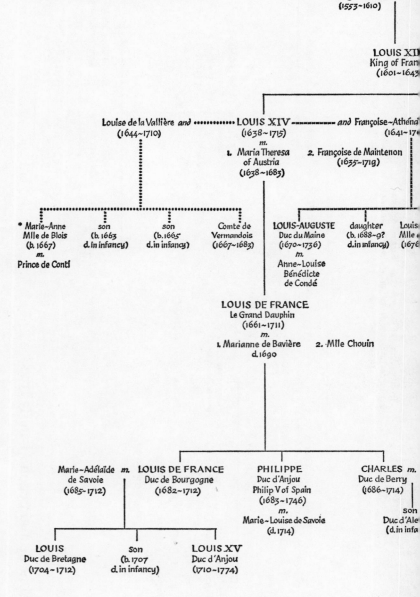

HENRY IV *m.* Mari
King of France
(1553~1610)

LOUIS XII
King of Fran
(1601~1643

Louise de la Vallière *and* •••••••••••• LOUIS XIV ----------- *and* Françoise~Athéna
(1644~1710)   (1638~1715)   (1641~17
                                         m.
                                    1. Maria Theresa   2. Françoise de Maintenon
                                       of Austria   (1635~1719)
                                       (1638~1683)

* Marie~Anne	son	son	Comte de	LOUIS-AUGUSTE	daughter	Louis
Mlle de Blois	(b. 1663	(b. 1665	Vermandois	Duc du Maine	(b. 1688~9?	Mlle
(b. 1667)	d. in infancy)	d. in infancy)	(1667~1683)	(1670~1736)	d. in infancy)	(1676
m.				*m.*		
Prince de Conti				Anne~Louise		
				Bénédicte		
				de Condé		

LOUIS DE FRANCE
Le Grand Dauphin
(1661~1711)
m.
1. Marianne de Bavière   2. Mlle Chouin
   d. 1690

Marie~Adélaïde *m.*	LOUIS DE FRANCE	PHILIPPE	CHARLES *m.*
de Savoie	Duc de Bourgogne	Duc d'Anjou	Duc de Berry
(1685~1712)	(1682~1712)	Philip V of Spain	(1686~1714)
		(1683~1746)	
		m.	son
		Marie~Louise de Savoie	Duc d'Ale
		(d. 1714)	(d. in infa

LOUIS	son	LOUIS XV
Duc de Bretagne	(b. 1707	Duc d'Anjou
(1704~1712)	d. in infancy)	(1710~1774)

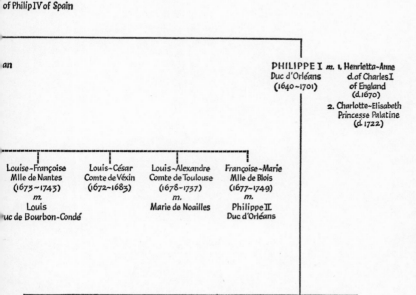

of Austria
of Philip IV of Spain

an

PHILIPPE I *m.* 1. Henrietta-Anne
Duc d'Orléans   d. of Charles I
(1640~1701)   of England
    (d. 1670)
2. Charlotte~Elisabeth
Princesse Palatine
(d. 1722)

Louise~Françoise   Louis~César   Louis~Alexandre   Françoise~Marie
Mlle de Nantes   Comte de Véxin   Comte de Toulouse   Mlle de Blois
(1673~1743)   (1672~1683)   (1678~1757)   (1677~1749)
m.   *m.*   *m.*
Louis   Marie de Noailles   Philippe II
Duc de Bourbon-Condé   Duc d'Orléans

PHILIPPE II   Marie~Louise   Anne~Marie   Elisabeth~Charlotte
Duc d'Orléans   (1662~1689)   (1669-1728)   1676-1744
and Regent   *m.*   *m.*   *m.*
(1674~1723)   Carlos III of Spain   Victor Amadée   Léopold
m.   (d. 1700)   King of Sardinia   Duc de Lorraine
Mlle de Blois

Elisabeth

* The birth date for Marie-Anne, Mlle de Blois (also known as Mlle de Bourbon)
is sometimes given as 1666. She died in 1739.

Index